HIDEAWAY:
LIFE ON THE QUEEN CHARLOTTE ISLANDS

Other Books by James Houston

HIDEAWAY

Life on the Queen Charlotte Islands

JAMES HOUSTON

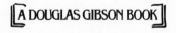

Canadian Cataloguing in Publication Data

Houston, James, 1921-
    Hideaway : Life on the Queen Charlotte Islands

Includes bibliographical references.
ISBN 0-7710-4276-0

1. Houston, James, 1921–   – Homes and haunts – British Columbia – Queen Charlotte Islands.   2. Queen Charlotte Islands (B.C.) – Description and travel.   I. Title.

PS8515.079Z53 1999   917.11'12   C99-931675-3
PR9199.3.H598Z47 1999

The publishers acknowledge the financial support of the Government of Canada through the Book Publishing Industry Development Program for our publishing activities. We further acknowledge the support of The Canada Council for the Arts and the Ontario Arts Council for our publishing program. Canadä

Illustrations, including map and endpapers, by James Houston

Typeset in Goudy by M & S, Toronto
Printed and bound in Canada

A Douglas Gibson Book

McClelland & Stewart Inc.
The Canadian Publishers
481 University Avenue
Toronto, Ontario
M5G 2E9

1 2 3 4 5   03 02 01 00 99

To Douglas Gibson,
a good editor
and still a friend

Haida potlatch

Contents

Langara Is.

ALASKA

Haida Village

Rose Spit

Masset

GRAHAM IS.

North
Pacific
Ocean

Port
Clements

Tlell

Queen Charlotte City

Skidegate

Sandspit

Cumshewa

Skedans

Tanu

Map
of the
QUEEN
CHARLOTTE ISLANDS
1851

Ninstints

Rose Harbour

HOUSTON

I

Running West

The first person to tell me to go and live in the Pacific Northwest was suffering from Arctic hysteria. And when he told me about the Queen Charlotte Islands, he was standing, shivering, thousands of miles away on south Baffin Island, deep in the Arctic. On that still day in the early spring of 1951, the hills around us looked as if snow had been dumped over the backs of elephants whose granite bellies plunged down into a thick layer of snow-covered ice that circled Kimmirut harbor. My first wife, Allie, and I, then freshly married, had traveled there by dog team from Frobisher, now called Iqaluit. It had been quite a trip. After a couple of days' rest, we felt nearly normal again, enough to go for a walk in the ice-cold Arctic landscape around the small jewel box of a harbor.

The Hudson's Bay Company post manager and his clerk had repeatedly warned us to expect a wild, human encounter. It didn't take us long to discover why. As we rounded a hill, we saw a man standing dead-still before us. He was oversized and wore a bulky, rusty-colored parka. He did not look at either of us. His eyes kept staring slightly upwards, as though he were looking for birds, or a religious experience.

We stopped and stood watching him, wondering who should make the first move. Finally, I called out, "Decent-looking morning."

It took some time before he looked down, then answered, "Yes." Suddenly, he turned and marched stiffly toward us, pulled off one mitt, and extended his large, chilled hand toward me. He had a reddish, bulbous nose in a frost white face. His dark eyes seemed too wide open and shone too brightly to appear normal.

"You're the Houstons," he said, then looked behind him, examining the sky again. "They've been expecting you."

"Yes," I asked. "We're staying with Geordie over at the Company and we've met the police and Arnold Ruskell, the Anglican missionary."

"I don't mean them," he interrupted in a hostile voice. "I mean . . . the others."

"Oh, the Inuit?" said Allie.

"There are no Eskimos around here now. They're out in their camps." He looked at her for the first time. "I don't mean the Eskimos." He looked expectantly up at the sky again. "I've seen them twice since Christmas – well, not them, but the shiny ship they're flying. It's stopped and hovered twice, just above the nursing station beside those rocks."

Allie secretly nudged me as he went on.

"Both times when the ship appeared, the big police dog team sent up a wailing and howling."

"What kind of ship was it?" I asked.

"A space ship, a UFO," he answered. "You've heard of them, unidentified flying objects. It was a small one, just big enough to hold maybe four to six of whoever they are. I imagine them maybe playing cards or something like that inside the ship while peeking out and deciding where to make their landing. If the sky's clear and you two go out about the time that Jupiter appears tonight, you'll probably see them all aglow as they approach you. The half-dozen whites around here, they're suffering from frozen brain, or they're snow-blind. They swear they've never seen them. But maybe you can.

"I've heard from the wife of one of the hunters down the coast," he continued. "Her husband trades in here. Like me, she says she's seen them. Yes, seen their space ships more than once."

Allie and I both shook our heads. "We've never seen one in our lives. But why don't you come over and visit us at the Company maybe tomorrow?"

"NEVER, NEVER!" he yelled. "I don't see eye to eye with any of the others around here – except some of the Eskimos."

"Then should we come over to your place?"

"NO!" he answered loudly. "No, nobody's allowed in the nursing station. But we could meet right here again. It's as safe as any place. We might see the space people come down low while we're talking. They're definitely interested in you."

With that intriguing final line, he strode away.

The next day had a slight breeze that was murderously cold. Light snow was sifting down and the clouds hung above us like a blanket of lead. I walked along the snow path and found the male nurse there again, motionless, blending into the face of the granite rock. This day he was wearing a huge, Russian-type fur hat with the earflaps dangling down.

"I got a message last night," he called out as I approached him. "Houston, you've made a big mistake. You've come to the wrong part of the world. They say you're looking for art. I heard that. Well, there's nothing much in the way of native art around here. Maybe a few little ivory scraps and cribbage boards left over from the Scottish whaling trade. That's the only kind of thing the Company still orders. You should get the hell out of this country," he said, his earflaps trembling. "Turn your dog team around and head back to Frobisher Bay."

He paused, then asked in a different tone, "Have you ever been up on the Northwest Coast? I mean the north Pacific Coast in real Indian country? That's the place where you should be. I know the north Pacific Coast." He shook his head. "Forget Cape Dorset. I've never been to Dorset. But I've heard those Eskimos over there are a contrary bunch. Some Company men say they've got fire in their bellies. They like to talk about Dorset's big shots, travelers living in their nomad camps not caring about the whites. Men like Pootoogook, Pitseolak, and their brother Kulula, who's dead now. Oh, you'll hear plenty about them and that dead brother if you go over there. He had an all-white dog team. He once rushed in over here, grand as one of the three kings of the Orient bringing in a big load of white fox skins to trade for a certain type of bullet that would fit his Company rifle. But would they trade him over here? Oh, no! The Company manager at that time told this big shot brother to get his fancy arse back to Dorset, the only place where he's allowed to trade. That made Kulula so mad, they said, that little bits of white foam formed on the corners of his mouth. The hard way he answered the manager scared the interpreter half to death. He says he didn't have the nerve to explain half of it."

He kept holding his mitt over his face to thaw his nose and prevent frostbite, and I did the same. "Yeah, if you go out to the north Pacific Coast," he said, "you'll see some real carvings, some really big ones, and some real dancing. But you've got to try and get on the inside track with those Haida or Kwakiutl Indians before they'll let you in to see their potlatching – that's their word for partying, feasting, and giving big gifts away. I had a Kwakiutl friend out there near Alert Bay. He took me to one of their feasts in an old, falling-down shed. Potlatching is still against the law in Canada, you know, because our government judges thought it too wild and wasteful and outlawed it. So the Northwest Coast Indians had to go underground because the Mounties were on the watch."

"Why?" I asked.

"Because an anthropologist had reported that lower chiefs would hold a feast and give away their fishing boats and every other thing that they possessed, then set their houses on fire just to prove to the higher chiefs at the potlatch how rich and grand and reckless they were. When I was there, a government doctor told me the Kwakiutl didn't have anything left of that fancy, real good, old stuff of theirs that you can see saved in museums in Vancouver and Victoria. The women had to make all new costumes for the feast that I saw. They cut up pieces of old navy blue blankets, then sewed on a wide border of red with white shell buttons along the edges.

"After that the men rushed out with an axe and split pieces of cedar firewood. By noon, they had the cedar shaped and carved into masks. Some of them were really big ones like the Whaa Whaa bird masks. They found some kind of house paint or enamel and made quick designs all over them. Then, with the paint still wet and dripping, they danced wearing the mask on that same night.

"Dear God, man, you got a right to see those masked dancers with their fringes flying in the firelight and their black shadows leaping after them. You got to hear the flutes whistling and the drummers drumming as they call the Hamatsa spirit into the house. That's all a part of the cannibal dance. You'll see with your own eyes a naked person attacked by that kind of a spirit who will bite until a bloody piece of flesh is torn right out of his victim's arm. After the spirit's appetite for human flesh is appeased, the spirit seems to be exhausted and other dancers catch him and drag him out of the shed. But the spirit still has strength. Amazing stuff."

The nurse coughed steam in the freezing air. "Now these Eskimos trading into this place, they do nothing like that. Early explorers said they've always been a peaceful people around here."

"Well, isn't that good?" I asked him.

"Maybe," he answered, his eyes bugging out at me. "But I like those wilder, West Coast Indians better. A woman anthropologist who went there to study them told me that those people were always wild and liked the habit of fighting each other, one clan against another, even when they were neighbors. But there was a big change, she says, when they first saw the white men. The Haida Indians used to call us iron men, not because we're physically strong – they're usually a helluva lot stronger – but because we brought them iron, knife iron to fight with and adze iron for making quicker, better carvings and totem poles and for quickly shaping bigger war canoes."

Bird mask

"Well," I said, "there's too damned much ice to do much canoeing around here most of the year, and there's no wood at all to build houses, canoes, or totem poles."

The male nurse snorted like a horse. "No sea otter around here either," he said. "Lust for sea otter pelts caused most of the trouble on the Pacific Coast."

"Why?" I asked him, though by now I was eager to end the conversation. I was getting really cold.

"Because those Indians living on the Northwest Coast, especially the Haida on the Queen Charlotte Islands, were glad enough to trade a prime sea otter skin for a hand's length of iron that they could pound and lengthen into a dagger or widen into a carving adze. They say those pieces of iron cost the sea captains, who had come around the Horn to trade, about two pennies apiece. A prime sea otter skin during the best of times could bring as much as a thousand dollars each in Canton to be traded to rich Mandarins. Some difference, eh?

"So the Yankees, the British, the Spanish, and the French all competed in the otter trade along the north Pacific Coast. Each ship rushed to get to the otter hunters first, trading rum, dagger iron, muskets, and blankets, causing all hell to break loose. You got bigger and bigger potlatches, and ever taller bigger totem poles began to rise."

"Sorry, but I've got to go," I said, shuddering inside. "But wasn't there the same kind of competition when the Yankee and the Dundee whaling captains arrived here in ships? They competed like hell for the big bowhead whales that would boil down into tons of oil."

"Yeah, but those men usually wintered over on this coast to be ready for the good spring hunting. They used the Eskimo men to crew with them in their six-man whaleboats sent out from the ships. And they became friends because these Eskimos around here are very friendly and generous people, easy to get along with. They'll share everything with you.

"Wait a minute, don't go. I've got more to tell you. The West Coast Indians were never kind like that." He shook his head.

"When foreign captains first sailed there, they almost never flew a flag – that would reveal who they were. If unknown, they could tell the Indians that someone else was to blame for the cannon fire and other bad things that had happened. When the Haida, in their big forty-man canoes, came paddling out to greet or maybe try to harm the traders, the captains would order their so-called tiger nets hauled up above their ships' rails so they couldn't be overwhelmed by a horde of Indians who might try scrambling aboard. They'd all heard tales of massacres. These Indians were tough guys."

"That's interesting," I said. "But I do have to get back." I started stamping my half-frozen feet. "I don't want to miss a meal," I explained.

"Yeah, I know. You're looking kind of gaunt. But I'll tell you this last bit quick . . ."

I realized that before me stood a man in isolation, desperate to talk to someone, almost anyone. This male nurse was in trouble with everyone in this tiny settlement. He was a man who had openly declared that he had seen flying saucers over Kimmirut, not once but several times.

"Wait, wait!" he gasped. "Hear about one Yankee captain sailing up the Northwest Coast. He was famous in his time as the meanest, roughest, drunken son-of-a-bitch in all of the otter trade."

I started to walk away, calling out, "Goodbye." I left him standing there.

Days later, while we were traveling across Baffin Island looking for the camps of Inuit carvers, I found that a seed had been planted. The thought of some day running west to see Kwakiutl and Haida art on the north Pacific Coast was never far from my mind. For more than a decade after that, I continued to read books, study, and observe as much as I could about Inuit art and the history of Inuit people with whom I was working and sharing an exciting life. But I also read as much as I could about the history of the Haida and other Indians of the north Pacific Coast, and especially about their art. Some day, I promised myself . . .

Dance blanket

2

First Glance

For nine exciting and rewarding years (described in *Confessions of an Igloo Dweller*), I lived in Cape Dorset and traveled to the thirteen camps that surrounded it. There lived the hunters and their families, moving on their ancient, nomadic, food-gathering paths. Slowly, from the late fifties to the late sixties, they gathered into the small central settlement that was increasing in size. It now had a new school, a nursing station, the West Baffin Eskimo Co-operative, and me, a Northern Service Officer at first, then the grandly named Administrator for the area of 65,000 square miles.

In an unlikely move (explained in my second volume of memoirs, *Zigzag*), in 1962, I leapt from the Arctic directly into the heart of Manhattan to become the Assistant Director of Design for Steuben Glass. I worked hard to adapt myself quickly to an utterly different world. Six years after being in New York, I was surprised to be invited by the Canadian Minister of Northern Affairs, the Honorable Arthur Laing, to journey throughout many Indian reserves of British Columbia in order to write a report on the possibilities of a redevelopment of Northwest Coast Indian art.

I had just remarried. My second wife, a Connecticut girl named Alice, is the daughter of a Yale professor, and I was eager to show her the wonders of the Indian world along with the mountainous beauty of British Columbia. Steuben Glass, generous as always, continued to pay me while we went off on this important journey. We were joined by Robin Kendall, the Deputy Minister of Indian Affairs for British Columbia. Robin was an ardent fly fisherman and we became lifelong friends, remaining so until his death.

Our first visit was to Victoria on Vancouver Island, where we saw two of the Hunt brothers carving a small pole, less than two stories tall, for the provincial museum. From Victoria our mandate was to go to all the reservations. Now British Columbia is an enormous province, more than three times the size of Italy. It has been described as "a wildly beautiful explosion of mountains, islands and fjord-notched coast." That coast runs from the Strait of Georgia, where it borders Washington State, all the way north to Alaska. Inland – and sometimes not very far inland – run spines of snow-capped mountains as tall as any on the continent, with some patches of cactus-dotted desert thrown in for variety. To me, an old Ontario boy, there is nothing to beat British Columbia for its beauty and variety. And we saw it at its best.

We traveled by road, boat, and plane to many other Indian communities that were known to have created art in the past. But we found that currently nothing was being done. Even Alert Bay, once famous for its abundance of creative Kwakiutl art, had nothing going on at that time.

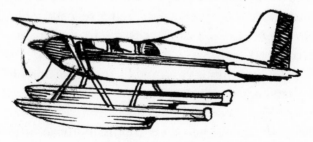

Floatplane

Bella Coola to the north was more interesting. As we came swooping in our small floatplane down into a long, steep-walled fjord, the pilot pointed up above our heads at a scattering of pure white dots that turned out to be at least a dozen mountain goats casually standing on the sheerest ledges. We landed in a wide, thunderous silver spray, then taxied in beside the dock at Bella Coola. Our small party was met by an enthusiastic Indian agent named Jerry Piper. I learned with pleasure that we were not far from the place where Sir Alexander Mackenzie, determined to be the first to cross the continent from sea to sea, had been guided across the mountains by Carrier Indians, and finally reached the waters of a deep inlet of salt water on the North Pacific Coast in 1798. Here, he had been met by people whom he described as bold and hostile coastal Indians. One of them had tried to choke him, and when Mackenzie drew his sword, the man jumped away and made clear to Mackenzie that he had already been struck with the side of Captain George Vancouver's bright saber. *Vakuba* was the way the Indians pronounced Vancouver's name.

Later that afternoon, in an old and shadowy hall at the edge of a forest, the Bella Coola Indians gave us a delicious smoked salmon feast. We stuffed ourselves with the delicious pink and pungent salmon and drank many mugs of tea. Afterwards, they performed Bella Coola dances made magical by a half-dozen seated elders who did their drumming on a long, hollow log. Whaa Whaa dancers, naked to the waist, leaped in the air, then squatted, peering at us in silence through their long-beaked, painted masks, then suddenly resumed their chanting. I tried to make rapid sketches of the dancers' every movement, with some success. Then for a special reason, they beckoned us all outside. To our amazement we found ourselves listening to an old recording of Bella Coola singers, on a hand-wound machine. We could hear singing and drumming, all of which had been scratchily preserved on short, fat, wax tubes, using a much older recording technique from earlier days. The Bella Coola spoke the name of Dr. Marius Barbeau, a famous French-Canadian anthropologist from Canada's National Museum who had visited early in the century.

We did not see the current artwork of the Bella Coola Indians, and we were told that there was little to none being created at that time. Their dance masks, they said, had been made at the turn of the century. Neither Robin nor Jerry, the Indian agent, nor any of the local elders we spoke with were able to offer further clues about current creation of art.

We then journeyed in a small boat to a heavily forested area and made a short rock climb. There we were shown old, deep engravings on several huge boulders. These were of two three-masted, square-rigged ships, from what looked to me like the eighteenth century, and beside them were a few typical Indian art images carved into the stones, depicting clearly the ovoid forms and other characteristics of the northern coastal style.

Ovoid curve – fish head

We stayed the night at Bella Coola, met more Indians there, and breakfasted with the agent before we flew out next morning. We soared north over the mountains to Ocean Falls, a pulp mill town where they receive an average of 155 inches of rain per year. Later, that mill closed. No wonder. I was told its workers said they could feel their skin puckering and their brains and bones becoming waterlogged. The Indians on that coast had the wisdom to live elsewhere.

In our small floatplane we crossed northwestward to the Queen Charlotte Islands. Because it was a clear day, we could see the long archipelago of 150 separate islands, large and small, running from northwest to southeast in a narrowing wedge. We landed on the water in front of the old landing pad on Skidegate Inlet. There we met the Indian agent, Robert Bell, a cheerful Scot with a West Highland accent, who drove his car to the water's edge to collect us. We went with him to the small house of Rufus Moody, a short, broad-shouldered man of few words living on the Haida Skidegate Reserve. Rufus led us to his workbench where he had several gray bricklike chunks of argillite and a water-darkened piece that he was busy working on. You could see that it was going to be a six-inch totem pole. Through his window, he had a good view of the sparkling blue inlet, with a background of tall, treed islands with snow-laced mountains rising beyond them.

When I asked Rufus questions, he gave short grunts for answers. He had been warned that we were coming but he didn't like being disturbed. Finally, his thoughtful wife asked us to have some chocolate cake that she had made, she said, especially for us. That, with a cup of tea, brought our visit to an end without further conversation.

Today, I sometimes see Rufus in a store or walking on the road and he is just as brief after more than thirty years as he was on that first day we met him. This can tell you something of the Haida attitude. They are content – or should I say determined – to keep more or less to themselves. White outsiders and Haida had hard, violent times more than two hundred years ago, followed over time by the disastrous spread of white diseases, and many have perhaps been slow to forget these things.

We heard from several sources that there was one more Haida carver by the name of Charles Adams who had done some work that we might wish to see. The first part of the road (and I mean the only road) north on Graham Island, the largest island in the chain, had been recently rebuilt and covered with smooth asphalt. Not a single car did we encounter, but there were bald eagles peering down from tall trees and lots of mule deer browsing beside the road.

"This is some sort of paradise," said Alice. "I've never seen a place like this."

When we were halfway between Skidegate and Old Haida, Bob stopped the car at a narrow, wooden bridge that spanned a river. He waved his hand. "This is the Tlell," he said, "one of the best salmon rivers in the world!"

We all four – Alice and me, Robin Kendall, and Bob Bell – got out of the car. We walked forward and leaned against the rail of the wooden bridge, staring at the long, curving sweep of the tidal river. It was flowing north on an outgoing tide. Its waters were as smooth and brown as buckwheat honey, carrying an outgoing parade of huge gray logs debarked by the sea. These had escaped from timber booms and slipped upriver on previous tides. They were on the move again, being swept north into the inland passage of the wide Hecate Strait.

"There she is," said Robin. "That's the Tlell, one of the best and least known salmon rivers on the continent."

"I'd give anything to live in a place like this," I told Alice. She, my new bride, glanced at me. Not knowing if I was serious or not, she hesitated to agree or disagree, fearing perhaps that I meant stay here forever.

Bell, the Indian agent for the Haida, coughed and said, "We'd have a drink, but the water's way too salty with this tide. The asphalt road ends right here at this bridge. Beyond, it becomes all humpy and bumpy, dust and gravel. On a dry day like this, it's sure to clog our throats."

"Should we take a nip from this wee bottle?" I asked, to general enthusiasm.

I looked along both banks of the tree-lined river, at the silver ripples where the river crossed a shallow ford beyond us, then back along one bank again until close to the bridge among some big fir trees I saw an almost hidden cottage with an aged shake roof and green-stained shingle siding. There was no smoke coming from the brick chimney and the windows stared back at us like dark, unseeing eyes. The place was obviously vacant.

"God," I said to Alice, "Imagine fishing here and writing books in a house like that, a hideaway on this lonely river, no phone, no radio, no Vietnam War news!"

Alice stared at me, then asked Robin, "When do the salmon start to run?"

"Very end of August and all September," he answered, "depending on the big moon tides. But don't start dreaming, friends. That simple cottage is one of the oldest buildings on these islands. It belongs to a very wealthy man who lives in Vancouver. He's mad for salmon fishing. He's not up here now, of course, but, believe me, he will be when the big coho start to run. He would never even dream of parting with a treasure of a house like that."

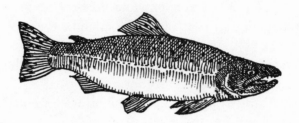

Coho salmon

3

In the Beginning

The Queen Charlotte Islands and the Tlell River had cast a spell over Alice and me. That lasted all through the winter of 1968-69. We waited through most of the following summer, then collected our rods, checked our reels, and eagerly flew west again with no idea where we would stay. This time, we arrived by floatplane at Masset, landing on the top of the north island, where we rented an old blue wreck of a car. It was the only one available in town, and we hoped we wouldn't have to sleep in it. We spent our first windy, rain-lashed spring night in the Singing Surf Motel.

When I asked about other accommodations on the islands, I was directed over to a house belonging to Dick Ward, the owner of the motel. He was a large, genial man with a wild shock of hair that was turning gray. He welcomed me in and offered me a beer, before he produced a large map and helped me understand the islands' ins and outs. He said there was good fishing on the Queen Charlottes, somewhere, every one of the 365 days of the year.

When I asked about the Tlell River, he said he and his friend, Teddy Bellis, a Haida Indian, were spending their time off in building a fishing camp down there. He added that he and Teddy would be happy to have us stay there the next night and to welcome us as their first guests, and he assured us we could bunk in there free. He admitted that there were none of the usual amenities yet, no electricity, no toilets, no running water, or food. But it was right on the river and the fishing should be good.

"Don't come too early," he laughed as he warned me, "Ted can't get there until nearly dark and that's when we'll start putting on the shingles above your heads. Don't worry, it'll be finished on time."

We fly-fished the Hiellen River on Graham Island's north end next day, where we took no salmon but released lots of good-sized cutthroat trout – except for the two we had for dinner that night before we checked out of the Singing Surf. It was raining hard when we ran for the car, threw our gear into the back seat, and headed south on the long, dark road hemmed in by a tall, straight forest. Alice counted more than seventy black-tailed mule deer caught in our headlight beams as they browsed along the edges of the clearing beside the road. Here the sunlight had created lush grazing, which was totally lacking on the forest floor beneath the thickness of giant spruce.

As we approached the Tlell River, we could see a faint battery light through the trees. We slowed the car and turned in. We could hear the sound of hammering as we turned off the engine and stepped out into the steady downpour of rain. When we looked up at the light above us we could see the dark outlines of two men up on the roof of a new wooden structure, where they were pounding in shingle nails with determination.

"Who's that?" they called down to us, shielding their eyes in the glare.

"The Houstons," I called back to them.

"Oh," said one, and started climbing down the slippery rungs of their homemade ladder. Dick Ward, the owner of the Singing Surf, approached us, followed by the other man.

"We've been trying to shingle that roof on the bedroom as I promised you last night. But, hell, with all this rain, the new floor's wetter than the devil in there. Tomorrow, maybe, but I don't think you'll be able to use it tonight. This is my partner, Teddy Bellis."

We all shook hands.

"Yeah," Teddy laughed, "everything is soaking wet inside and there's no bed, no chairs, no nothin'."

"Is the fishing any good?" I asked them.

They turned and looked in the direction of the river too dark to see.

Teddy nodded, "The salmon should be running in on this tide, yeah, probably good tomorrow morning."

"It's like working in a shower bath up there," said Dick. They were both soaked to the skin. "Time to call it a day. We're going to drive back to Masset, dry out, and sleep."

"That's almost forty miles," said Alice. "Do we have to do that, too?"

"Nooo," said Teddy. "If I were you two, I'd go south down the road about four miles and see if you can sleep at the Baron's *schloss*. But you'd be best to come back and fish right here in the morning."

"Who's the Baron?" I asked him.

"Oh, he's a character who lives not far down the road. He takes in guests sometimes – if he's in the mood."

"He's got a kind of farm," Dick added. "There's usually a porch light on at his place. Just open his gate and drive in. He may fire a rifle at you, but don't worry, he'll aim above your heads. Be sure to close his gate after you. He's a hard old nut, and he hates it if you let his cattle go astray."

Teddy climbed the ladder and brought down their kerosene pressure lantern. "If the weather's any good, we'll finish that damned roof tomorrow night."

"Sorry, can't do it," Dick told Teddy. "I've got a date."

"Awh, you and your dates." Teddy laughed as they got into the cab of their truck and took a long drink each from the neck of a stubby bottle. They shouted "Goodnight," and wheeled out onto the road.

"This hard rain doesn't seem to bother them," said Alice. "I guess that's the way you'd come to think if you were born around here."

We started driving south along the shiny, newly black-topped asphalt road for about six miles before we saw a dim light burning on our right. On the other side of the road was the black Hecate Strait, stark except for a silver parade of breaking waves.

I nipped out, opened the gate, and carefully latched it closed after Alice had driven through. The Baron's house was unusual for Canada, for it was shaped like a small chalet in the Bavarian Alps. It was stained dark brown so that it was hard to see even in the headlight beams. The tall, dark wall of forest was close behind. We got out of the car aware of a big dog barking furiously inside – or was it out behind the house?

"Hello," I called.

No answer.

Feeling like a pair of burglars, we stepped somewhat nervously onto the porch.

"Hello?"

Again, no answer.

When I was almost at the door, I saw the silhouette of a short, barrel-shaped man standing rigidly erect in the shadows.

"Who are you? *Vat* do you *vant?*" the figure demanded without moving.

"Oh, hello," I answered nervously. "Dick Ward and Teddy Bellis, they aren't finished building the space where we intended to sleep. They said you might have a room for rent for us here."

"*Vat's* your names?"

"Houston," I answered, "James Houston. And this is my wife."

He opened the door behind him and his big German Pointer came lunging out at us.

"Down, down," he yelled and caught his growling dog by its heavy leather collar. "Take off your boots and come inside. It's a filthy night *ut der.*"

He lit a second dim lamp in the main room. "My name's Gerlof. Joachim von Zadora-Gerlof." He clicked his heels together and we shook hands.

"This is my wife, Alice," I said as formally as I could.

The Baron, bowing, took her hand and kissed it. "I'm sorry, my wife, Christine, is not here to greet you. She's gone down to Victoria to see a medical specialist. You're wet," the Baron said to Alice. "Your bedroom *vill* be that one. Dry up, then come and have a drink."

When we returned to the main room, he offered us the best of Scotch and some biscuits with deer pâté and sour pickles.

"Your name is James Houston?" he said. "I've just finished reading a book by a man named James Houston about the Arctic."

"There he is, the author himself," said Alice, beaming. We were pleased to hear that someone so far away had actually read *The White Dawn*, which was my first adult novel.

"You wrote that book?" he asked. "Well, this is good luck. I liked your book very much. Earlier I was up in Alaska trading sealskins," he said. "I know the Arctic country. But business there was too slow, no money in it. I came here and brought up my wife, Christine. I built this house with my own hands. I couldn't afford any help. There's no good help around here anyway. We have two children, a boy – he's asleep right now – and a girl. She's away at school off island.

"In the morning," the Baron told us, "I must feed the animals in the pasture and the geese. Then I *vill* go to the river with you and show you some of the best fish pools. You can try the one just above the bridge or down at the bent tree. It is too bad Christine is not here, but I *vill* make you a sandwich lunch with a thermos of tea."

We thanked him and said goodnight.

In the morning after breakfasting on his own fresh hens' eggs and bacon from his own pig, the Baron found me staring at a plaque on the living room wall.

"That is the ancient order of the Knights of St. John of Malta. I inherited that honor from my family."

"In what country were they?" I asked.

"Sweden, mostly, but I attended school in Germany. It was not easy getting away from that war." The Baron looked out the window, silent, seeming to be remembering a great many moments of the war. "Once I made my way down to Spain, but I was caught, arrested by the Spanish, and thrown in jail. I was stationed at Berchtesgaden at the end of the war.

"See that epaulet in the frame on the wall?" He pointed. "That belonged to Field Marshal Hermann Goering. I had the honor to tear it off his shoulder." I must have looked astonished but he waved a dismissive hand and went on. "I spent time interrogating refugees. After that, I immigrated to Canada. I came here, hoping I *vould* not get bothered. Hoping my luck would change."

Alice looked at me. "We've got to go or we'll miss the fishing."

"We'll be back around four or five this afternoon," I told him.

The big dog had turned friendly and was nuzzling Alice and me in all the wrong places. Gerlof shouted harsh military commands in German. The dog hung its head and backed away in fear.

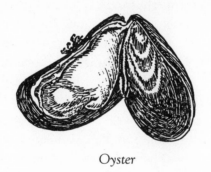

Oyster

4

A Place to Dream

In time, Alice and I got to know Baron Joachim von Zadora-Gerlof and his warm and charming wife Christine. She was an Austrian Countess. During the early seventies, Alice and I were among the few guests to stay with them. Joachim, short and plump, with a clipped white moustache and a bristling shock of white hair, will forever be a European. One of his many concerns was how he could possibly increase his tourist numbers, for he needed the money, but at the same time he hated the expensive and the all-too-revealing business of advertising his own particular hideaway.

The Queen Charlottes had a lot of typical hippies in the seventies, most of them from south of the border escaping the Vietnamese War. The very thought of "those people" was the greatest scourge of Gerlof's life. He hated to have them come anywhere near him, or even to see them drive past his chalet.

Pierre Elliott Trudeau was one of Canada's most memorable Prime Ministers. I greatly admired him for helping to save Canada during the 1970 October Crisis when René Lévesque had lit Quebec afire and his campaign to separate was on the rampage. About that time, Trudeau decided to marry Margaret Sinclair, a beautiful, young, British Columbian socialite from Vancouver.

The Trudeaus came north to the Queen Charlotte Islands to officiate at the opening of the new, small Haida museum, marked by the return of some early Haida materials from the National Museums of Canada. The Prime Minister's Office had made island inquiries and asked David Phillips, a local Masset resident, to arrange accommodations for the Prime Minister's party of six. David thought that Gerlof's Old World, Bavarian-type *schloss* would make a perfect setting for such important visitors. And, of course, the Trudeaus' stay would be the making of the Gerlofs' fortune, with publicity for their place across Canada and beyond.

So David, a perennial bachelor who later would run for Mayor of Masset, and some long-haired friends roared down the road to Gerlof's, thrilled to be the bearer of such overwhelming news. When they arrived, David and his pals leapt out of their ancient truck and tried to open the tricky lock on the gate. After fumbling with the latch, David climbed heavily over Gerlof's cattle gate and began to trot up the Baron's private lane to carry the joyful word to Countess Christine and her husband.

He stopped dead in his tracks when he heard a heavy deer rifle fired into the air from the porch of Gerlof's house. "Get off my land, you hairy bastards," Gerlof is said to have roared – although David said later that he'd forgotten the names the Baron had actually called him, for he was desperately busy climbing back across the fence.

As a result of this early encounter, the fabled Trudeaus stayed far away from Gerlof's place. David borrowed some special original Haida art, some decent rugs, glasses, plates, and cutlery and anything else that he could find, and decorated the log house at the end of Beitush Road, and then worked out a way to lend it for the grand occasion. Christine Gerlof always remembered missing a visit from the Prime Minister and his new wife with a disapproving shake of her head.

The tourist business at the Gerlofs' *schloss* never did become a big success, and Gerlof finally departed just like the historical wave of German immigrants who had tried to farm the Charlottes long before him. But it is widely rumored that the man we called "The Baron" went to Switzerland and struck it rich, in some quick, unfathomable way. He abandoned his place on the Charlottes and departed south for greener lands to enjoy his noble old age.

Gerlof usually thought of things a jump or two ahead of anyone. In my opinion, he had learned to think that way in order to survive the war. For example, one autumn day, I said to him, "We'd like to find a place of our own where we could stay a length of time writing, drawing, and fishing."

"I *vill* show you the best possibility." He narrowed his pale blue eyes, then pointed down the river not far from the Tlell bridge. "There he is. That's Graham Dawson. He owns the green cottage," he whispered. "That's Dr. Hamish McIntosh fishing with him. Go ahead, wade out and ask Dawson now. You *vill* probably never get a better chance, so catch him in the river."

I waded out across the incoming tide, false casting as I edged toward them. When they glanced back at me, I said, "Good morning," and stopped casting, for it's not at all polite to move too close to another fisherman. The sky was gray and it was windless, with the river running smooth. I took a pace or two upriver, but remained within talking distance. "I've been told that you are Graham Dawson," I said.

No answer for a while as he coiled his line into his old-fashioned casting basket, looked at his friend, the doctor, then suspiciously at me. He made another cast. "Yes, Dawson here," he said.

"I've heard that you own that green cottage behind us by the bridge."

"Yes, what about it?" the doctor chimed in with his Scottish accent as he, too, moved slightly closer to me and made another cast.

"I understand you and your friends only stay here for the salmon season."

"And come for the spring trout some years," added Dr. McIntosh.

I cast my fly again. "I'm an author and I love it here."

They glanced at each other in disbelief, but made no answer.

"I was wondering if I might rent your cottage, Mr. Dawson, during the off season, the late winter and early spring." I cast as the doctor did, toward a tail swirl in the water. "I think it would be a wonderfully quiet place to finish a book."

Dawson looked upriver at me again and over his shoulder at The Baron, who was sitting stiffly on a large log on the riverbank behind me. Saying nothing, Dawson made another cast.

"Don Harvie from Calgary is a mutual friend of ours," I said. Don was involved with the Glenbow Museum when I created the glass sculpture *Aurora Borealis* for its main hall.

"Oh, yes," answered Dawson in a more friendly tone this time. "I'll be seeing him later this month in Montreal at a board meeting." He paused, "Yes, you can write to me. What's your name again? Oh, Houston, yes. You could write to me and I'll take your letter under advisement."

"Thank you, sir," I said. "Good luck." I waded out of the river, casting as I went.

"Did he agree?" The Baron asked me.

"I don't know," I answered. "Maybe."

Later, I received a letter from Graham Dawson saying that he had seen our mutual friend while in the east and that I would be welcome to use the cottage. No mention of rent was made. I wrote him by return mail, thanking him and saying that my wife and I would be making plans to return to the Charlottes in early March. I made no inquiry about rent.

On our way out to the Charlottes that year, we were invited to dinner at the Dawsons' house in Vancouver. It was large, with spacious grounds, and had a darkly Scottish interior that would have you think that Queen Victoria was about to come grandly down the hall. We met Graham's wife, Dorothy, and his fishing friend, Dr. Hamish McIntosh, with his wife, Lorna. During drinks, the men, both being veterans, were interested to know the Scottish regiment in which I had served during the war. Our wives got on as well together as we did.

Next day we flew north from Vancouver to Moresby Island on the Charlottes with its small airport at Sandspit, crossed over Skidegate Inlet, and moved into the little green cottage in blustery, wet snow weather. We enjoyed a wonderful spring. The writing went well and the trout fishing, with big cutthroats, was the best I'd ever known.

When the writing was finished, we headed off to Scotland. I asked Graham on the way through Vancouver what I owed him for the rent. He looked at me and laughed. "How about an Eskimo carving?" he answered. "You know a lot about carvings, so you select the one you think appropriate."

"There's nothing simple about a selection like that," Alice said while we were flying east. Even in those far-off days, there were wonderful museum-types and painful airport-types of Eskimo carvings, with a hugely different price range.

I telephoned Graham during the summer and said, "We're hooked on the Tlell River and plan to come out and do some autumn salmon fishing. Would you allow us to rent the cottage when you're not going to be there? I'll bring you out the carving to cover last year's rent."

"Fine," he said, "we'll hope to see you here in Vancouver on your way north."

I took Dawson a carving of museum quality, one whose price today would have shocked both of us. Graham came up that autumn with his friend, Hamish, for they, with others, largely doctors, had formed a small fishing club nearby, with their new quarters looking out on the Hecate Strait.

After a riotous cocktail hour and dinner there, we three men went out in the dark to water the horses – as servicemen of our vintage liked to say – and I raved about how much we appreciated the cottage and its closeness to the river. "If you're not using it, I'd like to rent it again next spring."

To my shock, Dawson said, "Houston, it sounds to me as though you'd like to buy the place."

"You're damned right, I would!" said I. "How much?"

His price sounded more than fair. "I'll take it," I called out, then stumbled over a log in my excitement, and so did Hamish.

"Just one thing," said Graham. "I'd like to be able to continue coming up for one weekend a year, sometime when I'd hope the salmon would be running. I'll take five thousand off the price if you'll agree to that, and we'll invite you to another fishing place we have on Lake Pennask."

"One weekend a year? Sure," I said. "That sounds fine to me."

And so a Vancouver lawyer drew up the papers. I wrote out a check, and the deal was done. That was a quarter of a century ago and it's worked out fine. Some Septembers we've remained there and all have had a great weekend fishing together. Other years, Alice and I would make short journeys into Alaska, or to the upper Skeena River, or down to visit friends in Vancouver or Seattle. That remote green hideaway in the middle of nowhere soon became – in winter, summer, spring, or fall – the most important annual zigzag in our much-traveled lives.

Not long ago, I caught Alice doing a dance step in the kitchen in early autumn and I asked, "What's that about?"

"Oh, it's just being back in the cottage," she laughed, "being close to the river again."

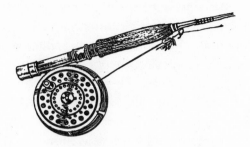

Fly rod and reel

5

In the Middle of Nowhere

We have owned our fishing cottage since the mid-seventies and our going there each season is joyfully anticipated. When the shad run in the Connecticut River is over and the pleasantly cool spring weather of New England begins to heat up, I start to dream of other non-hot, non-humid climates that I know, and of another river, this one on the Northwest Coast of Canada, a whole continent away.

Now, as veterans, we prepare ourselves for our journey west by driving together to a store called Fin and Feather in nearby Rhode Island and excitedly buying perhaps two dozen new, old-fashioned, feathered flies, the very kind I used to tie more than a half century ago: Brown Hackle, Royal Coachman, Trout Fin, and the like. We'll have to wait until we reach Vancouver or Victoria before we can find the Umpqua flies we'll need. Oh, yes, we'll want a dozen new, nine-foot, tapered leaders, too. But in spite of all the visual temptations, we won't buy much more equipment. Lord, no! We're both of Scottish descent and feel that we've got all the fishing gear we'll ever need – good, light, graphite salmon rods and even lighter trout rods in sturdy cases with the right weight reels to match. Why, hell, every fisherman knows good equipment only improves with age. I wish that could be true of humans also.

Finally, on a much anticipated morning, usually well before sunup, we prepare to depart from Stonington. Having removed the best of our sentimental household treasures (not worth that much, but almost impossible to replace), we phone our house sitter, throw the bolts, and carefully set the burglar alarm. Then just before leaping into our loaded car, we shout, "We're off, dear friends!" in hope that our best friends and nearest neighbors, who loosely surround our old eighteenth-century house in Stonington, will hear us and roll over in their beds, wake their partners, take a pill, and find some way to celebrate our annual, pre-dawn departure.

We choose to go by way of Boston, clearing customs in Toronto, then flying west across the continent. That flight arrives too late to fly on to the Queen Charlotte Islands, recently renamed Haida Gwaii by the Haida people. That delay always causes us to remain a day or two in Vancouver. This is in no way a hardship, for Vancouver is truly one of the grandest cities in all of North America and we have good friends living there. There is a colonial, British air about the place (you can find kippers for breakfast and tea is served at four) and today the shops have wonderful Northwest Coast Indian and Inuit art. The restaurants, once very dull, are now spectacular. In appropriate shops we buy other suitable coho salmon flies and build up our excitement. We know that the Tlell River is perfect for us river-wading fishermen. A few twelve- to fifteen-pound coho nicely grassed, as the Scots say, meaning without the help of a hand net or a guide, and caught using only the lightest tackle and the smallest flies, will set us dancing for the rest of the year.

For this second leg of our journey, we rise early, have breakfast, and taxi from the hotel to the nearby Vancouver Airport. We check in and hurry to the one and only airline that flies north. It's an hour-and-a-half flight along the Coast Mountains, one of the world's highest and most spectacular snow-capped mountain ranges. Then the flight takes a seventy-mile jig west out over the Pacific to the old military airstrip – now much improved – at Sandspit on South Moresby Island, and we land in a different world. We board a shaky bus heading to the inlet, and round the peaceful shoreline leading to Alliford Bay in hope of crossing on a British Columbia government ferry. It's Indian-manned, small but sturdy. However, the ferry crew always takes an hour off for lunch, exactly coinciding with the time that the airport bus arrives with passengers hopping up and down, so eager to cross north to Graham Island where almost all of the population now live.

But relax, this is another world you've entered, a place where you have lots of time to talk to friends you meet again in the line of cars or trucks. Who cares if the weather is misty, bright, or raining as you cross the inlet? Just wrap yourself in the blueness of the mountains. Watch the soaring flights of the geese, the eagles, and the ravens before you dock at Skidegate Landing, on Graham, the northernmost of the 150 islands that make up the long, thin archipelago of Haida Gwaii.

Once there, we hurry to retrieve our slowly dying island station wagon. We kick the tires. We peer through the foggy windows of the damp and mildewed interior, then try the key to see if it will still work in the lock. Our car sullenly resists because of the long season of winter rains and rust. Forget rain. Who cares about a little dampness? Once you're fishing, who minds if it rains or shines? I go back and struggle to open the rear hatch of the station wagon, then reach in and grab two hand-tall Sitka spruce that are growing there and show them to Alice before I throw them away from the places they've grown in the earthy carpeting on the floor. This is normal, healthy stuff for the Charlottes. The dampness during those soggier winter months is said to provide tree growth here that is greater and stronger than in any other place in North America, some say the world. Anything that's got the will to live will flourish in this cool, damp, island climate that is endlessly warmed by the Japan current, but not warmed enough to melt the summer snows off the long, central spine of the Mosquito Range of mountains.

The moon is waxing and we talk excitedly with old friends about the trout and salmon they have observed schooling in the estuaries. Late in the season, a lot of these will swim up the river to pass our small green cottage. We hope they'll move in daily, a few hundred on each tide, without doing it all in a rush on some night when the river has been grossly swollen by rain.

We go into the local store and the newer Skidegate Haida Gwaii co-operative to stock up and buy fishing licenses – not nearly as homey a task as buying them from old Mrs. Richardson in the early days when she was almost our nearest neighbor. We can never remember what we had enough of last year in the cottage, so we make lots of strange purchases like chutney, soy sauce, flashlight batteries, and toilet paper. Every year we are reminded that prices are wicked on the Charlottes compared to costs on the Lower Mainland. The car soon sags with food and Hochtaler or Schloss Leiderheim dry white wine from British Columbia's Okanagan Valley, jug wines that are reasonably priced and go down nearly as well with salmon as the Chilean and Californian imports do. We fill up with gasoline. Sold by the liter now, it nevertheless costs an awful lot.

As we drive north on the one main island road, we cut through black spruce shadows and bright patches of sunlight, and frighten two bald eagles off a road-killed deer. I start breathing deeply, smelling the trees and longing for the hideaway.

Tlell stretches for several miles along the handsomely repaired logging road now called the Yellowhead Highway, which was named after a fast-flying flicker and one of the earliest and most famous Iroquois Rocky Mountain guides with an eastern company of explorers. Tlell has been declared an unincorporated (all but invisible) village. Left behind is moldering evidence of ancient houses of the Haida chiefs. Wooden houses, like totem poles, last only about a hundred years in the heavy rain.

After half an hour's driving, Alice says, "Let's stop and hear the local news."

We turn into Wiggins Road and hop out at the home of our friends. We hear all the local scuttlebutt about the fishing, Haida happenings, new outrageous love affairs, old feuds, huge winter tides, and the cold violence or damp softness of last winter's weather. Our friends most generously insist we take with us some backstrap, venison filet mignon off a deer.

Knowing we'll talk with them tomorrow, we set out again and soon see the white wooden bridge that crosses the Tlell River. Just a fly cast away stands our house at the start of Beitush Road, first cut by earlier German settlers. We open our white gate and squish along our path of deep moss. The ground around our house is covered with fallen pine cones. On dry days, it can be like walking on a bowl of Grapenuts cereal, crunching cones at every step. Two red squirrels are leaping around between the forest and our house. They're smaller and seem perkier than our eastern red squirrels, and they have distinctive red tufts growing off the tops of their ears. We tread very cautiously as we step up onto our front porch, for it has long fed an army of carpenter ants that come out in droves to sun their wings just one day a year. The porch used to sag and creak beneath our weight, but it feels better now after a local hippie's son, a self-trained carpenter, fixed that problem several years ago. I poke around the back of the house and find the hidden key, then peek through the window before I unlock our red front door.

We begin to stagger back and forth retrieving our luggage, then all the bags of food and drink. Thoughtful friends of ours have been in ahead of us to start the fridge and freeze water in the ice cube trays. One of them has placed a pure white slab of fresh-caught halibut on our cutting board beside a bowl of fresh-laid eggs. Some neighbors, eh? Some country!

We sit for a moment, staring out the window, wondering again at the soothing quality of this tidal river. We're home. Yes, home. I think, *put up the fly rods, hang out the hip boots and the waders, shake out the rain gear, open the fly boxes. Tomorrow morning's coming soon.*

There's a damp smell of must and mold inside the cottage. A shriveled mouse carcass lies in a trap, its round black turds scattered casually around it. A large and lively spider is busy wrapping up a big blue fly, tightening it in its web in the corner of the windowsill. We fling open the doors to let in the rich aroma of spruce and ferns.

After unloading the car and checking the amount of water in the well, I'm drawn away from going upstairs or even looking in the fish room. I want so much to go outside and feel again the soft, familiar yielding of the moss beneath my boots. I look around for delicious King Bolitus mushrooms the size of golf or tennis balls – our small property is famous for them. Then I check to see if the deer

that nimbly hop our fence each night and the flights of migrating
fish crows have cleared all the Saskatoon berries off our one large
bush – no, not quite. Alice is a gardener, but she doesn't have a
garden at Tlell because we're almost never there when that garden
should be planted. Mercifully, we have generous island friends, good
fisherfolk, and gardeners who revel in the rich soil and abundance
urged on by the winter rains.

Inside the cottage, we attack the few remaining problems to be
solved. First, turn on the electric pump – it's comforting to redis-
cover that you have tap water, a working toilet, and a shower.
Next, turn on the electric heat and melt away the winter's dampness that seems to grip the inside of the cottage. Fill all the shelves
again with this and that: HP sauce, granola, coffee, and much
more. It will be at least three weeks before we shop again. Grate-
fully, we discover a large box of Huqwa tea left there by one of last
year's guests. Finally, we shake our sheets and blankets hard to rid
them of tiny spiders, then put on our shaggy-looking sweaters and
corduroys, stretch, then stand together in our slippered feet, admir-
ing the river as it flows just below us along the bank, less than a fly
cast from the window. Of course, no salmon are coming up yet, but
they soon will be.

I'll wait until the next morning before unpacking my sketch-
books and watercolor boxes, the pens, pencils, paperclips, lined
paper, erasers, Scotch tape, scissors, reference books, and more.

Alice removes the glass bits from two bottles of tonic water that
exploded in the cupboard last winter during an unexpected freeze.
Then, while she begins to sweep the pine needles off the porch and
to shake out our musty seat cushions and pillows, I slip our fly rods
out of their cases and lay them on the two wide, thick cedar planks
that form our dining table. Beside them, I can spread the reels,
lines, leaders, and fly boxes while still keeping my eye on the river.
The two joints of each of our trout rods fit together smooth as silk.
The reels set in their footings and I screw them tight, then draw
out each line thick and heavy, forward weighted to allow us to make
long casts. I attach new nine-foot, one-pound-test leaders.

"What kind of a fly do you want to start with?" I call to Alice.

"Oh, get one from my fly book," she answers, still flogging the blankets on the porch. "One of those hand-tied gifts from Robin, an Umpqua. Yes, a new one, with its gold-washed hook."

I tie on a Size 8 hook using my best knot, then go through the same operation with my rod, fastening on a small Brown Hackle. It's not a new fly, but it's still in good condition. I touch up the point of the hook with the sharpening stone. Alice asks me to clear the table of fishing gear and open the wine. We have the delicious choice of fresh venison or halibut for dinner.

Brown Hackle

6

Histories and Mysteries

Of Canada's ten provinces and three northern territories, British Columbia – shortened to B.C. – is easily the most beautiful and versatile. Its whole extensive thousand miles of coastline is edged by the Pacific Ocean, which gives much of the province a soft, lush, salty ocean smell, particularly in its southern reaches near the Strait of Georgia at the southern end of Vancouver Island amongst the San Juan Islands where it borders Washington State. North, beside Alaska and the Yukon Territory, and far inland there are huge, rugged spines of snow-capped mountains.

My favorite portion of B.C., of course, is the Queen Charlottes, that graceful green archipelago of 150 islands that have risen about

eighty miles (just over one hundred kilometers) beyond the mainland, west of the port of Prince Rupert located at the wide estuary
of the Skeena River. The British named them after Charlotte, the
wife of King George III. The Americans defiantly called them the
Washington Islands. These days, the Queen Charlotte Islands are
starting to be known as Haida Gwaii, the ancestral Haida Indian
name. Today, they stand as Canada's most westerly group of islands,
with nothing but the mighty Pacific Ocean rolling between
Graham Island and Japan.

Archeologists have discovered that a much earlier culture once
lived on these islands long ago. They left little but small flint tools
and firepits as evidence of their ancient presence here. Much later,
the Haida, as part of a group of Northwest Coast people, seem to
have appeared, probably using some kind of sea-going vessel to
follow the Pacific Rim and thence offshore onto this fertile chain
of islands warmed by the Japan Current. In the Haida oral tradition,
it is remembered that those earlier, less sophisticated people were
willing to marry into the Haida Raven clan, and Haida men, in
times of female shortages, were allowed to accept these women
from the older culture. But Haida women, it is said, were forbidden
to join the camps as wives of the earlier people. This practice of
intermarriage or some other unknown events caused the earlier
island inhabitants to disappear.

The Haida themselves gave every indication of being a relatively sophisticated people when they arrived on these islands of
Haida Gwaii. We know that they carried with them a superior
sense of design. Unfortunately, their earliest designs were usually
created in wood, and only a few made in hard stone have survived.
The few stone carvings that have been found, those created over
several thousands of years, had been made with the elk horn pick
and hammer technique. They had forms that were similar to
present-day formalized concepts of Haida art, displaying the ovoid
curve and other highly stylized features of design. Later, various
Haida poles were noted in the journals of sea captains who first
visited these islands in the 1780s, and a few drawings were made
of them by seamen at that time. They also noted that the Haida

practiced painting on their houses and canoes, on masks, frontlets, and boxes.

Stone hammer

Haida have elaborate myths and legends. Over the years, in the absence of a written language, they have depended on their art and storytelling to carry their complex culture forward, to record their history so that it would be passed down to their future generations. The belief in supernatural, physical, and mental exchanges between the humans and the animals showed their basic belief in the close connection between the animals and the Haida nation.

It is believed by some that the Raven clan came to these islands countless centuries ago from the north, following around the Pacific Rim to the Aleutian Islands, and entering Haida Gwaii through Alaska. The Raven clan were the first Haida group to arrive, and brought with them weaving skills and the awesome power of story-telling. The families of the Eagle clan are said to have come in their long dugout canoes from the south and to have dominated the southern reaches of these many islands. They may have arrived some time later than the Raven clan, but they are said to have brought with them the songs and dances, as well as their superior creative carving skills. For the most part, these two clans have survived and flourished together to such an extent that it became a social rule agreed by the chiefs that any person from one or the other clan must marry a person from the opposite clan. This reduced the chances of inbreeding and of war.

Women, to some extent, held the upper hand. This was a matrilineal Haida society, for the children followed in their mother's family lines instead of the more common, almost worldwide practice, where children of a marriage follow in their father's family line. In the Haida system, the mother's brother, the uncle, played a vital role in teaching her sons the ways of their clan.

It is said that the first very small scraps of iron, useful in creating arrowheads, had reached the Haida through distant Siberian sources trading in the north, as it had with the Tlingit Indians in southern Alaska. We can only speculate how eager that must have made the Haida to contact and trade with other strangers bearing pieces of this magical hard material.

We know that the next people to discover Haida Gwaii were explorers trying to map the globe – the Spanish, English, French, Portuguese, and, in time, the New Englanders – sailing there from around Cape Horn. These crews were impressed when they saw the boldly decorated Haida houses, totems, and huge canoes, but most especially by the beautiful sea otter capes that their chiefs wore. The Haida were at first willing to give these to the visiting sea captains as a token of their friendship, and the chiefs and captains practiced the important habit of adopting each other's name to ensure their safety on board ship or in the houses on shore. The result of that early practice is still evident in some of the Haida names today.

When these foreign ships continued on across the Pacific to the important Chinese trading ports at Canton and Macao, the sea otter pelts that they brought with them were a stunning revelation to the wealthy Chinese, and to the traders. The Mandarins in the north so desired these warm, impressive pelts to trim the double and triple layers of the heavily embroidered silk costumes they wore in their cold country that they would trade almost anything for them, and that fact changed almost everything for the Haida.

An all-important sea otter trade was begun. Foreign ships' captains sailed into the coastal bays to trade with the Haida chiefs who had built their individual houses or small clusters of houses on the beaches, for the Haida relied on the sea to provide them with all the food they needed, and turned their backs on the land. The Haida traditional method of transportation has always been by sea. They had canoes – war canoes, freight canoes, fishing canoes, small women's canoes, and children's canoes. The ocean was almost everything to them, more important than their ownership of land, which was mainly used to provide wood for their houses, their canoes, and the creation of poles. And, of course, the land was the source of an endless supply of firewood, in addition to providing berries and game in season. But the constant, over-riding importance of seafood caused the Eagle and the Raven village chiefs to select an area of the sea that usually lay out before their houses and to declare it exclusively theirs for fishing. They claimed a certain distance that was as far as the eye could see to the horizon, and the specified area to the south and to the north.

This abundance of easily gathered food from the sea that their servants dried and stored in boxes for use over the winter gave these household chiefs the leisure time to contemplate and commission artist craftsmen to create artforms of the highest levels of perfection. In medieval Italy, art was encouraged in much the same way by the popes, doges, and noblemen.

Goat horn spoon

Famous artists were hired by chiefs of the Northwest Coast to come, be housed and fed, and receive other rewards for staying a year or more while they carved extraordinary poles on orders from the chief. He, in turn, would indicate exactly which animals and supernatural beings should appear on a commissioned pole to remind visitors of his proud historical family order. The large cedar poles were often carved as house poles to be attached to the house so that all those entering or leaving would do so through the ancestral animal's mouth. Sometimes poles were carved to the height of two men to be used as mortuary poles that would support on top a cedar box into which the dead were folded. Such original burial poles may still be seen standing on the small southern island of the Charlottes' group called Ninstints. It has also been known as Skung Gwaii or Red Cod Town, or Anthony Island.

The sea otter trade brought with it many new and useful tools – iron chisels, saws, and hatchets for carving, crooked knives and harpoon points, cord nets, foreign blankets, clothing, and above all copper, which the Haida valued for its luster, malleability, and glowing beauty. They valued it far more than they valued gold or silver. "Coppers" were hammered into the shapes of shields and were about the length of a man's arm. The Haida looked upon such shields as large banknotes of greatest worth, which were given names as they passed from one owner to another and acquired ever-increasing value. Examples of the names given are "47 slaves" or "5,000 blankets." They were accumulated riches essential for a chief to give away at important potlatch feasts, whether a chief was paying off his debts or avenging himself against some rival chief by showing off his greater generosity and wealth. In other words, the Haida chiefs had developed kingly practices not unlike our own, or indeed our own competition in throwing more lavish weddings than the Joneses. Among the Haida, the potlatch was sometimes called "feasting with mine enemies."

When the sea otter trade had run its course, the ships' men left behind such ravishing sicknesses as tuberculosis and venereal diseases, and a serious addiction by the Haida to our trade rum. This was followed by the gold rush of 1851 where as many as eight or ten three-masted, square-rigged ships could be seen anchored in Gold Harbour on the West Coast of the Charlottes. The wild prospecting was not a financial success, but it further disturbed the original vestiges of the Haida way of life. Late in the century the worst thing of all happened. Smallpox descended, wiping out whole communities. It is believed that 70 to 80 percent of all the Haida died as a result of these illnesses in the nineteenth century. The many Indian villages on the islands were soon abandoned, and their populations from the south fled to Skidegate, and from the north to Masset, where missionaries of various faiths were eager to convert the Haida. Land forts owned by the trading companies began to appear, as soon as they thought the Haida had been subdued enough to make it safe for them to live among them.

The British, then the Canadian governments had long believed that the trouble with the Haida was that they were determined to cling to their old animistic beliefs. So they encouraged German farmers to immigrate to the Charlottes and join with the foreign missionaries to try and turn these people into Christian farmers. It seemed to work at first, but then the German farmers found that even they, experts though they were, could not profitably farm the Charlottes for reasons of high import and export costs and soggy pasturage. The missionaries stayed on long enough to all but eliminate the Haida language and change many other Haida values. Then the missionaries, discouraged by each other, began to disappear.

World Wars I and II passed, and then the draft notices for the war in Vietnam caused a number of young Americans to flee across the border. Some of them had heard about the remoteness of the Queen Charlotte Islands, the slim chances of anyone bothering them, and the overwhelming abundance of wild food – salmon, deer, ducks, and geese – and free wood with which to build their temporary (and often highly imaginative) houses, and to heat them. They came tumbling into Haida Gwaii, found the magic mushrooms, raised their own marijuana, and stayed on, many of them to this day, after marrying young Canadian women.

Then a great ruckus occurred over the savage clear-cutting of forests in various parts of the Charlottes, especially Lyell Island. This caused the hippies to scream in protest and the Haida to rise up and defend the southern portion of the islands. Various logging roadblocks appeared. Drum-beating protesters, including Haida elders, defied the logging companies' permits to cut. The police were frustrated. With care, they removed the hand-to-hand chain of protesters that included old Haida women. In the end, those arrested were released. Staunchly supported by Canadian lawyers and the world press, the Indians immediately formed a force effectively run by three very vocal Haida. Negotiations continued in

Victoria until Gwaii Haanas Wilderness Park on South Moresby was established. This new park, where no logging will ever occur, contains about 15 percent of the southern portion of Haida Gwaii. Many persons here believe that the next project the Haida will undertake will be to gain the fishing rights around the entire archipelago. The whole future of the Charlottes remains a mystery, but the islands feel the effects of Haida Indian power. Besides the right to create a park on the southern islands, the Haida won a huge grant of $38 million.

The whole question of first people's rights will remain a thorn in the side of Canada until entirely new arrangements can be made. Who came here first is even now in serious question, with the discovery in the USA of a dozen ancient European-style skeletons. My belief is that we are all Canadians together in this country of ours, some rightfully – and some wrongfully – receiving far more benefits than others. Until we can come to some kind of consensus and truly become equal partners, Canada will continue to have a serious ongoing problem that will weaken our image around the world.

Raven screen

7

Bridge Cottage

Our small green cottage, according to the local historians, was built in 1928 for the legendary Mr. Dyson who planted the great oak at the fork of the road leading to Port Clements. This house, too, was sturdily planted on the river's bank that led down to the coastal waters. Even at that late date, the rivers and the sea were still the easiest and most commonly used forms of transport.

Mexican Tom, a folk hero in these parts, was the first to open an overland trail, while the Haida continued to round the island in their boats. The trail was eventually widened from a footpath to accommodate a horse and rig. As modern times approached, those who might use it decided to build a plank road north to the village of Port Clements on Masset Inlet. This was a major undertaking. The work was to raise log butts to the height that was considered necessary, taller in the hollows, then lay six-inch-thick cedar planking that was fourteen inches wide, not crossways, as we might do it now, but straightforward, two planks set three feet apart to accommodate a light vehicle's tires, like a set of railroad tracks. It did create the earliest attempt to make an inland island road.

When it rained, which on the Charlottes can be quite often, the narrow, saw-cut planks became slippery and the Model T Ford that Mr. Dyson owned would easily and often slip off. The solution was to carry as passengers a pair of hearty loggers who could lift this horseless carriage back up onto the plank road. In every sense, in those days you wanted light traffic. Today, if you drive slowly along the much more recently constructed road just north of our place on the Tlell, you can look down to your left, and there below you will see the last remnants of that earliest plank road.

It seems to Alice and to me that almost everyone on the Queen Charlotte Islands, still here or now elsewhere in the world, claims to have lived at some time in our cottage. Well, hell, why not? We've heard that the hippies used to sunbathe naked on our front moss lawn. That may have inseminated the house and grounds, for the poor old girl has clung passionately to her riverbank and her memories, refusing to slip away into this obstreperous tidal river, even though she's more than seventy years of age.

We have a cherry tree that bears no blossoms and a rhododendron that has thrived in our best patch of sunlight by the river gate. In the afternoon when the sun is warming the bush, we two have held competitions to see how many thumbnail-sized frogs we could count on the leaves. This is no easy matter, for each one of these tiny adult frogs seems differently colored, from shades of green to brown, to orange, and copper. These frogs, with their various forms of camouflage, cleverly match the leaves or buds of the rhododendron and are all but impossible to find in the moss or grass. The frogs in our garden in summer have complicated, ovoidlike designs like heraldic symbols that cannot fail to remind you of Frog, the communicator, a frequent subject of Northwest Coast art.

These small frogs love light or perhaps the promise of warmth from the sun, for if we leave a light on at night, we will in no time find that dozens of frogs have hopped up and squatted on our cedar plank porch as though waiting to be invited in. Even if they are not, several of them will somehow manage to hop inside, perhaps through the crack under the front door.

The Haida claim Frog is the communicator between the creatures of sea and earth. Frog in Haida myths and carvings has always been somewhat of an enigma to outsiders. Frog is a sub clan crest, but also Frog seems to have much to do with shamanism. Numerous rattles of the northern style show on their top, beyond the rattle's handle, a shaman said to be sucking power from a frog's tongue.

8

Salmon Fever

We decide to go to bed early and sleep long and peacefully, but I arise as usual at five, well before light. Oh, what a day this will be! I pull on thick socks and step into my short, rubber boots, then hurry through the pre-dawn blackness, pausing once to listen to the river. The thick moss beneath my feet feels soft and deep. It's squishy from the night's rain. The tide will soon be seeping up the river, bearing with it the first eager schools of grilse and trout. *Well, I think, the adult salmon will not run here for several hours. Oh, forget the salmon. This is the best time of my day for writing, a time, if there's ever going to be one, for serious work, a chance to put down early morning thoughts and enchanted dreams before the daylight weakens them.* That has been the thought that roused me, the one that drove me out of our warm bed.

I cross the small square porch and enter the hideaway, the little cabin that is my study. Closing the thick, cedar door behind me, I turn on the light and start the coffee. Settling down at my desk in the thinly padded, straight-backed chair, I pause again to smell the scent of the red cedar as it begins to blend with the smell of Colombian coffee. Moths would hate this hideaway of mine. But raw cedar in the morning seems to sharpen my senses. I count out and number ten pages of lined foolscap that I am determined to fill. I check my story outline, but it's already in my head. I angle all the pages to suit my awkward-looking, left-handed writing style and begin. I don't know how to use a typewriter. But, hell, wasn't every other author writing by hand not very long ago? Some of the best literature we possess was scratched out with goose quill pens long before some of Alice's rustable, breakable, irreparable typewriters, now worthy only as museum pieces. They've all been replaced by computers. Alice likes to try and frighten me when we're in this wilderness of ours by saying, "My electric typewriter's rusted and the letters 'M' and 'H' are stuck forever. Are you prepared to write those letters in by hand?"

Forget all that nonsense, my boy. You're on to Nootka Sound and John R. Jewitt and the taking of the ship Boston. *Concentrate on the feelings, the details and the violence in this book,* Eagle Song.

I study Maquinna's portrait and I start to write steadily for an hour before a movement in the forest catches my eye. I'm surprised to find it's light, and dawn is seeping through the trees. A small, plump doe has just hopped into our yard. She looks toward me for a moment before she drops her head and browses on some mushrooms. I've got five-and-a-half double-spaced pages written. That's not much, but for the first day here, it's not bad. I look at my rough outline for this chapter again. Just rounding out the character of Maquinna should more than fill the remaining paper. Then coffee and juice up to Alice and we'll go try the upper pool.

Wait! Look! Just along the Tlell, near the smooth-flowing bend of the river, a large salmon has leaped clear of the water, flashing its silver side at me before it flopped back with an audible splash. I wait and watch. Yes, it does it again, or was that a second fish? *Is this the first school of coho riding up on the morning tide?* I close my eyes and try to visualize the salmon, their elegant, dark backs, their shining sides flashing as they ride in fresh from the ocean. They're already four kilometers or over two miles above the estuary, with sixty more long, curving miles of river calling them to glory upstream. *Well, it will still be a while before the real run gets here. Why don't you settle down and finish up this key chapter.*

I return to the writing, but with a difference – I've drawn the draperies. But now, want to or not, I'm listening. I hear another tail strike the water harder, closer now. Slap! *That was a big one, and there's another. Oh, my God, am I going to let this main run pass?* I glance at my watch, and then the paper. *Only four pages to go. Awh, to hell with it, I'll finish them later.* I start up. Slap! I pull open the draperies and look out. Big, bright circles are spreading on the river just below the hideaway. I sit down determinedly and jerk the draperies closed. *There, only these few more pages, then maybe . . .* Slap, slap! *Jesus! There's a lot of salmon tailing going on out there.* I close my eyes and watch them in my mind's eye, sliding past the hideaway like half-seen ghosts riding the incoming tide while I sit here like a helpless Volvo crash dummy waiting for the action to start.

My determination snaps. "To hell with the book," I say aloud, throw down my pen, run out and around our cottage to the front porch where my fly rod and waders are hanging. On the way, I catch a glimpse of Alice. She's very slow to rise most mornings, but on days like this one she's too damned fast. I spot her with her blue bandana hiding her unbrushed hair, already up to her hips in the river. She's stripping line off her reel, making long, false aerial casts across the pool. Alice loves to sleep late every morning she can in civilization, but not on a morning like this, not on this river. I see her let her straight line flow with the tide as I struggle into my waders. I see a big rise that I hope is well beyond her casting range. But no. *She's good at long casts, but can she reach that fish before I even wet my line?*

I hoist the suspenders over my shoulders and pull on my fishing jacket and snatch my long rod off its wall pegs. Then, trotting down our path, I fling open the white gate, cross the road, and plunge down through the wet salal bushes toward the river's gravel bank. Zing goes Alice's reel.

Lord, she's already got one on, her rod bent almost double. It's got to be big by the way it's taking out her line. The fish circles the pool. Now she's hand-hauling in her line. The salmon jumps. It's big, all right, and bright, just in from the ocean. The fish turns and starts to make its first long run upriver, moving fast with the tide.

Now Alice is leaning on the fish, and she glances quickly back at me, laughs with delight. She is feeling the old excitement as she tries to slow down this fish by using the heel of her left hand to hand bump her reel. All the weight forward line is out and probably half her thin, strong, nylon backing as well. Now Alice is in a panic. So am I. She and this big fish are moving downstream. I don't cast my line, of course, for fear of tangling with hers if the fish turns.

"Don't let him get into the pilings," I shout.

The salmon slows its run, then turns back and runs straight toward Alice. That's about the worst thing that could happen. Alice is desperately hand-hauling in the line, trying to take up the slack while letting it fall in limp hanks into the river, then trying hard to reel it in before this fish circles or jumps again, before it starts its second run.

"Robin's Umpqua fly worked fine. There goes my fish again," she calls. "Is this leader new? Is it strong?"

Her reel sings as the big fish starts back again toward the old bridge pilings. Alice's new Sage rod bends almost double as she tries to slow the fish, tries to keep him in deep water away from the perilous snags. At least we're the only people on the river and she's got the whole pool clear for the fight. This fish may be more than twice the weight of her new, eight-pound tapered leader.

I'm worried Alice will lose this fish, so I try to think of something else. I sit down nervously on a large, gray bleached log and watch the last of the morning fog move down the river, rising to hide the tops of the tallest spruce before it fades and disappears. Alice is a good fisherman, but she can be overly cautious. Now that she's gaining control, she will take her time with this big coho. She'd like to beach this first big fish of the year, no doubt about that. The fog has now faded. We can see towering thunderheads, their edges turning pink in the morning sun before the west wind starts tearing them into pieces. The river has turned to molten gold.

"Don't overdo it," I warn her. "That hook will be working itself loose in that fish's mouth."

Alice has been playing this fish for about twenty minutes. She starts slowly backing out of the river and up onto the flat gravel beach. "Come and help me," she calls.

It's not the style to use a net or gaff for salmon on the Charlottes. If one fails to take a salmon or trout out of the river, we think that fish deserves to complete its journey.

There is another jump, another bright flash of silver as this salmon makes its last, strong run. Alice's reel gives a short scream, then slows. She waits, tight-lined and cautious, then begins to reel in all the backing and some of the green line as she edges farther up the beach.

"Don't hurry," I advise her. "Don't try to beach him until he turns over on his side, then reel in as you go carefully back into the river to be near him." It's more fun instructing your wife than writing books!

"Keep your line tight and point your boots out Charlie Chaplin style behind him. If he's quiet, reach down and slip four fingers under his gill, clamp your thumb down tight, then slide him quickly up the beach."

"He's heavy," Alice calls to me in a breathless voice when they're both well away from the river. She stops to admire the torpedo-shaped symmetry of this big salmon before she searches and finds a clublike beach rock and administers the *coup de grace*.

"Congratulations," I call to her. "He's a damn good fish." Then I hurry across the bridge to get a closer view.

"It's not a he. It's a she," Alice says, for she has popped a pair of bright orange eggs out from behind the salmon's anal fin. "Look, there's another good rise," she points. "This pool is all yours now, dear. I'm going to carry her up and brine her eggs to make caviar. We'll ask Noel and Barbara to dinner, and Benita and Borge and Bill Ellis and Fran, who can drive up from Skidegate together."

Alice lifts her fish by the gills. "Remember, dear, only one salmon allowed in our house at any one time. Be sure to release any you catch today." She gives me that *La Giaconda* smile of hers and whispers, "See you later."

Alice, carrying her rod and salmon with its tail trailing on the beach, disappears into the salal bushes. I continue casting, but nothing comes near my fly. Soon I hear the music of Vivaldi drifting softly down the riverbank, spreading its magic glory over the upper pool. I forget the fishing and lean against the log again, watching the smooth flow of the river and the effect of the morning sun as it strikes the tallest trees. Then I head back to Alice's better coffee and to admire her salmon, which she has neatly boned and split in two, besides preparing its eggs. Alice comes from a family of professors and biologists. Out of the window, I see a mature bald eagle come and land on a spruce branch that hangs out over the river. It's waiting for the tide to fall, watching for trout or smaller salmon that are exposed crossing the shallows of the ford.

Fish knife

9

The Bridge of Cries

The Tlell River has long borne the passage of fish, animals, bugs, birds, and humans. During the Ice Ages, in fact, much of the Queen Charlottes escaped glaciation, which makes it biologically unique. Scientists tell us that, as *The Canadian Encyclopedia* says, "there are numerous plants here found only on the Charlottes or in distant lands such as Iceland and Japan." But of all the living species around here, I would guess that none of us overviewers have enjoyed the river more than the ravens, the eagles, and perhaps the gulls.

The length of the Tlell River as it twists and turns through the mossy boglands like a shining snake measures well over sixty miles or 100 kilometers in length – and that's some snaky trick on this, the largest of all the archipelago's islands, which is only seventy-five miles long.

The only wooden bridge that crosses the Tlell is close to our house and offers the best view of the river as it flows south to north through a wooded wilderness without another single dwelling in sight. This bridge is repainted white every few years by the Department of Highways, and we're prepared to swear that the bridge acts as a sort of border, a demilitarized zone, a warning line to separate the territory of the eagles and the ravens. That doesn't mean that either fail to raid boldly across the bridge and enter into enemy air space. Indeed, they often do. But, believe me, you can see it makes the raiders nervous and uneasy. They know damned well when they've crossed onto the wrong side of the line. Yes, the northern, two-mile stretch of the river from our view to the Hecate Strait belongs to the white-headed, white-tailed bald eagles, while the southern reaches of the river are clearly controlled by ravens.

Here on the Tlell River, the bald eagles are our most majestic birds, sitting or soaring proudly as they survey their river kingdom with the turn of their snow-white heads. Young eagles, even when they are as large as their parents, still wear their immature head-dress of brown, and fly shakily with less assurance. These young eagles are aerial acrobats who will soar across the bridge into enemy territory and even dare to try and perch there. But soon an adult raven will appear, dive to land ominously close to the eagle, and before too long will be joined by a second raven. The immature eagles quickly get the message and go wobbling back through the air above the bridge to seek the safety of their own side.

Sometimes when the fish run is late and both these birds are desperately hungry, I've seen them land together on either side of a dead, beached salmon or part of a deer carcass and threaten each other, neither daring to take a bite. Then, suddenly, together they turn and join forces to drive off the new arrivals, half a dozen big, aggressive black-backed gulls. But normally the ravens and the eagles do not suffer hunger on this river because there is usually plenty of food to satisfy everyone, except perhaps those ever-hungry gulls.

The eagles within our view are a contemplative lot that enjoy sitting in a towering spruce alone or in a pair, twisting their heads to stare in both directions along the river. When they've had their breakfast, they just relax, enjoying their domain. They have several special perches closer to the water near our cottage, lower perches that they use when they plan to make a dive for fish. Bald eagles are not at all like osprey, gulls, or ducks, birds with oil in their feathers. In this respect eagles are more like blue grouse or domestic chickens, vulnerable to water. Oh, they're hunters, all right. We watch them swoop down and grasp a live salmon in their talons. Sometimes their prey weighs more than they do and, unable or unwilling to unlock their needle-sharp claws, the eagles will almost be dragged under. Only then, after they have been nearly drowned, will they – soaking wet and looking more like bedraggled chickens – swim toward shore with a flopping dog paddle. If the eagle is successful, it will hop on one foot, dragging the squirming salmon across the shallows of the rocky river to eat the best of it on the shore, leaving the head and tail for the always hungry ravens and gulls.

Their close neighbors, the ravens, rarely go in for crazy stunts like that. They enjoy their meat, perhaps one might say, a little ripe or even, like Limburger cheese, a little high. Ravens follow the Pacific salmon farther up the river where the fish spawn, turn red to purple, grow thin and then die. Both eagles and ravens eagerly wait for these tasty fish remains left behind by nature to fatten them for winter, and they are joined by the quickly assembling gulls and sometimes by black bears.

Herring gull

Eagles, American bald eagles – all kinds of good and bad words have been said about these birds. This eagle, *haliaeetus leucocephalus*, is the very symbol of democracy throughout the United States. This is also the supernatural Haida eagle on their totems. And how many other eagles have, from the days of ancient Rome, ruled the world's heraldic roosts? There have been the double-headed eagle that reigned on the crests and flags of imperial Russia, the German eagle, the Polish eagle, and that dramatic snake-snatching eagle on the Mexican flag.

Once when I was fishing for salmon with our Calgary friend, Don Harvie, wading in the river we experienced a huge downfall of rain. The whole surface of the river was lashed into a white frenzy, and fly-casting at that moment was impossible. Fortunately, we were fishing in the upper pool close to the Tlell bridge, and we quickly scrambled in under its protective cover and watched the downpour wavering in silver sheets.

We had not been there for long before the rain began to slacken. Out of the dark woods on the riverbank came a small white poodle, soaking wet, disoriented, and looking, as we had, for someplace to escape the rain. Searching for its owners, it sniffed the ground. As we watched, this small lap dog looked up, then dashed toward us.

Suddenly, we saw a mature, white-headed eagle swoop down from the protective branches of a Sitka spruce. Fanning its wings and spreading wide its white tail feathers, it put on its brakes, and with yellow-footed claws thrust forward, it came in, adjusting its wing flaps for the attack. The white poodle, perhaps feeling the fanlike breeze from the eagle's pinion feathers just above him, sensed the danger and dashed toward us.

We both thought the dog a goner. But the eagle, realizing that it would have to fly into and under the dark, traplike bridge, saw us as well and decided to break off the chase. It threw its whole weight backward. The magnificent power of its wings went into reverse. Then, like a helicopter, it rose into a vertical climb that allowed it to clear the bridge, then disappear into the haze of falling rain. The small, wet dog sat trembling close beside us, nervously looking out and licking its chops.

"Phew! That was close," said Don.

I've always thought it a sheepherder's myth when I've heard or read accounts of eagles snatching farmers' lambs, but since that day I've been a believer.

Bald eagle

In the lower forty-eight United States of America, the bald eagle was once plentiful. Then this grand bird all but disappeared, pushed farther and farther west by the relentless spread of civilization. But on the far Northwest Coast of Canada and in Alaska, the bald eagle continued to flourish because of the scarcity of humans and the almost year-round abundance of seafood.

The Europeans coming into British Columbia, which they called New Caledonia more than a century ago, were Scots – and also English, Irish, Germans, French, Chinese, Japanese, Italians, Scandinavians, Russians, and a sprinkling of other immigrants – and were great meat eaters. They took up ranching beef and sheep, raising poultry and pigs, and growing grains, fruits, and vegetables. In most parts of the province they could usually catch all the salmon they wanted, for the spawning run of the salmon often extends hundreds of miles up a number of rivers from the coast. Any man could pretty well sustain his family on the natural abundance of seafood and venison, wild birds' eggs, and berries from the forest. Of course, they traded a lot among themselves.

Unlike the Indians, however, these newcomers felt that they needed a few civilized things that could only be bought with money: twine for nets, iron nails, tin buckets, fish hooks, kerosene lamps, cloth for their clothing and bedding, boots, and above all, guns and ammunition. Trapping was never worthwhile on the Queen Charlotte Islands, and the once valuable sea otters had been utterly exterminated by the time white settlers arrived. So how were these settlers going to get the cash they needed? The sheep-raising German immigrants were among the first to try serious farming out on the Charlottes. They soon reported that they saw the white-headed eagles swoop down and try to grab their lambs. That was enough. "*Achtung, achtung!* We need help!" the islanders cried, and they started writing and dispatching citizens to Victoria, the seat of British Columbia's provincial government, demanding that officials put a bounty on the eagles. One dollar per eagle would be enough. The government agreed, provided the farmer sent in the eagle's feet – not just one foot, mind you. They were on to that trick. The government demanded two feet per eagle bounty. Two, if the reward was to be collected.

This political boondoggle went on for a number of years on the Charlottes, marked by the vastly greater number of small, .22-caliber rifles and cheap shotguns ordered at the trading stores, and a terrible slaughter of the eagles, so that the lambs could frolic undisturbed. But then a strange thing happened. Slowly the flocks of sheep began to die. From hoof rot, most say, brought on by the animals standing around in the flooded salt marsh pastures during the high moon tides. Finally, the bounty on eagles' feet was no longer paid.

I'm pleased to say bald eagles are back, and they're off the endangered species list now. They once more perch majestically and they look as wise as always. But the sheep and their shepherds are long gone. You can't blame the eagles, though, for sometimes mistaking little white dogs for those deliciously similar lambs.

I O

Raven, the Creator

There is a Haida Indian myth that declares the world first came into being on the islands of Haida Gwaii. Long ago, this assembly of rising mountains lay beneath the sea. It was Raven, the creator, who, when flying over the endless ocean through the utter darkness, decided to raise a rock. When he had done this, he landed there on what was to be the south end of Haida Gwaii. He caused the land to rise and spread north, growing into countless islands, large and small. Raven rose again and flew around and around this lonely place, looking at the snow-peaked beauty of the islands' central spine of mountains and its moon-shaped beaches backed by tall, dark forests cut through by shining lakes and curving rivers. It was impressive. But there were no animals, no birds, no fish, no humans, nothing.

Finally, as Raven flew over the long, sandy point of land stretching north that he called Rosespit, he saw an enormous clamshell lying on the beach. Curious as always, he flew down and landed by the giant clam. When he listened he could hear faint voices inside. With his powerful beak, Raven pried and partly opened up the clam. Out of it came five male humans, each of them no longer than your finger. They looked up in fright at this strange black bird, then fled away to hide in the forest. As they ran, they grew taller with each step, until, as they reached the protection of the newly protruding rocks, they found seafood, and grew as tall as men.

The reef named Ki'l on the south end of the Charlottes near Houston Stewart Channel consists today of several flat, exposed rocks. The early myths of Haida Gwaii declared that when no other land was showing in all the oceans of the world, a great supernatural being gained control and began to raise the rest of the dry world. When that work was done, he lay there quietly on the small rocks at the south end of Haida Gwaii near Ninstints. This supernatural being cleverly disguised himself as a mass of sea cucumbers and still observes the world in that form from there.

As the legend unfolds, Raven was still lonely in his dark world of sea, land, and air. When he flew near the Gwaii rocks, a barnacle shell called out to him, "Raven, Raven, there are women clinging just beneath this reef."

Raven flew north again to Rosespit and found the young men he had released from the clamshell. He urged them to hollow out a cedar log and shape it into a canoe, then demanded that they paddle south to meet with these strong young women, who, sure enough, were to be found beneath the reef. When they met, they sang and danced and made love together until they had peopled all the countless islands of Haida Gwaii.

Raven has done his work so well that nowadays when most travelers come to know of this remote chain of islands called Haida Gwaii, they long to see them – all of them. Some of the islands seem endlessly fog-hung in mystery, with a whole history that remains unknown to us. I have found that sometimes you can place your foot on an island and feel that no human has ever trod there before. Some ancient forests in Haida Gwaii show no signs of trails, for human paths so quickly disappear, hidden in tangles of deadfall and spreading alders, bushes that the big trees soon overshadow and destroy. For the most part, deer, bear, birds, and other smaller creatures do not live in these dense forests, but may use them as a hiding place, a safer place to rest. There is little food for them inside a forest. They prefer to forage along the wooded edges of the ocean beaches, around the lakes, or, like the elk, to live in the open pontoon marshes where the sunlight makes the food abundant.

Raven, it is said, was the one that used his shamanistic powers to lead the caribou that were said to have crossed over from the mainland on the permanent ice perhaps fifteen thousand years ago. They thrived on these islands until sometime early in the twentieth century. There were some smaller animals: river otter, marten, fisher, mink, and squirrels. Others such as the black-tailed mule deer, black bear, beaver, and raccoon were said to have been imported later, brought here by the Haida in their canoes to increase the amount of food and fur to sell to traders. The sea bird life around the islands was and is abundant.

Among the sea creatures that Raven created was the sea otter. This much sought-after creature had an adult pelt as long as your arms can stretch. These gentle, playful, and very photogenic animals thrived in the floating kelp beds that drifted in the bays and open ocean off the islands. Thrived, that is, until the sailors discovered that one pelt sold in China in the eighteenth century earned the equivalent of seven years of a British seaman's pay. Still, it's little wonder that the Haida have recently refused to have sea otters reintroduced around Haida Gwaii. Sea otters, whose pelts have minor value today, tear up fishermen's nets, which are now so costly to repair.

Sea otter

Male ravens, after mating, remain for the rest of the year a restless lot, good at vocal imitations of each other. Some of them seem especially gifted at mathematics. Early in the morning, semi-relaxed in the comfort of their own territory south of the bridge, they start their scholarly mental exercises. "Croak," calls the tenured professor. I check my watch. It's exactly 5:18 a.m. "Croak," answers his sleek female student from a tall tree two kilometers away. "Croak, croak," calls the professor. His student rearranges her feathers and clears her throat before she answers, "Croak, croak." The professor, in his most precise voice, calls "Croak, croak, croak," and his eager student quickly answers with exactly three well-measured "croaks." Now the professor ruffles his black robe and calls four times. After several minutes of panicky hesitation, his student answers, croaks one, two, three, then pauses for some time before adding the final fourth. The professor gives a distinctly different, perhaps pleased, academic grunt, then clearly demonstrates five measured calls. There is a very long pause. Then the rattled student screams three times in a much too rapid, high-pitched sequence, waits, and calls three more times before she leaps from her perch and flies away. "To hell with your ancient numerals, Professor. I'm going upriver and get laid."

I sit up in bed when I hear the old professor's feathers press the air as he flies fearlessly low between thick spruce branches and our window, heading south to catch that stupid student and teach her to count correctly. Here on the Tlell River in early morning, the whole environment throbs with education and quivers with the thoughts of procreation.

Out on the porch of the hideaway as the morning light increases, I watch a pair of mature eagles staring up at the female raven student as she does aerial acrobatics with a fleet of young males. The eagles call out scornfully at the wing-touching sky dance and call, "chat, chat, chat" in their strangely high-pitched soprano voices, so completely unsuitable for such regal-looking birds. The ravens, too, perched like Supreme Court judges, watch the act in their dignified black robes, appraising this sexual caper, each remembering its own wild youth and the lives of its clever parents that had lived before this white bridge had ever been built.

You don't have to wonder when early spring has arrived in British Columbia. You only need watch *Corvus corax*, the raven. Many Haida Indians believe that if you carefully listen to this big bird, you can hear it making accurate predictions of the weather. The raven has a deep, rich, bell-toned call and is known to have extraordinary powers to reason and to communicate with other ravens. Raven has long been called the trickster, for good reason. I lie abed some early mornings and listen to these birds purposely mispronouncing raven words to one another.

Ravens often work in pairs. One bird acts as a decoy, limping skillfully to attract eagles, gulls, or hungry raccoons away from a salmon carcass that the falling tide has deposited on the riverbank. During this hopeless chase, the other raven stuffs itself. Ravens that have joined forces in this way are often seen coming together to strut around their newfound prize, defying the big blackback gulls that usually outnumber them. The raven when hungry is a great one to march about on its powerful feet, searching out small frogs, berries, eggs, insects, and mussels. Sharp-eyed ravens may be seen waddling with their confident, wide-toed strut through the rich, multicolored moss, snapping up prey with their strong, quick beaks. When it has eaten enough, the raven buries the rest and remembers, of course, exactly where!

Spring drives ravens sexually mad. You can hear the passion and excitement in their voices. After a staid and somber winter, you can see them start to tumble through the sky like some circus gymnast who has seen a female trapeze artist stunting for the first time. It is then that they do overwhelming somersaults for the object of their love as with blatant courtship gestures they first try to, oh, so gently, caress one of her wing tips as they whirl around her croaking, "Spring is here, here, here, my dear!"

Ancient tribes, both European and Asiatic, linked the raven with the powers of magic. They liked to think of them as evil birds, as ominous as vultures or wolves. Most North American Indian tribes viewed ravens in a very different way. In the eastern woodlands, on the Plains, and on the Northwest Coast, the tribes spoke of ravens as great tricksters, which indeed they are. Indians of the Northwest Coast, however, believe Raven is a supernatural trickster. They thought it was always difficult to know what curious deceit he planned to play, as in the following story:

At first, the whole world was cloaked in darkness, and it was difficult for all the animals and humans to find food enough to eat, or even to move outside their houses in the blackness.

Raven had heard of a great sky chief whose house was hidden in the darkest clouds above the earth. Raven heard that this sky chief was the one who guarded the light and would never let it go. So Raven ate a lot of fish eyes, bugs, and worms to make him strong. Then he flew straight upward until he came to the house of the sky chief.

This house had a very large smoke hole in the roof. Raven dove down through the hole and started searching. He searched everywhere to find the light, while everyone in the house was sound asleep. But the grandchild of the sky chief heard Raven and awoke. The child started crying, whimpering that he wanted to play with the light. Finally, the sky chief rolled over and said to the child's mother, "Oh, let him take the boxes out and play with them, if he must. But tell him to be quiet about it." Then the chief lay back and went to sleep.

When the mother and child took the painted boxes from their hiding place, Raven hopped out of the blackness, snatched one of the treasure boxes and flew away with it up through the smoke hole. The small grandchild was so surprised that he forgot to cry. After all, Raven was very hard to see when all the world was cast in darkness.

Raven landed on top of the chief's totem pole, then skillfully untied the strong rope cords that bound the lid onto the box. Tipping the lid aside, he reached in with his powerful beak and he lifted out the moon. Raven was so excited that when he flew up and placed it in the sky, he knocked off some small pieces, which became the stars.

Raven quickly flew to the house again and untied the cord around the second larger box and drew out the flaring sun. It was so hot that he had to fling it quickly upward into the sky. Daylight came in a growing, glowing dawn and spread its glory throughout the world. All the animals and humans ever after have lived to see the sun rise and set, then rise again, while the moon goes on brightening the night.

Raven steals the moon

It's been a long time since I visited Langara Island, called Quuskai, with Teddy Bellis's friend, Dick Ward. We spent a day and night there. It's a lonely place, off the northwest corner of Graham Island, that makes you think you're standing at the end of the world. But those crazy people who love spotting rare birds think they are in heaven here. It's one of the remaining strongholds of the peregrine falcon in the world. And among the rare species that will set birders dancing are colonies of ancient murrelets, Leach's storm petrels, fork-tailed storm petrels, common murres, Cassin's auklets, rhinoceros auklets, and even tufted puffins.

Teddy once told me what he had learned about Langara from his mother, Nora, who was from Haida Village. Raven, the supernatural, had landed at Langara at a time long gone. Her story told that this raven, on the shores of the inland lake, had laid some very special human eggs. Because Langara was such a lonely, storm-tossed place, almost lost in autumn mists and winter fogs, the raven warmed the eggs all through one rainy spring. But still these human eggs refused to hatch for her. Finally, the raven gave up warming them and flew away. A Haida chief, with his great sea canoes, landed at Quuskai and built a great house with a famous pole to declare the family's lineage. But in time this house, too, was abandoned, and the pole fell. The raven's eggs slowly began to turn to stone.

These eggs may still be seen near the soft holes of the nesting place at the edge of Langara Lake. But beware of going there when the moon is full, and the eggs cast long shadows that may cause harm to humans.

Raven

Without these supernatural ravens calling to me through the early dawn, this world of islands, Haida Gwaii, would seem a much too silent place. Could it be true that their supernatural Raven, like Frog the communicator, could have landed here after he raised the islands of the world to tell us his special message that we're not yet wise enough to understand?

Indians along the Northwest Coast equate the supernatural Raven with God. They choose Raven as the Creator, the one who had the power to raise all the islands, making them lands above the seas.

Never Insult a Raven

Would you like to have an example of a really grisly legend about the Raven clan? It's a piece of Haida history. Could you handle a dandy Canadian Indian western that has not yet been used in any kind of film? Try this – and know for certain that if I were a much younger person, say not yet seventy-five, I'd never give a plot like this away to anyone.

Working Title: *A Raven Woman Scorned.*

Opening Shot: A sturdy Haida house with a tall entrance pole near water's edge on Haida Gwaii.

Action: Through the open mouth at the base of the totem, a proud Raven chief, dressed in a black cape, uses his hand to display all of his immediate family, relatives, and captured slaves.

Camera Pans To: The family gathering on a high, rock island where they had built a small but sturdy wooden fort, a safeguard against surprise attack.

The Story: These Raven people were visited by a large canoe from the Eagle clan. With the Eagles was a character named Shaman Batons, a young minor chief who, in his own much smaller canoe, paddled slyly on the offside of the Eagle dugout. Shaman batons are healing sticks. The man only carried this given name, but was not a true shaman.

Rising in the center of her grand canoe, an Eagle woman of the highest rank gave a strong oration to the Ravens who stood watching her suspiciously from shore. The main part of her speech declared that Shaman Batons was a good man seeking a wife, a young woman of rank, from among the Ravens, as dictated by the Haida custom that a member of one clan marry a person from the opposite clan.

After hearing the Eagle's request, the Raven chief agreed to allow this Eagle man to marry a young Raven woman. So Shaman

Batons landed his canoe in peace, as the selected Raven girl was brought to him. But just as the girl stepped into the canoe, Shaman Batons let out a fierce curse, then jabbed the girl with his pointed paddle, causing her to fall into the water. He then paddled swiftly away, leaving the Raven girl abandoned and shamed by this young fool in front of everyone.

Keeping face was as necessary to the Haida on these islands as it was to the people on the other side of the Pacific. Revenge needed not to be swift, but etiquette demanded that it must surely be carried out, to wipe away this unforgivable insult.

Both large and small Eagle canoes reached their home shore at Dance Hat Town and all sat together around the firepit, laughing at or criticizing the outrageous insult they had dealt the Raven clan. In time, they decided to try to improve the situation. In the spring, Shaman Batons sent a ranking cousin to speak to the Raven house chief on his behalf. The cousin said that it all had been an accident, that Shaman Batons had meant no offense to the Raven house and wished to return bearing gifts and ask forgiveness so that he might be allowed to gather his bride-to-be.

The Ravens were still angry, but readily acknowledged that Eagles had to go on marrying Ravens, as must Ravens continue to marry Eagles. So once again, the Ravens lined the beach in front of their fort, while Shaman Batons lay low behind the Eagles' grand canoe. This time his respected uncle spoke for him. The Ravens were suspicious, but finally agreed to accept the gifts and to once more allow the girl to marry Shaman Batons.

Finally, Shaman Batons stood up, revealing himself, then stepped into the shallow waters and, accompanied by three other young Eagle warriors, marched proudly up the beach to the Raven house where many were gathered inside. Once they stepped through the entrance, the enraged Raven chief made a quick hand signal, causing his vengeful warriors to draw their hidden daggers from beneath their capes and murder every man in the Eagle party except Shaman Batons. Shaman Batons had been allowed to survive so that the Ravens could force him to be a slave, to perform all of their dirtiest and most miserable chores.

Expecting reprisals from a nearby Eagle Lodge, these Ravens moved en masse, taking along their slave Shaman Batons, to the small fortified island at Torrens. The only trouble was that this island had no fresh water, which meant the Ravens had to send out a party to sneak over to the mainland in the dark to gather water. Learning of this, Shaman Batons' people cunningly lay in wait.

One night the watching Eagles saw the Raven chief creeping ashore for water. They sprang out, surrounded him, and at dagger point forced him down the beach till he stood waist deep in the waters of the inlet. As his horrified people watched the moonlit scene from the nearby island beach, the Eagle warriors closed in and forced him beneath the water. As the tide turned red, they triumphantly held up his severed head to show the watchers that they had taken their revenge.

In answer to this murderous insult, the Ravens grabbed their Eagle captive, Shaman Batons, forced him out onto the beach, then stretched him like a log and slowly cut him in half with a two-man crosscut saw which they had traded off a white man's ship.

This never-to-be-forgotten event occurred at the beginning of the heavy mists of winter and was endlessly discussed around the household fires, and led to further reprisals. Will you believe me that the marvels of Haida carving are often formalized illustrations of their important myths and legends? And wouldn't this make a marvelous horror movie?

Haida canoe man

12

First Contact

When Captain Cook set out in his ship HMS *Resolution* on his last great voyage of Pacific discovery, in July, 1776, he was accompanied by a young ship's officer aboard HMS *Discovery* named George Dixon who had been on all three of Cook's voyages, starting as a midshipman. To be one of Cook's midshipmen was something special. Cook, a laborer's son who had learned the ropes the hard way and advanced in the Navy on sheer merit, insisted that his soft-handed gentlemen midshipmen do the same. So they had to dress in tarry clothes and work high in the rigging like common seamen until they had learned their trade – if they survived. In later years, of course, that harsh, effective training made them an elite group in the Navy, where their professionalism was greatly respected.

History is a little vague about the nature of Cook's contact with the Queen Charlottes on this last voyage that was to end in his violent death farther west in the Hawaiian Islands. *The Canadian Encyclopedia* notes that he "visited" Haida Gwaii in 1778, while heading north from Vancouver Island in search of the Northwest Passage. We will never know whether he planned to return to the islands to develop the sea otter trade there. What we know for sure is that while anchored for a whole month off Nootka Sound on Vancouver Island, Cook and his crew had earlier carried on a lucrative trade in sea otter pelts with the local Nootka tribe and traded additional otter skins from other northerners. We also know that this apparently made a great impression on the younger George Dixon.

Dixon quickly resigned from the Navy and persuaded investors in the City of London (the term "merchant bankers" has a long history) to back him on an expedition to the land north of Nootka to trade for sea otter, setting off in 1785 in a ship named after George III's wife, Queen Charlotte. After disappointing trading on the Alaska coast, they wintered in Hawaii. Returning to the North American coast Captain Dixon approached Haida Gwaii from the northwest, passed Langara Island, then sailed east through what is now called the Dixon Entrance, and was first to circumnavigate the islands. When the tall white sails of his *Queen Charlotte* appeared on the horizon, Haida history would be forever changed.

On July 24, 1787, having found this wondrous archipelago and named it after his sovereign and his ship, Captain Dixon gave the order for the *Queen Charlotte* to drop anchor, and a dozen Haida canoes came offshore to meet him. One of the first Haida towns to be visited was Skung Gwaii on Red Cod Island at the southern tip of the Queen Charlottes. There the Haida sea hunters showed no fear at all, and the chiefs were notable for the long, handsome sea otter capes they wore. A brisk trade for otter pelts was soon set into action by Koyah, a powerful chief who did the bartering for all his subjects. Dixon did an immense trade in sea otter pelts, which later sold at a profit of ninety thousand dollars in Canton. For the time, it was a record success.

Dixon gives an account of landing with a party of his ship's men in order to take an excursion in the woods. He encountered a fortified rock which he supposed would serve these people as a place of refuge in case of invasion. The walls were naturally perpendicular, about forty feet in height. The top was flat, about twenty yards wide. It was inaccessible on all sides except by a long pole ladder erected by its side. This fort the Haida used when their northern neighbors came to molest them, putting their women and children onto it before hauling up their ladder. Then their men did battle with the invading Indians.

Later, a visit from another ship, *Lady Washington*, led to amicable trade between Haida and whites for two years. It was widely noted in captains' journals that if the trading chief's wife did not approve of poor trade items her husband had received for otter, she would not hesitate to attack and beat him for his lack of trading skills — perhaps diminished by the rum the sailors freely provided on such occasions. On his first visit Captain John Kendrick wrote in his journal how two canoes came out, each paddled by a crew of thirty

Haida. Kendrick confessed that the size of the canoes made him feel apprehensive, since the biggest canoes were much more than half the length of his ship, and the paddlers easily outnumbered the twenty men he had aboard. He put up what seamen call tiger nets or boarding nets to prevent a swift attack.

Flintlock pistol

But after a while, the chief held up a dozen sea otter pelts. This Haida chief and his men seemed sociable enough, so Kendrick, who was prepared to take risks to trade with the Haida for sea otter, allowed them aboard – first in small, then increasing numbers. Soon enough, the Haida made it clear that what they wanted desperately from this foreign ship was iron knives, and iron hatchets. Kendrick had discovered this from past experiences with Northwest Coast tribes. Instead, he produced iron wood chisels along with accordion music and trade rum to soothe then excite the customers. His sailors didn't want to endanger their lives by selling knives. The wood chisels were less dangerous, simply flat pieces of iron, one-quarter of an inch thick, an inch wide, and five inches long, partly grindstone-edged at one end. Kendrick demanded in trade one sea otter pelt for each chisel, the chisels being worth at that time a half penny in Boston, while the large sea otter pelts traded to the Chinese in Canton were often valued at more than one hundred dollars. Both sides believed that they had won in the deal.

But when in 1789 the ship returned once again under Kendrick's command, a tragedy occurred that in some ways affects us all to this day. Hostility grew between the Kunghit Haida and this new foreign captain, whose mood was not improved by the fact that he drank heavily. Pilfering of minor items from the ship by Haida soon led to quick and violent reactions. The incident that triggered open hostility – comical though it sounds now – was the theft of Captain Kendrick's underwear, which had been hung on the ship's lines to dry. Kendrick ordered the two chiefs, Koyah and Skulkinanse, then aboard his ship, to be seized and held as hostages until his underwear was returned. Although all but a few items were handed back, he forced the chiefs to have their remaining otter skins brought aboard and sold to him at a ridiculously low price which was determined by Kendrick himself.

Captain Robert Gray, on a later visit to the area, added further details of the incident from native accounts. His journal discloses that the Ninstints people claimed that Captain Kendrick seized Koyah, tied a rope around his neck, and whipped him. The captain painted Koyah's face black and cut off all his hair, then took from Koyah a great many otter skins and bound him and returned him to shore. Because of this, Koyah was no longer accepted as a chief, but seen as an *ahliko*, meaning one of the lower class. The villagers now had no clan chief but many inferior contenders, which only led to further trouble.

It seems a curious truth to us, but if a Haida chief was captured by a raiding tribe and was enslaved by them, and that captured chief escaped and was able to return to his own former house and people, his clansmen whom he had formerly ruled would utterly reject him. His chieftainship was denied him, they said, because he lost his rank when he became a slave. That chief could never regain his rank or expect to hold a high place in that house or clan again.

In June 1791, Captain Kendrick returned to trade at Ninstints. The captain had been drinking and this time carelessly allowed at least fifty Indians on board to trade without first arming his crew. The Haida seized the keys to the arms chest and forced the crew below decks. The vessel was immediately thronged with natives, as a woman standing in the main rigging screamed to urge them on. The officers and seamen all held below were without weapons save the few pistols belonging to the ship's officers. Captain Kendrick stayed on deck, endeavoring to pacify the natives. At the same time, he edged toward the companionway to insure his escape into the cabin. All the time, one Haida was wielding a huge marlinspike he had stolen, holding it over Kendrick's head, ready to strike the deadly blow whenever the order should be given. The other natives, with their iron daggers in their hands, were waiting for the word to begin the massacre. Just as Captain Kendrick reached the companionway, a Haida jumped down, landing on top of him, making a pass at Kendrick with his dagger, which only went through his jacket. The officers by this time had their pistols held in readiness and would have ventured on deck except for their fear that their captain would immediately be killed.

Kendrick made a sudden dash to his cabin. There he snatched up a musket and a pair of pistols and rushed back on deck. His officers followed, carrying the remainder of the arms they had collected. The natives, on seeing this defense, all jumped off the ship into the water. All, that is, but the woman, who still clung to the bowsprit chains, continuing to urge on the warriors, until her arm was cut off by a seaman's saber. The woman fell. As all the other natives made a swift retreat, she attempted to swim away, but was shot in the water.

Though the natives had carried off the keys to the arms chest, it did not happen to be locked. The crew immediately flung the chest open, grabbed arms and ammunition, and kept up a constant fire as long as their musket balls could reach the swimming natives. Then, placing the small cannon in a whaleboat, they chased the natives ashore, where the crew continued to wreak havoc by killing every Haida within sight.

Swivel gun

As more and more ships came to trade, the Haida chiefs raised their prices, and the game of treachery to reap more sea otter pelts and more chisels was on. Of course, the foreigners never learned to hunt sea otter in the drifting beds of kelp. That skill was possessed entirely by the Indians. If the captains wished to go ashore to view the remarkable, often colorfully decorated chiefs' houses, the chief aboard would sometimes offer to trade his name for that of the sea captain, the chief's name being a guarantee of protection against harm ashore, while the chief asked to be given the captain's name to protect him while aboard. The foreign captains soon forgot the honor of being given a Haida chief's name, but the Haida chiefs did not forget. The result was that many Haida today still bear the names of ship captains, mates, and even some early missionaries.

Far more dangerous than the Haida attempts – sometimes successful – to capture these foreign ships, and the all too frequent return of cannon fire that destroyed some villages, was another totally hidden horror. It perhaps came to the Haida in the form of blankets contaminated by smallpox, that terrible disease against which the whites had built a degree of immunity. During the nineteenth century this scourge went drifting unseen through the 160 Haida towns and killed off perhaps 80 percent of the total Haida population. Those who remained alive fled in big canoes from their southern houses and traveled to Skidegate, which was then called Sea Lion Town. There the missionaries had arrived to save their Haida souls, they said, and to give to the Haida children an English-only education.

So in roughly a century after George Dixon's sails were seen for the first time, the whole unique pattern of life so elaborately created by these Haida people was gone forever. The sea otter had been totally annihilated here and the hugely profitable Chinese trade for otter pelts was gone. The heavy mists came down once more to hide these all but shattered Raven and Eagle clans for many more years of uncertainty.

It is not going too far to say that these violent attacks led to two centuries of bad feelings. Fortunately, no such tragic event ever occurred in the Canadian eastern Arctic, which has meant that there whites and Inuit have been able to live with amiable feelings flowing both ways.

13

Rosespit Magic

Within sight of Alaska, there is a rain forest on the northern end of Graham Island. The scenery there is especially beautiful, along the Hiellen River near Tow Hill, with enormous, almost bear-sized wrappings of bright green moss around the strongest branches that are dappled with subtle shades of gray. A velvety rich carpet of moss stretches over the ground and fallen trees. This northern rain forest has a permanently dark and ominous look. From sturdy tree trunks, wet, black, broken limbs project out as though their only mission was the suspension of these extraordinary clumps of moss. Some growths caught in the narrow beams of sunlight glow like huge, exotic fruits that seem to wait in the silence, dreaming of the past – or are they worrying about the future?

North Beach, as it is called, stretches for miles, forming sandy, hard-packed tidal flats curving off up to Rosespit Point like a scimitar. When a big moon tide returns, exerting its greatest power to draw back the water at low tide, the Haida and others will be there for clamming. We gather our special narrow spades and buckets, pull on our hip boots, and walk down to the water's edge when the tide is at its lowest ebb. The razor clams make a small, wet hole in the sand like the indentation from one's little fingertip. If you've experienced this kind of clamming before and you're really quick, you'll dig and catch clams, some a hand's span long. They live beneath the sand and can retreat faster than you can believe. Clamming is a learned art. It is for some Haida a feast as well as a livelihood.

During the proper season in June, out beyond the low tide, you may find the hand-sized Dungeness crabs are mating. You quite often catch a copulating couple with a single dip of your net, but the law today demands that you should wisely return the females to the sea to keep the crab stocks from falling.

Agate Beach lies near the foot of Tow Hill, that ultimate natural fortress of Haida defense. Located on the north end of Haida Gwaii, it is famous for its agates washed up on the tide, especially after each violent Pacific storm. Here a geological wonderland exists. There always seems to be a fresh supply, if you can train your eyes to be as quick to spot them as the young Haida who may have been there before you.

During the time of the Roman Empire, agates were so rare and thought to be so magical that ordinary persons in the north of Russia were not even allowed to search the beaches for them on pain of death. Agates were to be found on the northern beaches and in the shallow waters and were considered far more valuable than gold. Closer to our house, on the long beach that faces east to Hecate Strait, is a good place to hunt for agates. They are sometimes of the pure, dark golden honey color that can be tumbled in a rock mill until they glow the way neck pendants should.

A Haida friend on the Charlottes once gave me an agate weighing more than half a pound, but it was somewhat streaked and not of the highest quality. It is very rare to see an agate of that size today. But who knows what the sea tides will expose tomorrow!

Haida Gwaii seems full of natural treasures – a lost pinion feather from an eagle's wing, a raven's quill that can be cut into a wonderfully useful pen, pale agates, silverish abalone shells, and a whole mountain of black argillite. What a place to live and enjoy!

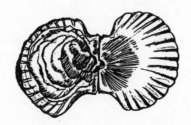

Blue mussel

14

Silver Treasures

The Salmon people, Teddy Bellis explained to me, are the ones who return to our Haida rivers each year, swimming or walking just beneath the water on the tide. They give their flesh only when all is right between us and those underwater people so that they and we may live here peacefully. When children throw stones into the river, the Salmon people turn away, believing it is we, the adult Haida, who insult them. That's how it was told to me by Teddy.

"I don't like to see any kids throwing stones into the river," Teddy said, "especially at the time of year when the Salmon people are coming in to visit us. At that time, the females are laying their eggs and the males are spreading their sperm over the long nests to fertilize them, so that their young and our young may live and grow, enjoying the gift of Salmon people's flesh."

Sports fishing on the Pacific Northwest Coast has long suffered a bad reputation among fly fishermen in eastern Canada and the United States, largely from those who have never tried it. They believe that the Atlantic salmon, *Salmo salar*, is the only worthy fighting fish in the salmon family. Oh, how wrong they are! There are five kinds of salmon on the Northwest Coast and it is true that three of them will not touch a fly. But this does not apply to coho, or silver salmon as the Alaskans like to call it. The Latin name is *Oncorhynchus kisutch*. Nor does it apply to the steelhead, a rainbow trout, *Oncorhynchus mykiss*, now classed as salmon, that runs into the sea. Both of these are grand fighting fish, often eager to take a fly. In the Tlell River or on the Yakoun River, the coho usually weigh about ten to twenty pounds and, taken with a light fly rod and line while wading the rivers in those glorious surroundings, provide some of the finest fishing imaginable.

Early in our time on the islands we were invited by our friends to travel across to Rennell Sound to fish for large chinook salmon. In Canada, they are called spring salmon; in Alaska they are known as king or tyee salmon, meaning "chief" in the Chinook jargon. They, *Oncorhynchus tshawytscha*, have a wide range and a world record weight of 126 pounds, but they will not take a fly. The sheer size of this huge salmon, with the most delicious dark red flesh, attracts all Atlantic fly fishermen – especially those who have fished the Restigouche and the Miramichi in New Brunswick, the Humber in Newfoundland, the Grande and St. Anne's Rivers in Quebec. But when they hear of all the heavy hardware that is nec-essary – with a net, a deep line, or with a heavy lure, the fish having first been attracted upward with a flasher – they snort and turn away from West Coast salmon fishing. That keeps them fishing on their now all but empty eastern rivers; this salmon shortage is a dis-aster that took place after the long, secretive Danish Greenlandic salmon-killing orgy that occurred off southern Greenland for a dozen years. This all but ruined the Atlantic salmon spawning worldwide, especially in Canada, Great Britain, and Europe. Only Russia, and to some extent Iceland, escaped.

Rennell Sound on the West Coast of Graham Island on the Charlottes is not often seen because the choice of overland travel on a rough logging road or around through the narrow, twisting tidal channels makes it just too difficult to reach. Having done it both ways, we much prefer going by water, but you need an expert person who knows the tides and channels, as well as all the reefs, to take you there.

It is significant that none today, no Haida Indians or other islanders, live on the West Coast of the Charlottes. The storms there are just too violent when they occur, and that is all too often. The good of it is that it protects that whole environment. But if you're in a boat out there and the weather starts to turn on you, be prepared to leave quickly, for there are no good harbors in that sheer wall of mountains dropping straight to the ocean floor, and the whole Pacific Ocean is brewing up giant waves to the west of you.

Rennell Sound itself is an impressive sight, with great gray pillars of rock that are said to moan and groan like a huge church organ when the west wind decides to play. Along the immense shoreline, hills rise into bare blue mountains. A lush growth of a mixed forest – spruce, cedar, and hemlock – covers the lower elevations. The ocean stretches north to west to south as far as the eye can see.

There is a small rock island just south of Rennell Sound that the navy during World War II decided to use as a gun emplacement against enemy attack. They poured a strong concrete base and housing for the gunners. It worked well until a terrible wave swept into the landing area, devastated the gun, and drowned the entire crew.

By contrast, one sunny day when we were there, the Pacific lay like an endless pond of clear green ice. Suddenly, surprisingly close to us, we saw a gray whale rise and blow. This whale must have come up from southern California where the whales have grown used to seeing humans, because it was very close.

Alice and Benita landed and went in to explore the beaches of that small island, while Borge and I continued to fish. We took two fair-sized spring salmon and a red snapper. Later, on the main shore of the Sound, we gingerly netted a number of tennis-ball-sized sea urchins from beneath the clear blue waters where they clung in colonies to sheer rocks. Sea urchins are considered a great delicacy in both Paris and Tokyo, but they are almost never eaten in Canada or the U.S. Why? Because they're an unattractive rusty brown in color and are covered with porcupine-like quills that are long.

We went ashore to eat, tending to the sea urchins first. Cut in half with a sharp knife, their insides gleam bright yellow. You spoon them out of their shells and eat them raw. They're as delicious as the best of oysters, with a uniquely different taste. After the sea urchins, we lit a small fire and cooked a two-kilo red snapper, wrapped in foil moistened with tinned butter. It was just enough for the four of us. We saw a good-sized black bear searching along the upper edge of the tide line and later several small dark mule deer came out of the forest to graze. The sense of being one with the Sound and the great abundance of bird life there is almost overwhelming. On summer evenings such as that one, we wonder why we ever chose to live on any other coast or island in the world.

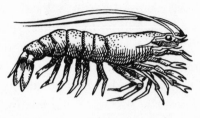

Shrimp

It's almost impossible to hire a guide to fish on the rivers of these islands. I believe that comes about, in part, because the Haida are proud folk who don't like the idea of being anyone's servant. Good luck finding a Haida woman who wants to clean your house, for example. Then there's the difference between the Indian and non-Indian sense of time. If a sports fisherman is willing to pay enough money to hire a guide to take him out, and they definitely agree to meet and go at, say, 7:00 a.m., that fisherman means 7:00 a.m., not 10:35 a.m., when the guide is likely to arrive. This casual disregard of time is a point of pride with the Haida. They laugh about the consequences, referring to theirs as "Indian time." Anyway, if you are fortunate enough to go out with a friend there who is a knowledgeable steelhead or coho fisherman on any of the five main rivers, you should watch his tactics carefully and listen to his advice. Remember, a big winter steelhead, which may weigh in at twenty pounds or more, is anything but an easy fish to take.

If you're casting over waters likely to hold steelhead, a pool, or rill on a coastal river, keep your eyes open. Not so much for fish; you'll sense them, feel them. But watch out for any sign of human life you might detect behind you in the woods or across from you lurching on the river's edge. If it turns out to be a fisherman – and no one but a fisherman or a Fisheries officer would be crazy enough to hang around that river on an icy winter morning – you should start moving right away. Let your shoulders droop forward, giving off that fisherman's air of utter hopelessness. Shake your head as though there's not a fish left in the whole damned Pacific Ocean. Pretend you're freezing cold and heading back. Keep a sly eye on this other angler. Ask yourself is he a local or a dreaded off-islander? Both types can be bad. A local will be glad to tell anyone who'll listen exactly where he saw you fishing. Off-islanders from as far away as Germany can take out their maps and point out to their friends in Hamburg or Baden-Baden exactly where they saw you take a steelhead and the Baden-Baden Fishing Club can afford to come over in force the following winter. They're tough. They don't shy away from icy steelhead rivers. Yes, on a public river, private knowledge of the pools is the only true advantage you've got for coho – which flies are best, and when the winter tides are just right for steelhead taking.

We had a famous New York Episcopal bishop come west to visit us. For some reason, he preferred fishing at a point where I don't believe anyone had ever caught a salmon on the Tlell River for almost thirty years. Well, he persisted in casting various flies over that luckless pool and in two days, alone, without a net or a guide, he grassed two large salmon. Maybe it proves the goodness of some bishops. Or is it the power of prayer? Now that spot upriver is called, with reverence, "the bishop's pool."

Who's to protect what has been called "the king of fishes"? One of our greatest fears is the rapid decline of salmon stocks. We hear endless howling in the press from our youth, whose wandering passions have been set ablaze by paid professional environmentalists. They have caused these kids to drive spikes into our trees until the Japanese refuse to buy them because of the damage the hidden spikes cause to their costly milling equipment. These kids proudly chain themselves to trees until they're hauled off by the police. The young will often do things that they wouldn't dream of doing when they've matured by ten or twenty years.

But who really fights for the salmon today? Well, for example, the U.S. and Canadian fishermen's unions fight a lot against each other. They roar their messages loud and clear that each should have a bigger, always larger share, while they scoop up in nets what they consider their holy right to take, until the last of the dwindling, unseen, wild salmon populations are gone.

If salmon were like the plump passenger pigeons that we exterminated to feed to our pigs, or like the plains buffalo, gone now in their vast herds of millions of animals, we'd be yelling all over North America. We'd be seeing it all with our own eyes as the TV cameras recorded the tens of millions of fish dwindling to the thousands, until it would make you sick with shame. Are we North Americans just going to sit around and wait, refusing to foresee this final disaster as we did with the Atlantic salmon and the Newfoundland cod, both now almost gone? Will we wait until there are too few fish to spawn in the rivers or until the spawning grounds have been made completely unsuitable? Only then will we on the Northwest Coast start to seriously wring our hands and no doubt blame the Alaskan fisheries, while they point their fingers at Canada.

Yes, that's exactly what we're doing out here on the coast, while sports fishermen blame the commercial fishermen, and in turn the commercial fishing fleet guys curse the farming of salmon and say it pollutes the waters and the taste of ranched salmon is no damned good. There has to be something vastly wrong with those two ideas. Would these same people have been against the domestication of beef and pork, turkey, chicken, and lamb for their tables? We have an ever-increasing population around the world that must be fed, while we mindlessly destroy the natural stocks.

Just think of the northern rim of the Pacific Ocean, the United States and Canada, Alaska, the Aleutians, China, Korea, and Japan, and those thirty-mile (fifty-five-kilometer), rogue drift nets that silently float out in the Pacific, guided by their sonar fish-locating devices. Tell me where in God's name are the last of our world's wild salmon populations going to hide? Don't tell me fish farming isn't going to work. It's already working in Europe and North America. Salmon has been on almost every restaurant menu in the Northern Hemisphere for more than five years. By all means let's clear up the last of the farm fish pollution problems before we lose all of the wild breeding population. Sports fishing in Alaska and in B.C. earns vastly more money for state or province than that earned annually by those two commercial fishing industries put together. Why do we allow the netting of the last of those priceless fish that are spawning the last of their golden eggs? To help preserve our future, there should be catch and release of sporting fish and the use of single, barbless hooks. Everyone must help to save the fish that we, with our nets and commercial sonar honing devices, have all but destroyed.

Beaver feast bowl

Early spring, with a light fly rod in many of the rivers of the Charlottes, is just the time and place to take a Dolly Varden. That's an amazingly beautiful, speckled char that most like to call a sea-run trout, and that gets its name from a character in a Charles Dickens novel famous for her wonderfully colorful, printed dresses. These fish, *Salvelinus malma*, were aptly named after the other Dolly Varden more than a century ago at a time when fishing with a fly was definitely a favorite sport. The Dolly Varden can weigh two pounds with a record weight of up to thirty pounds, but is most commonly caught at much smaller sizes. It is a game fighting fish with a delicious flavor on a well-warmed plate with lemon and dill.

Alice seems to have a special knack for catching Dollies, even though she carefully releases them. I believe she picks her flies from a feminine point of view, thus choosing the right kind of finery to tempt a colorful Dolly Varden.

There are some enormous halibut off the West Coast of Haida Gwaii, and when I say enormous, I'm not fooling. I'm not sure how the commercial fishermen take in their halibut. But I do know that taking a large, flat fish like a halibut can present real problems if you're fishing from a small canoe or a collapsible Zodiac, which is nothing more than a pumped-up rubber life raft.

When I asked a Haida friend of mine how to do it, he said, "James, it's no real problem. Take a .22-caliber rifle with you. When you get one – say, maybe a hundred-and-fifty- to three-hundred-pound halibut – up to the surface, shoot him in the head before he has a chance to turn you over."

That sounds like a terrible fish story, doesn't it? Well, it isn't. Huge halibut are not unusual out this way. Fresh, ruby red spring salmon are great, but fresh, virginal white halibut steaks are about the finest fish you'll ever have the chance to eat – except perhaps perfectly smoked black Alaskan cod. Drop by and see Noel Wotten, the painter. He's got photos of a three-hundred-pounder to prove this whole halibut fish story.

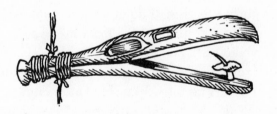

Halibut hook

15

Teddy

Teddy Bellis, my best friend from across the river and our closest, almost only, near neighbor, was a Haida. Like his all-important mother, Nora, he was of the Raven clan. While growing up, Teddy had to be taught secret Raven ways by an uncle who was his mother's brother and, of course, a Raven.

Before he married Dorothy, a lean, elegant, part Cree woman from Northern Ontario, Teddy was said to have been a great ladies' man. He certainly looked the part. He was always smoothly tanned, winter or summer. He was a smiling, good-humored man with an expressive face and a big, typically Haida head and blue-black hair. His sensuous strength was covered over by a slightly padded softness of clear skin which women have admitted they liked. Teddy was a great storyteller, but he was also a remarkable listener and would surprise you years later by quoting your words exactly.

Teddy was remarkable, too, in being much more open with strangers than other Haida I have known. He was always delighted to invite young European cyclists and hikers into his lodge, where he let them take potluck, and use their sleeping bags. He almost always refused to accept money when it came time for them to leave. In fact, Teddy hated taking money from anybody for any reason. "It's a crazy way to run a lodge," Dorothy often told me, but she, like Teddy, did it joyfully.

The way he put it was this: "I don't want any money from these young people who come hiking here from far away, to go on our logging trails or bike or kayak around these islands. I like to listen to them in the evening, talking and laughing around our long dinner table. These kids are from England, France, Germany, Sweden, Japan, Switzerland, and other places I've never been, but from them I've come to know their countries in a kind of Haida way. I know them through their voices, through the way their eyes shine, the way they move. Old people see life through their own past, but these young people, they're trying to find the now, the future. That's exciting."

I told Teddy, "I hope they'll know what to do with it at important moments when the future steps in front of them, then jumps away."

During this period of his life, Teddy was a logger and drove a truck for MacMillan Bloedel, a huge logging company on the north

Pacific Coast. A lot of Indians make their family's living at logging, in spite of all the bad publicity you hear concerning that particular essential Canadian industry.

Teddy, being of the Raven clan, had developed a long-time friendship with a real live raven, so close that he and that raven used to share his lunch. Teddy claimed that this familiar raven spirit of his got hungry around noon as Teddy drove along the logging roads beyond Juskatla, near Ghost Creek and Hoodoo Bay. This is not just a legend; many Haida and other loggers have watched this special raven as it flew evenly along the road beside Teddy's truck level with his elbow, keeping exactly to the truck's speed, going uphill or down, regardless of whether the truck was empty, or loaded with logs. Teddy would look at his heavy golden Japanese watch – which he was proud of because he'd bought it in Vancouver for $7.95 – and shout, "Hell, cousin, it's only eleven-thirty!" But the raven would just keep flying on, eyeing Teddy inside the driver's cab. Teddy said it was a kind of sharp-eyed raven's stare.

"Okay, okay," Teddy would yell at the raven. "It's humpback salmon, cold, with Prince George cheese on Dorothy's home baked bread this morning." He would take a bite, then hold the sandwich out. The raven, not missing a single wing beat, would reach out and snap a good-sized beakful. Then Teddy would take another sizable bite and this supernatural raven, by prior agreement, would finish off the sandwich.

That raven stuck by Teddy on the logging roads until the day that he retired. Not long after that, Teddy had a massive heart attack and died. The replacement driver, an Indian, said that he saw the raven when he passed the tree where it had always waited for Teddy. The raven didn't move from its perch. It was there for a few more mornings, but refused the new driver's offer of his sandwich and disappeared. The new driver told others, "The raven knows that Teddy has gone off to the other world," and said he wondered if the raven had gone there, to look for his friend.

One morning during the autumn salmon run, Teddy and I agreed to meet each other early. As it turned out, we did just that in the middle of Tlell's small wooden bridge, halfway between his house and mine. The bridge that morning had an overnight slick of ice called blacktop. Such unseen ice has tricked many an ardent lover speeding back home to Masset or to Queen Charlotte City after a night of reveling. These folk, with slackened passions, were heading home, alas, to get some sleep.

A small red car came ripping up the road and both of us waved to the driver to stop him. He waved merrily back at us, then slammed on his brakes. As he hit the ice-slick bridge, the little red car slithered from side to side before it reached the road on Teddy's side. There it left the road, clipped off a sizable post, and rolled violently to rest.

We ran as hard as we could and looked inside. There lay a youth whom Teddy knew. He was minus his front teeth, but smiling gamely at us.

Teddy said, "Dorothy always says you shouldn't move an injured person, but she's gone off to the hospital. I'll go and phone her."

When I went around the car to see how much damage was done, the boy crawled out.

"You all right?" I asked. "You could have killed yourself."

"I might as well have done it," the lad said. "When my brother sees his car, he's going to kill me anyway."

That year, I had a new pair of palm-sized binoculars, the smallest and most powerful I had ever seen. I had bought them during a visit to Taiwan in 1978 after a midwinter lecture in Tokyo for the international World Wildlife Fund.

"Some swell glasses!" Teddy said when I showed them to him. He adjusted the focus and looked north for life along the river. "They're great," he said, and he seemed to have to force himself to pass the glasses back to me. "Lots of salmon rising down there at the bent tree pool, but with this big moon pulling so hard, you might as well stay here. Those fish will be coming up here while you'd be walking down. Let's look at the river on the other side of the bridge."

We stepped across. The thing I love about all those miles of river is that in the morning, you can usually look north and south for a mile or more and never see another person fishing there, except maybe my wife. For a great salmon river these days, that's almost unthinkable anywhere else in the world, except on Russia's arctic coast. That's a new place to fish Atlantic salmon, if you wish to risk your neck flying there along that desolate coastline in one of their ancient Russian helicopters. Here in Canada, with the stroke of a pen in the mid-sixties, Premier Bennett took this once private salmon river away from the members of the Dunes Fishing Club and made all of British Columbia's waters public. That was not long before my time. But the cost of airfare to the islands today has made this river almost private again.

Looking south from the bridge along the leaden-colored river that reflected the foggy morning's sky, I saw not a single rise. "They're not up here yet," I told Teddy. "Maybe they won't come up to this bridge today, but probably they'll come up tomorrow."

"Wait a minute. Some are here," said Teddy. "Can't you see 'em?"

"Where?" I asked.

"Right there!" He pointed. "Five of them moving into the pool."

"Where?" I said, looking hard.

"Well, you can't see the fish, but look at those narrow, ripply little patches. Count them – one, two, three, four, five – and look, here come two more."

I was learning how to count salmon that were hidden beneath the honey-colored waters. With Teddy's help, I was seeing them well enough to count them, not by a fin or rise, but by the subtlest ripple, so that one can stand near a river's edge and see them. The ripple system works well here because the bottom of the Tlell has algae thinly coating the stones and pebbles that make it a greenish brown. The river also reflects the trees in varied shades of darkened green. And, of course, the dark backs of the salmon reflect exactly that same color, making them almost impossible to see unless something spooks them, causing them to give you an instant flash of one silver side before they disappear again.

"You want to come fishing tomorrow?" I asked Teddy.

"No, no thanks." He smiled. "I don't fool around with fish like you do. I go out in the strait and use my family net. By the way, Alice asked me to help you take down that old brick chimney that's standing in the middle of your house. So tomorrow, after you're finished playing around on the river, I'll come over here and help you." He pointed again. "Do you see those salmon moving along just below your hideaway?"

I hurried back and got my rod and boots and went down the bank to cast a fly near them.

"If you get one, you holler and I'll come back over and we'll take the chimney down today."

"Sure, and you stay for lunch with us," I said. "But I want you to promise right now that you'll take money for doing that job and also for fixing our pump."

"James, I'm your neighbor. I've never taken one damn nickel from you and I'm not starting now. Say, what's that riding up the river?" he said, to change the subject. "Lend me those pretty little glasses of yours." He took a look. "Sea canoe, sea canoe," Teddy called out and pointed.

I could see a big, gray glaucous gull calmly riding up the incoming river standing on a large, gray drifting log.

"Yeah, sea canoe! That's what the Haida call out when they see a gull perched on a logger's stick. You remember that." Teddy looked at the outside of the little binoculars. "Say, these are the nicest damn glasses and the smallest I've ever seen, the smallest that any Haida has ever seen around here!"

Well, the end of the story is that the old brick chimney got taken carefully down and carefully taken away for some unknown future use. The pump was fixed, and the roof, where it had dripped, was boldly patched – all done, of course, by Teddy. I'll bet anything that Teddy parted with those fancy binoculars I insisted on giving him. He'd have given them at some large winter potlatch feast to someone important to Teddy. Hell, who needs ordinary money in this strangely different world where rare gifts and rank and prestige count the most?

One very early morning, I got a clear view of the deer that I was hunting. It was standing stock still, like a wooden carving, hard to see because it had that special blended color of a mule deer with a very small set of horns. It looked delicious, so I shot it.

After a minute or so, I heard Teddy's voice call to me across the stillness of the river. "You must have got it."

I answered, "Were you waiting to hear a second shot?"

"No," he said. "I was just listening to you sharpen that knife that your son gave you."

"Teddy, you've got ears like a raven. I mean, for a guy who's getting old."

He laughed and I started cutting up the venison.

During more than twenty years that we have owned the cottage on the river, we have invited many friends to visit us here – some from the eastern seaboard, and others from Europe, and even some from that never-never land of films in southern California. And the retelling of their experiences has become legend. After their visiting, they occasionally contact us, perhaps phoning at cocktail time, reminding us that it was the wonderful fishing and the closeness to nature that continued to impress them. Their visits had impressed us, too, because of the pleasures of fishing with them on that river and our before- and after-dinner discussions reflecting on the differences between the rush of life in the big cities and our quiet country repose.

Most friends of ours had never had the luck to really know a Haida Indian like Teddy firsthand. I mean, well enough to sit down and have a drink with him and hear how he thought the last few years had produced too many bears and that they should wear a bell on one of their hip boots. We'd never seen so many good-sized black bear tracks left on the wet, clay beach near our cottage after they'd crossed the river at low tide. He explained that black bears mostly wouldn't hurt you, but on the other hand, it was better to give them a warning signal that you were on your way along the riverbank, because bears are fond of fishing in exactly those same good places that we fisherfolk so greatly favor.

Teddy had black argillite stone and made me a gift of a seal that he had carved. He said he had carved the seal because he thought that sometimes I was lonely for the Arctic, and he knew that it had been one of my most beloved homes.

Some Haida are shy with strangers, but not Teddy. He seemed to enjoy almost everyone, and knew a wide variety of visitors to the islands. He purposely made acquaintances with people, like a bird watcher who collected sightings of all unusual birds. Years later, he could remember their names and many small, unusual details about their characters, their drinking habits, and dress.

Our friends usually arrived somewhat haggard off the daily plane at noon. We'd pick them up after they'd ferried to Skidegate, show them the small Haida museum, then drive them to our cottage. Once there, we'd sort out luggage and see who would sleep in which beds, double or single, and who would stay in sleeping bags on the sofas. Invariably, we would all go out to admire the majestic sweep of the river as it curved grandly northward toward the sea, often with pink salmon performing a ballet of rises before their eyes. We would offer our guests tea, coffee, or whatever. Many of them would choose whatever.

Then those wishing to shower would rush toward the only bathroom, while others simply headed upstairs to change their clothes before searching for ice and mixing favorite drinks. Standing on the porch, we'd sniff the clear evening air along with hints of salmon or a venison roast. Together we would revel in the coming evening.

At about that time, Teddy could be seen ceremoniously crossing the Tlell bridge, headed toward us, bearing a large platter. Teddy was one of Haida Gwaii's most distinguished persons, almost always smiling and quick-eyed. He would shake hands with each of our guests, most of whom had never known an Indian, let alone a legendary Haida. Before Teddy would accept a drink, he would call out loudly, "Alice, would you like something special to go with drinks before dinner? Would your friends like some smoked dog?"

The new arrivals in the room would go dead silent.

"Oh!" Alice would exclaim. "Thanks, Teddy, we'd love some of your smoked dog."

The guests would gulp down the remaining liquid in their half-empty glasses, then move fast to pour themselves another longer, stronger drink.

Teddy would whip away the cloth that he and Dorothy had used to cover their present, a neatly arranged special Indian board of hors d'oeuvres on an ancient Hudson's Bay meat platter. Teddy, a heavy man, would then move gracefully among the guests, saying, "Would you have some smoked dog? It won't bite you."

When he found he had no takers except Alice, Dorothy, and me, he'd say, "You folks are missing something damn good. Dog salmon is by far the best of all the salmon for smoking."

This is the precise instant of relief that everyone seems to remember best. Then Teddy would take a hearty drink and pass the platter again.

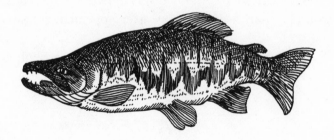

Chum salmon

Teddy had several cats, some chickens, and an old black Labrador bitch named Sassy, who was overweight and sometimes bad tempered. She came and lay on our porch whenever Teddy visited, but she'd rise and bark angrily at me if I went outside. With Alice, she was only a little more civilized.

One year, we had two adult land otters fishing in the river near the bridge. They had grown quite large feeding on an endless diet of young trout. One night, Sassy must have heard or smelled the otters up on the bank, for I heard her go barking and charging down through the salal bushes to the river where there was a convenient tangle of fairly large tree roots worn smoothly gray by the tides. The otters must have had a home in there, for we heard a quick and noisy fight before the otter or otters retreated into their stronghold. Sassy stayed and barked at them all night – and I do mean all night.

When I went down to fish next morning, Teddy came down to see me. Behind him, hanging her head and with a badly torn up nose, was Sassy.

"I guess she just couldn't handle the two of them," said Teddy. "Old Haida say that land otters are the trickiest, most dangerous supernaturals of the lot. Oh, I heard her raising hell down there by the river and I thought of you and Alice, but Sassy had to try and settle something with those two, and I don't know whether she won or lost."

At first, we didn't know either, because we saw no trace of an otter on the river for over a week, but then Alice saw them out our window and called to me. The otters raised their heads. They looked around. Then a new young otter appeared, followed by a second one.

"I'm glad they won," said Alice. "But still I'm sorry about poor old Sassy's nose."

16

Lost in Winter

The Canada Council had invited me to fly west from my winter base on the eastern seaboard to the Yukon Territory to give a reading from *Frozen Fire*, the most recent book that I had written. There may be few of them, but they are very hearty people in the Yukon.

Most of them possess a wild zest for cold, clear air and the vast, mountainous silence of the North. When living in Manhattan, one almost forgets that there are still such magical, distant territories, with bushy-bearded men and heavy-chested women who would choose to live in no other place in the world.

On my way back from the Yukon, I took the chance to head west, stopping off at our place on the Tlell. In those days, when I went to our fishing cottage in winter, long after the autumn salmon run was over, I sometimes felt inspired there and able to write more than in any other place. Since I have never learned to use a computer or even a typewriter, it has become my habit when traveling to carry a sheaf of short, lined foolscap paper and a few black ballpoint pens. These hotel-type pens write well enough and allow me to scratch out my mistakes with equal ease.

The first full day after I arrived from the Yukon, I was in my best form. With no fish nor friend nor kin to interrupt me, I wrote thirty foolscap pages, which amounted to two chapters of *Spirit Wrestler* in a single day. Of course, that was a first draft, but still, thirty pages, that's one helluva world's record for me, and it underwent very few corrections.

When I got up next morning after that bold outpouring, I felt sluggish, weary-eyed, and word-worn. There had been a big fall of wet snow outside. It was still drifting down like white goose feathers in slow, zigzag patterns against the dark green forest. I had not turned on our electric pump for fear of leaving water in the line to freeze and crack the pipes when I was gone. That would cause a ton of trouble, not to mention money. So I lowered a pail and hauled my water from our outdoor well to wash my face, brush my teeth, and make the coffee. I used the deep woods and a large fallen log for my toilet. I admit that it was damp and miserably chilly – not Arctic chilly, but brisk enough to sharpen the mind. It provided me with the chance to peer carefully around at the blackened piles of forest deadfall softly topped with snow.

Before numbness set in, I hurried inside again and fed our stove with kindling and set it roaring with some axe-split chunks of cedar. I stood rear end to the flames as I drank coffee and ate last night's cold trout and cheddar cheese on toast before I sat down at my wide plank table and stared out the window at the miracle of gently falling snow. Then I tried to thrust myself into Chapter 9. It wouldn't work. I had accomplished three times my usual work the day before, and now I was drawing a complete blank. I hoped more black coffee might jump-start my thinking. But no. *Awh, to hell with it,* I thought. *Take a holiday!*

Looking down the river, I could see that the icy white edges had been swept away by the incoming surge of tide. The nearly full moon had drawn tidal water flooding up from the estuary to weaken somewhere well beyond the bridge. My thoughts turned to Wiggins Road. I could drive to its end and walk from there to a huge, grounded log where the river at high tide flooded the salt meadows. This was near the field that Richardson's cattle used to graze, that same place where the sandhill cranes came in the spring to do their ritualistic whooping and their dancing. I pulled on my thick stockings, my hip boots, heavy Scottish sweater and oiled canvas Barbour jacket, the knitted navy hat, and drove to the end of Wiggins Road.

I had not been casting long before I saw a tall figure coming toward me from what appeared to be a small new house on the upper slope near the road. This bearded stranger wore chest waders and a French beret, and carried a fly rod. That was a rare sight on the Charlottes at that time. How was I to know that this man would turn out to be one of the best friends I ever had?

"Noel Wotten here," he said as he stepped into the river just the proper distance from me and started to false cast out line. "Who are you?" he asked.

"Jim Houston," I answered, "from the green cottage by the bridge."

"Oh, sure," he said, "I've heard of you."

Good or bad, I wondered, noting that this man was making powerful, long, flat casts, laying out his fly exactly right and allowing it to drift close to the opposite bank.

"Any strikes today?" he asked.

"No," I told him, "nothing yet."

A few moments later, he hooked a good-sized cutthroat trout, carefully played it in, and released it very gently.

"There's a few steelhead around," he said, "but mostly they're up in the bush right now."

His comment meant that there were big winter fish in the river, but farther upstream. The Tlell River, which curves snakelike north from its multiple small sources, travels a lot of miles before it reaches its estuary and spreads its waters out to sea.

"I wish to God I could go up there today," he said. "I know a really good place. But I promised to meet a guy. We're going to split some cedar shakes. I'm roofing a new part of my house. Do you know that kind of cedar rail corral on the right-hand side of the road where the Bitterlicks let out their horses to graze? Well, that's the best place to start walking in toward the river. It's good for steelhead this time of year. I hope we'll go up there together to fish sometime."

We took a few more casts, and then we wandered up to his place for coffee laced with rum and ate some cold venison. The river had been so cold for wading that it numbed our legs and, unfortunately, somewhat higher, reminding me of Baffin Island dog team travel some four thousand miles northeast of Haida Gwaii, but still in Canada.

I thanked this newfound fishing friend of mine and went out and got into my mud-splattered, robin's egg blue Chevrolet. *Now I'm feeling refreshed and up to it again, ready to go back to my writing table, rebuild the fire, and settle into Chapter 10.* But then I thought, *Hell, I'll just go and make sure I know where that corral is, before heading back to our place.* I found it easily and stopped the car and sat for several minutes asking myself that burning question, *Which is the greater good, getting on with Chapter 10 or climbing over that corral as Noel directed, then walking in and casting to that huge steelhead that's waiting for me in the shadows?* I looked at my watch. The light was fading.

Slowly, somewhat guiltily, I opened the car door – slowly, mind you. The urge to tackle Chapter 10 had not utterly left me. But . . . I gathered my fishing gear and climbed awkwardly over the slippery cedar fence, first brushing it clear of snow. No one had trekked in this way today, for the path was smooth and solid white. I took my fly rod apart so it wouldn't catch in the hanging branches. Once inside the trees, there was a heavy sense of silence. The falling snow had turned the forest into a hazy, dreamlike place of darkest green and brightest white. I kept on walking, my mind totally concentrating on finding the river. After a while, I lost my sense of direction, but looking backward, I could see my footprints strong and black, for the snow was wet and ready to melt. *That's all right*, I thought, *after fishing I'll just follow my own trail back to the car.*

It was almost three o'clock – not too much time left for fishing. It gets dark early here in winter. I had studied the upper river on a map a year or so ago and knew the water must be close. When I reached it, I nearly slipped in, for the snow-white bank was soft and undercut, and the narrow stream appeared suddenly and shiny black. I was careful, for I feared I might step into a snow-covered hole. Being alone, I shuddered at the thought of falling in and having the icy river fill my hip boots, adding weight that would almost surely keep me from crawling out.

I am not much good at tight roll casting, which is a special fly fishing technique used when you don't have much room behind you. When done with skill, your fly rises up immediately behind you and rolls over your head and into the water, eliminating the long back cast that would snag your fly in here amongst the trees. I had no idea where the fish would lie and wished my new friend was with me. I made a few casts before I got my fly hung up in the bough of a fir tree. Then, by jerking the line too hard, I lost one of the beautifully tied Brown Hackles that Robin Kendall had given us. That caused me to give up, there and then.

The darkness was closing in around me, but, as in the Arctic, the evening light was reflecting upward off the snow. I took my rod apart and trailed myself back along the river, certain that I knew exactly where I should turn north.

Then, feeling there was no need to retrace my exact steps along the possibly dangerous riverbank, I made the mistake of taking a shortcut. To save time, I took a course heading straight toward the car and encountered a large deadfall of trees high with soggy snow that was almost impossible for anyone but an expert logger to climb across. I rested after I had awkwardly rounded the deadfall and pulled off my soaking woolen gloves. I had cut the thumb and index fingers out of these to make it possible to feel the line when fishing. Now those fingers were turning cold. I hurried forward in the near dark, searching the snow for any sign of my incoming footprints. I turned this way and that, certain I would find them. About half an hour later, it was almost totally dark and I angrily resigned myself to the fact that I had screwed up, I was lost. Jesus, how had I done it? I'd been lost in the Arctic, but that was not within a half mile of a road.

Stop, stand still, and listen carefully, I said to myself. *That asphalt road is close to me.* I knew I could hear if a car or truck went past. But not a sound. Hell, on that dark winter road at night, it was probable that no vehicle would pass till morning. I may have been close to it, but still I was lost. I stood dead-still in the darkness. Soon the first stars would appear, but would they help me? Because of the trees that stood tight around me, I would most likely not be able to see stars, except the few directly above my head. The only stars in the constellations that might really help me were Jupiter, the first star in the west, and the North Star. But without the Big Dipper, I would not recognize it through the dark sea of evergreens above me.

Uncertain now of my direction, I started walking. Then I stopped. The snow had started falling again in big, wet flakes, but many more of them, melting as they touched my face and ran down my cheeks. Suddenly, I had an image of the river running deep and black, with its cut bank of mossy whiteness right beneath my feet. I stepped nervously back, suffering from a novelist's imagination. Still, it had stopped me dead in my tracks.

I stood still while I thought of trying to light a fire, but everything was soggy, soaking wet. *Never mind the fire,* I thought, *this is not Arctic cold, and a little wetness won't hurt you. You deserve this, you dizzy bastard, for not properly marking your trail.*

I settled my problems by leaning against a tree, listening intently, hoping to hear some familiar sound. I heard several, one probably a deer passing through the woods not far from me. Another perhaps an owl whose night vision must have detected me. The forest was growing cold. I felt shivers scurrying up and down my spine.

Alice would be safely on the farm at Escoheag, thousands of miles southeast of here. I wish I had brought her with me. When I was too late returning, she would have gotten Teddy and they would have come along the road honking the big truck horn and calling to help me regain my bearings. What time would it be on our East Coast farm? Three hours later there. *And what time is it here*, I wondered, but I couldn't see my watch face. *Well, what are you going to do? It's too wet and cold to sit down, so are you going to lean against this tree all night?* I asked myself.

There it was happening again, that old bad Arctic habit of talking to myself aloud. *Oh, why the hell not*, I thought. *I'd shout like hell if I thought anyone was close enough to hear me. Maybe someone was.* I let out several yells, then listened carefully, but no one answered. No truck passed, no sound at all, just silence and the image of the darkened trees now closing in around me and the uncertain touching of the falling snow that made the ghostly branches drop small chunks of snow, leaving their branches swaying.

It was a long night. Toward dawn, I saw that I had developed a small, dark path from marching fourteen paces out, then fourteen paces back to my tree. I wish I could tell you in what direction out was, but I really had no idea. Then I leaned against my tree again and stared into the darkness, then walked, stopped, and listened again. *Did I sleep? I don't think I slept one wink.* Closing my eyes sometimes, I rested before re-restarting my short, twenty-eight-pace journey. My feet were growing numb and my hip boots were noisy and clumsy to walk in. But rolled up high, they were an additional source of warmth, a place to put my hands to warm them.

That night seemed to last a million years before I noticed a faint change in the light above the trees. *Thank God! That had to be dawn, so it had to be east.* I wanted to go northeast. I gathered my fishing gear and started out, keeping the rising light on my right shoulder. Before I had gone far, I heard a heavily loaded logging truck go rumbling past me along the road. I hurried through the new snow, still seeing no sign of my incoming path. But soon the forest opened and I turned into a group of alder bushes. Through them, I could see the corral fence and the old, snow-laden car. I climbed the fence and swept the car windows clear. When I turned the key, the engine wheezed, moaned, groaned, then stopped. But finally on the fifth or sixth try, it started. I backed out onto the asphalt road and followed the wide, black truck tracks toward home.

I was there in less than fifteen minutes, still shivering cold. I laced hot water, beef bouillon cubes, and rum together. Oh, Lord, how good it tasted as I stood over the electric heater, spreading honey on the Dutch baker's famous four-grain bread. I scarcely noticed as my shivers faded away. Slowly climbing our narrow stairs, I piled blankets on our bed and slept throughout the day. It was dark again before I rose.

At six o'clock, I called Alice – nine o'clock her time on the farm. "Did you catch a fish today?" she asked.

"No," I answered, "not today or yesterday, but I've got Chapters 8 and 9 done and I've found a new friend out here, a damn good fly fisherman. He's promised to take me up to the Yakoun River tomorrow. He says there's good steelhead fishing there. So I'll stay close to him and try to learn good places on that river. I'd certainly hate to get lost up there, you know, in winter! It can be damned cold these nights!"

"Have a good time," she said. "The cat and the dog, they miss you. And Big Virgil, the ram, is battering at his gate. And I think the ewes are all wooing him, encouraging him! Goodnight, dear."

Fish scales

17
Old John

Old John was Teddy's father-in-law. A Cree Indian from back east, he lived now across the river from our green cottage in the warm care of his daughter, Dorothy, and Teddy. Sadly, John was ninety-three years old when crowds attended Teddy's burial in the small local cemetery located in the forest just beyond our house. And one year later we all were together for the washing and raising of Teddy's tombstone.

Old John was thin and bent, not weighing more than ninety pounds, but he was cheerful and he was game. You could see it in his jumpy, crooked walk, and the way he crossed rough ground like a much younger man. He had a prominent nose and deep, shadowy caves beneath his cheekbones, while the pupils of his hooded eyes were dark and weasel-quick. He usually neglected to put in his teeth, and you could easily see that when he smiled.

I quite often met John on the river, and we would fish together in the early mornings when the salmon were first coming up from the ocean into the pools. We each had our favorite areas to wade and cast. I'd usually hear him climbing straight down the somewhat treacherous bank from Teddy's house, shielded by the bushes and invisible for almost all of his slow passage. If he paused and took too long, I'd call his name, wondering if I'd mistaken a deer or black bear for him.

"It's me," he'd call out in his high, cracked voice with its hint of merriment. "I'm just stopping to catch my breath and eat a few of these berries." Then he'd emerge and lurch unsteadily across the rough stones to the sandy river's edge across the salmon pool from me. "You seen anything today?" he'd call.

"Yes, two of them have been rising in the pool this morning," I'd answer, hip boot deep in the river, hopefully casting a wet fly over the calm, mirrorlike surface darkened by the tall fir trees that stood on either side behind us.

Old John wore short, rubber boots and carried a good but battered spinning rod and reel that I had given Teddy. "Dorothy knows a French guy – a patient of hers at the hospital. He gave her this new fish lure – told her to give it to me. I don't like the look of it too much, but Dorothy snapped it on my line last night, and I can't get the damn thing off. So here goes. I'll give it a couple of tries."

"Do it!" I'd call across the pool to him. "It may be good."

Old John had probably been good at reel casting in his earlier days when he lived in the east near Thunder Bay, Ontario. But he told me he wasn't comfortable with this fancy spinning rig that Teddy had given him and wished he'd brought his old rod and reel from home. I watched him sort of wind up and give the heavy new lure a two-handed thrash like a man swinging a baseball bat. Then he'd struggle to retain his balance. The lure went out and landed with a heavy plop. He started to reel it in.

"I've always loved fishing," he called over to me, "ever since I was a little kid."

"Me, too," I answered. "There's one!" I cast my fly toward the spreading circles of the rise. "That fish is closer to you, John. Try it."

John reeled in, then gave a kind of shuffling dance and underhand pitch and his French lure soared out and splashed in near the rise. As he started reeling in, the salmon struck hard, waited a moment, then started its run upstream. I quick-hauled then reeled in my line to clear the pool so we wouldn't become entangled.

"He's a big one," John called out to me as he stumbled upriver, bent forward as though the salmon was dragging him over the stones.

"Hold on to him," I yelled. "Keep your rod tip up and let him tire himself."

What the hell was I saying to this wise, old man who had been fishing Cree-style long before I was born?

The fish jumped. It was a big one, with bright silver sides, showing us that it had just run in from the ocean. They are the very strongest, hardest-fighting kind of salmon. This one looked like it was close to twenty pounds. The fish turned and made a strong run back downstream toward John and he reeled in as fast as he could.

"Don't slip," I called, fearing he might fall and break a hip. "Hold him back," I shouted. "Don't let that fish get in among those old bridge pilings or he'll break the line."

God, it's awful the way one excited, half-assed fisherman feels he must instruct another!

Old John was hobbling backward now, trembling, reeling hard to retrieve his line. I was already out of the river, hurrying along the bank, fearful that he would go down in the slippery wetness of the tidal rocks and ruin himself. I was sure that something bad like that might happen. The big fish lay sulking, regaining its strength in mid-pool, then jumped again, and turning, made another long run downriver. John, holding the rod in both hands, went stumbling after his salmon.

"This goddamned fish is playing me," John called out, his cracked voice trembling. "He's winning."

"Hold on to him," I called. "I'm coming over."

The pool was too deep to wade across, but luckily the wooden bridge was close to us. I left my rod slanted upward against a log and ran up through the salal on my side, crossed the bridge and went down through the bushes on John's side, heaving worse than a winded horse.

"Jesus, Jimmy, I'm glad you came over. My wrists are about falling off of me."

"Here, let me take the rod," I gasped.

"Oh, no," he said. "I ain't letting go of this one. If you could just kind of hold me around the middle so I don't fall down, that'll give my arthritis a chance to settle down. Then I'll take this salmon in myself. He must be getting tired," gasped John. "God knows, I am!"

I held one arm around his waist and the other underneath his wrists, but didn't touch his rod. I could feel him trembling hard. I thought of my own father, which I didn't do as often as I should. Then the coho made one last jump and ran around the pool and upstream again. But at the end of the run, I saw a flash of silver just beneath the surface of the water. The salmon had rolled on its side, a sure sign that it was getting tired. John must have felt this, too.

"I can bring him in myself now, Jimmy," he said. "Let me be."

But old John was standing knock-kneed and trembling, with the cold water sloshing inside his low rubber boots. I let go of him as he had asked, and he jammed the rod butt tight against the leanness of his body and very slowly, painfully cranked in on the old-fashioned Mitchell spinning reel, whose worn surface showed the scabs of winter rust.

Now we could see the big salmon in the shallows not far in front of us. It set John's reel squawking as it turned and made one last, brave-hearted run, but it was mercifully short. John began to reel in again. The fish rolled over on its side, its big gills red and gasping. Real Northwest Coast fishermen think it unsporting to use a net, so to help John I eased out a few feet into the water and took a stand behind his salmon while he kept an even pressure on the line.

"Jimmy, could you grab that fish for me?" he asked in a kind of whisper.

I slipped my fingers under the big salmon's gill, clamped down hard with my thumb, and slid it flat across the pebble beach until it was well away from the river.

John was gasping when he came up to me. "That Frenchman's newfangled fish lure that Dorothy gave me, it didn't work too bad now, did it? I'm going to sit down on this log right here. If I was still a smoker and a drinker, I'd sure be doing both – right now!"

This past year near Christmas, we called Dorothy and old John. They were in Thunder Bay, Ontario. When I spoke to him, I asked, "Do you remember that big salmon you caught that morning when we were fishing together?"

"No," he said, his ninety-six-year-old voice sounding a lot shakier than it ever had. "I don't remember any one fish . . . but I sure do remember that river, Jimmy, and I remember you and Alice!"

18

Remembering

Sometimes when it is raining on the river and my mind wanders away from any writing, my thoughts go drifting back to times long past, times that probably got me out here in the first place. Remembering when I was young, before the Second World War against Hitler, when I used to spend every summer and as much autumn and spring as possible away from Toronto at Lake Simcoe near Beaverton and Cannington, the place where my grandmother and my father had been born. It had long been Indian country, and my grandmother had only good things to say about the Ojibwa. "Snake People," she called them, a name that might have meant a band or clan within the Ojibwa nation that lived near us on the lake. Or she may have been referring to the people who lived on Snake Island.

My grandmother told me that when she was young, her mother had told her stories of when some of the Scottish settlers, especially the new ones, suffered hard times in the winter and were all but starved by early spring. "Sometimes the Ojibwa used to sneak up to the settlers' cabins and leave some fish or deer meat or maybe smoked goose carcasses and wild rice to help them through the spring, so the children wouldn't starve."

Once I came into our own summer kitchen at sundown, when no one else was in the summer place we called "the cottage." I saw some fresh green ferns spread out on our white pine table, and on top of the ferns lay a twenty-pound lake trout. We never discovered how that fish got there. We didn't know any cottagers who knew how to catch big trout in that season. In the end, we assumed that one of the Snake People must have come in quietly and left it as a gift for my grandmother, for that was just the way the Ojibwa were. They remembered the old times, too.

There were two fieldstone pillars that supported an old iron gate leading off the road that led to our cottage. The gate was only closed for one day of the year, from sunup to sundown. That was supposed to prove that the little road to our cottage and the cottages of my uncle and our only neighbors, the Wilsons, was private. The importance of the two narrow ruts down through long green mowed sward was that they led directly to the lake.

My sister, Barbara, and I used to climb on those pillars and pretend we were a pair of rampant lions out of some fairytale that had been read to us. But as we sat quietly, one on each pillar, we were really waiting and watching for our old friend, Nels, to come along the gravel road. Nels was our hunting and fishing friend who had taught us some valuable Indian ways. The best time to look for him was right after breakfast. He would be coming home from fishing then, carrying a sack and walking on the grass at the side of the gravel road, shambling like a light-footed black bear, head down, as though he searched for tracks in the dew. At times, Nels seemed to disappear, as if by magic, in the big dark pools of shadow beneath the now long gone elm trees, only to reappear suddenly in the morning sunlight. When we climbed down off the pillars and ran to greet him, he would stand still as a tree stump, then put down his bag, clap his gnarled hands together, and hold them out to us in welcome.

Nels was pleasantly plump and always deeply tanned. His clothes were so sun-faded that they blended onto him until they seemed like skin, a part of him. Nels wore thick, gray, wooly pants, even in summer, and wide gray police suspenders to hold them up. His shirts were always buttoned up tight at the neck and wrists to keep out the cold in winter and the mosquitoes in summer. Except on the very hottest days of summer, Nels wore thick, ribbed, woolen socks pulled over his trousers up to his knees. On his feet he sometimes wore moosehide moccasins, and over them he wore a pair of low rubbers purchased by his brother's wife, the writer in the family, from an Eaton's mail order catalogue. These rubbers kept out the dampness and gave him foot comfort, he said, in winter and in summer.

Nels let his hair grow much longer than most people did at that time, and he wore a tweed peaked cap well forward to shade his eyes, which were quick and bright. To me he always seemed more than a hundred years old. He usually had a stubby beard, for he shaved maybe only twice a month, when the moon was half full and again when it was full. I sat and watched him shave the heavy graying stubble off his face using his old brass safety razor given to him by someone after World War I. He always sat on an upturned wooden bullet box to shave, and he never used a mirror, just felt his face after each stroke. He used cold water and some yellow laundry soap to lather up. I never told him when he nicked himself and drew a little blood. I heard my father tell my mother that Nels said he had used the same five-cent safety razor blade for over three years, and he just sharpened it up once in a while by running it around the inside of a drinking glass. He told my father that he thought it would last forever.

Money didn't play any real part in Nels's life. It seemed to me that he never had any money, that he didn't need any money. He was, I believed, a person who lived way beyond money. I used to imagine that if anyone gave him money, he would just laugh and throw it away. But, of course, that couldn't have been true. He had to buy ten-cent plugs of tobacco and a fifty-cent pound of tea every now and again, and maybe a bar of Sunlight soap every few years. But in my mind he lived unhampered and unaware of all the commercial corruptions of this world, as calm and self-sufficient and as well-protected as a porcupine.

Nels not only cut up and smoked plug tobacco, he also chewed it. He gave me my first chew of tobacco and told me to be careful not to swallow it. I was surprised that it didn't make me sick at all. It tasted awful, but it was well worth it, because it made me feel so great to be sitting there fishing, with Nels in one end of the boat kind of singing to himself in the Snake language, and me in the other end spitting brown tobacco juice over the side as though I, too, were a hundred years old.

"Jesus, Jimmy!" he would say. "If your mother see'd you chewing that wad, she'd kill me. And you, too. For God's sake, don't dare tell her!"

One soft summer morning when the small-mouthed bass were

just about to start biting in the clear water, Nels and I could see them floating near our hooks and sinkers dangling far below us. The bass looked like ghostly shadows, waving their fins like wide-spread fans. The whole lake stood icy-still like a huge green mirror reflecting the tall, spreading maples that lined the shore. Across the lake along the horizon line of water, vast thunderheads hung motionless like the mountains one sees in dreams.

I sat in Nels's old, unpainted rowboat and tried to imagine what it would be like to walk or float among the towering gray-white clouds. Even before I felt the wind, I could see it running toward us from across the lake. I could see it coming, making driving patterns on the water's surface like leaping minnows. Then I heard it swishing through the maples, turning their big summer leaves over to show their silver undersides in a way that always forewarns rain.

"Son-of-a-bitching wind!" I said aloud, for Nels, unlike other grownups, didn't mind my swearing.

Nels didn't like the west wind any more than I did, for it meant an end to our day's fishing. He shifted his weight around, putting his back to the rising breeze.

"My old granddad," Nels said, "would have told you that that was Nanabush's brother doing all that winding."

I pricked up my ears when I heard the name Nanabush, for Nels wouldn't usually talk about him, at least never when you hoped he would. Nanabush, he'd told me, was some kind of an Ojibwa god, a giant that had lived a long time ago and had done some good things and some bad things. I had never heard that West Wind was Nanabush's brother.

"Yes," said Nels. "Once the west wind blew until this lake stayed rough all summer. Nanabush got so mad about the way it spoiled the fishing that he got ready to go out and kill his brother, West Wind.

"His grandfather, who was old and wise, said to Nanabush, 'Oh, don't kill him, he's your brother. Just break off one of his horns, and then he won't be able to blow so hard.'

"Well, Nanabush went out and broke off one of his brother's horns and then came back to the lake. West Wind got mad about his broken horn that wouldn't blow at all, and he told the other three brothers, East Wind, North Wind, and South Wind, not to blow another breath of wind.

"The lake lay still as death all that summer. Its face became covered with dust and dirt, old leaves, and dead fish. The Ojibwa were afraid to go near the water because of the awful smell.

"Nanabush had to run around to all four corners of the world and talk nicely to each brother, asking them to start blowing, but gently this time. And they did. The lake cleared and became fresh again. The *people whose moccasins have puckered seams*, as the Ojibwas call themselves, drank the water. The kingfishers screamed again and fished, the raccoons washed their faces, watching fish that jumped with joy."

When Nels had finished talking, he pulled up his old anchor. I asked him to tell me more about Nanabush, but his mood for talking had passed. While gnawing on his pipe, he reached for the oars, half-smiling at me, then half-snarling at West Wind. Nels always ate the stem off his pipes, which was quite a trick, for he had only three lower side teeth and two upper teeth to do it.

Crayfish

On another morning in those distant days, I walked with Nels to the railroad crossing. Coming along the tracks toward us, we saw a small group of Ojibwa women. They were searching for medicine roots and healing herbs. Nels pointed out to me one young woman with a child in her shawl. She was with two grandmothers, one fat and the other thin and bent. Both were also wearing shawls. These two old women were pointing out the different plants, telling the young woman which ones made the best medicine, I guess.

When the round old lady saw Nels, she left the others and came along the railroad tracks toward us. She found a good place, sat down on the bank, and beckoned to us. Nels and I went and sat beside her. I don't remember whether they spoke Ojibwa or English, maybe it was half and half. They were difficult to understand when they talked together, for their voices mixed and flowed like maple syrup and gravel.

The old woman pulled three roots from the ground and thumped them against her knee to clear the earth away. She gave one root to Nels and one to me, and ate the last one herself. The brown root tasted strong and bitter. After eating the roots, the old woman said something to me in Ojibwa, then hugged me to her side and went on talking to Nels. I will always remember her. She felt soft and warm, her clothes were brown as partridge feathers, and she smelled of wood smoke.

Later I was going to go out and find other roots, but my grandmother said I must never eat roots unless the old lady showed me the right ones. I often looked for her at the railroad crossing, but I never saw her again.

Next spring, when I asked Nels about her, he told me that she had died. He said she picked roots to make other people healthy, but nobody picked them for her. Then he shook me by the shoulders and said, "Awh, hell, Jimmy! She was an old, old lady. Old ladies, and old men, they die."

In the Great War – that's what they call the First World War, which ended three years before I was born – Nels and his brother and a lot of other Ojibwa from around the lake volunteered for the Canadian and American armies and a number of them became famous snipers. I was proud to have these great deer-hunting marksmen for my friends. I used to lie in bed on cold, moonlit nights in autumn, when the hounds were baying in the deer swamp, and imagine that

I was a German soldier about to raise my head and look over the trenches and through the barbed wire across No Man's Land. Then, magically, I could see Nels and his brother lying in wait for the soldier; I could even see their sharp dark eyes and the barrels of their deer rifles glistening in the moonlight. I'd duck my head under the covers, shiver with excitement, and wait to hear their guns go off. Sweet Jesus, I wouldn't want either one of those hawk-eyed brothers putting their front sights on me. I had seen Nels's brother take aim high in the air with his deer rifle and shoot a goose out of a flock of Canadas. It fell so far and hit the ground so hard it bounced off a furrow of a plowed field.

Those mornings that I went roaming with Nels I will remember for the rest of my life. It seemed to me then that the only education I wanted or would ever need I could gain right there from him, sitting in that old, fish-smelling boat of his or stalking through the woods. From Nels, I learned such invaluable things as the two little nervous clucks a ruffed grouse gives the instant before it thunders into the air, or how to whistle to a groundhog and have him whistle right back and stick his head out of his hole to see just who was calling.

My father used to make frequent train trips to western Canada, and when he returned it was always at night. My mother would drive with us to Toronto's Union Station where, in high excitement, we would take turns hugging our father and repeat it when we all arrived home. It was amazing how fast my mother and father would then rush us off to bed. In the early morning, my sister and I could scarcely wait to displace our beloved mother and jump into the warm bed beside our father. There we would watch him make his wonderfully quick line drawings and listen to him tell of all the Indian things that he had seen, and the strange tales that he had heard.

Once, when we were older, he told us of a young Ojibwa man, a hunter, who had been arrested for something like getting drunk or making his own liquor. This man was being held in a small country jail, waiting for the district court to come and try his case. The jailer said that this Ojibwa hunter was at first a very helpful prisoner, and could often beat him hollow at checkers. But slowly, as the hunting season came, the young Ojibwa grew restless and despondent. All his skill at checkers disappeared. He spent most of his days staring out between the iron bars, looking up at the empty sky.

On the best night of autumn, when the hunting moon was full, the jailer said that he and his wife could hardly sleep because of the endless calling of the wild geese as they flew south, crowding the night sky with their long, thin wedges. It was then that they heard their Ojibwa prisoner singing a long, sad chant.

In the morning, when the geese were gone, the jailer took the prisoner his breakfast of oatmeal porridge, an apple, and a mug of tea. He found that the man had escaped, had flown away with the geese. Only his body remained, hanging in the cell.

My father told me about that flying man more than seventy years ago. But even now in autumn, when I hear wild geese calling, I think of that Ojibwa man and try to imagine the shape of his soul. It must be a wild trembling thing, birdlike perhaps, yet man-sized, proud and many-colored, bursting to be free.

"That's an old-fashioned story," you will say. "Ojibwa, and other natives, aren't like that anymore."

Then tell me, I ask. Why do young Indians and Inuit have the highest suicide rate of any group in North America?

I was looking recently at a world map with CULTURALLY EXTINCT PEOPLE shown in capital letters. I began to think of those people: the Kamchatdal of the Kamchatka Peninsula, the Beothuks of Newfoundland, the lower California Indians, and others. I wondered how and why did they become extinct?

Some of my earliest memories are of Nels's daughter, Minnie, who used to help our family when we were summering at the cottage. At that time I was probably five and she must have been about sixteen. But I then just thought of her as a bit older, and certainly one of my best friends.

When Minnie was standing, rolling bread dough in our kitchen, I would sneak up and pull one of her apron strings. She would whirl around and kick off her shoes in a race as I darted out the back door. I thought I could outrun her, but she'd catch me easily just before I tried to duck through the small hole I'd made in our cedar hedge. Minnie would lift me up and hug me tight, then bite me hot and gently on the ear. Then, laughing, she'd set me down and retie her apron, saying, "You gotta get faster!"

My sister, Barbara, would call to our mother, "Jimmy's bothering Minnie again!"

Then Minnie would call to our mother, "Don't worry, Mrs. Houston, I don't care." And both of us would rub our bare feet in the dew that still covered the morning grass.

Right after the Second World War, in 1945, I left the army and went up to our cottage on the lake, feeling glad and lucky to be home again. Sad to say my father had died, but I still had my mother and my sister. When I asked about Nels and Minnie, I was told that they were fine.

I went in to Beaverton, the nearby town where lived my very favorite aunt, Mary Ritchie. After dinner, there was something going on uptown, probably the first of July, Dominion Day. There I met an old girlfriend of mine. She had grown up, it seemed to me, with longer tanned legs, shorter blonde hair, and even shorter snow-white shorts. We celebrated with friends our seeing one another again, then went out onto the main street where we decided that this rediscovered girlfriend could see much better if she was riding on my shoulders.

As we and our friends went whooping down the street, with me kind of hoping that we would not meet my mother or my favorite aunt, I suddenly saw Minnie. She had stopped dead-still to stare at me and I stopped and stared at her.

"Is that really you, Jimmy? My God, you've grown. I guess even if you started running again with that young Dorothy on your shoulders, I'd have trouble now to try and catch you."

Dorothy climbed down, saying, "Hello, Minnie. I've been away.

I haven't seen you since before the war," and together we caught up with all of Minnie's news.

Dorothy and I walked more sedately along the small, crowded street, and soon enough we met my mother and my favorite aunt, who remembered her and greeted her almost as warmly as they did me. The war was over and it seemed to me that all the best was yet to come. At that time, I had no idea that it would include living among the Inuit in the North and the Haida on the Queen Charlottes. But I still miss Nels and Minnie.

19

Gifts from the Orient

One morning in Tlell during early spring, when the whole world seemed in tune, I rose early and walked slowly south along the river upstream from the bridge. The air was hung with lazily moving curtains of mist that shifted through the black fir trees like slowly blowing smoke. I was searching for those strange-looking odds and ends that are stranded along the beach by the tide. That morning there were the usual strangely shaped knots of driftwood, a dully shining salmon's carcass argued over by a pair of herring gulls, and a piece of rough-hewn timber turning a handsome gray-white as it dried, still holding rusted nails.

As I wandered on, eyes searching the beach for shells, bear prints, deer tracks, raccoon and otter paw marks – anything – I heard an unfamiliar, raucous call. It came from the salt marsh just beyond the river. I made my way cautiously to a thin stand of alders, and peering through them, I received one of the great thrills of my life. Standing tall and gracefully slim as ballet dancers were two sandhill cranes – in Asia they're called Manchurian cranes – close relatives to our all-but-extinct whooping cranes, which summer in Saskatchewan and wisely winter south in Texas. These two chest-high birds were so enchanted by each other as they stood face to face that they took no notice of me. Their bright red head patches seemed to glow as their long beaks ritualistically stabbed the air. But here were thoughts of loving, not of fighting. The bird nearest me crouched, paused, spread its great white wings, leaped high in the air, then flapped gently down to perform a perfect landing. The other mating partner leapt even higher, making the first notes of their magically liquid bird cry. The background of the mist-softened meadow edged above by the tall forest reminded me of an ancient Japanese painted scroll unrolled in a museum only on the rarest occasions.

After a while, the two birds seemed to perfect their dance, continuing their haunting calls until they flew off so close together that their wing tips touched, searching for some utterly remote river bend where no voyeur like me could watch or try to sketch their mating.

The Charlottes are home to smaller birds, too. One of the strangest thrills in the world of birds is to see a dipper, *Cinclus Mexicanus*, which looks like a sort of wren, when it's at work gathering underwater eatables. It runs in the shallows, hunting, with the water well above its head. You are likely to see this bird in action when you are wading and casting across the narrower places toward the opposite riverbank. I've often seen this gray sharp-tailed little western bird hopping through bushes on the river's edge, but only rarely have I seen it doing its underwater feeding tricks.

Nature has a thousand thrills, it seems to me, that it chooses to keep hidden from all but the most curious and attentive human eyes.

One day, I heard a hard thump against the window of the hideaway – hard enough, I thought, to have broken the windowpane. I looked, but seeing nothing, I rose up from my chair, jerked open the door, and walked around the cabin. There, below the window, I saw a trembling, iridescent motion. It was a good-sized bird, with wings widespread, head with the beak turned to the side, whitish eyelid down, apparently dead. The dark crested head first attracted me, and then the most unusual kind of deep, glowing Prussian blue on the wings and tail feathers that one so rarely sees. The bright feathers merged into black in the neck and head complete with light streaks around the bill, making the whole bird a triumph of color, shape, and design. Before me was *Cyanocitta stelleri*, Steller's jay, named after the famous Arctic navigator George Steller, who made so many discoveries around 1741 on the Alaskan and Siberian coasts before he starved to death.

Back at my desk, I was making plans first to make a drawing of the bird, then to display his bright tail feathers inside the cottage. But when I looked outside again, the Steller's jay, the same size as a blue jay, was sitting up and looking around. Then he stood and took several groggy hops before he lurched into the air and flew away. We put out bread on the porch railing and two Steller's jays came to eat next day. But we were never really on their list.

Barbara and Noel Wotten, on the other hand, had a number of Steller's jays come and visit them each day. These birds had a huge problem to overcome at Wotten's place, for there lived two fat and sassy cats well known to have an eager appetite for birds. Exactly how it was worked out between the Wottens, the cats, and these Steller beauties is not really known to us. But the positive results were that the cats would rest a foot or so beneath the boldest of the Steller's jays. At first, the cats and jays eyed each other with mistrust, but finally the birds took the chance and daringly hopped down almost between the paws of those two fast and sharp-clawed cats. When we next came, we watched them acting casually toward the jays, with no apparent thought of an attack, although any other kinds of birds that dared come in range would immediately be thought of as a perfect meal. Had Barbara and Noel trained this peaceable kingdom? Or had some secret pact been formed between the cats and these bold rare jays?

If so, that pact is still holding strong today. I would advise you to go and visit Sitka Studio for yourself and at the same time buy from the Steller's jays' feeding place one of Noel's beautiful watercolors of a Steller's jay, or a salmon, or perhaps some of Noel's Tlell River hand-tied salmon or trout flies.

Crested auklet

The Queen Charlotte Islands is the place to go if you are interested in sea birds, including Cassin's auklets, rhinoceros auklets, crested auklets, eider ducks, and even horned puffins. Go right after one of those huge, North Pacific storms when there are restless flights of sandpipers, soaring gulls, and sea ducks like surf scoters riding the waves for pleasure. Then you can walk the beaches and search for those handsome collector's items, Japanese or Korean hand-blown glass net floats. These quickly done craft delights vary in size from grapefruit to cantaloupe, and occasionally to basketball size. They come in thick, smoky grays, subtle blues, and haunting gray-green orbs. Each has a fast-closed, rough glass punty that marks its end and usually has lots of bubbles and rough glass cords in the glass, indicating that they were blown for immediate, functional purposes and are only accidentally beautiful.

Often, these thick, hard glass floats are still encased in their original strong web of netting, antiqued by years of bobbing in the salt water while leaving the sea of Japan or elsewhere, then slowly crossing the vast Pacific Ocean to beach somewhere on Canada's or Alaska's most westward island shores.

The second and much easier place for us to look for floats is on the beach near our house after a storm has washed them around and into the Hecate Strait. We wake some mornings to the rolling thunder of the dying waves. Then Alice and I rise and hurry out early. We hope to run the beach and prevent some more avid collector from having the chance to race along in a four-wheel drive dune buggy and snatch these Oriental treasures from the beach before we arrive.

I know you're probably thinking of an eastern beach or a West Coast southern beach with lots of other cottages strewn around. But that view is wrong. It's not like that here.

This beach is only five minutes from our cottage. We walk first down a narrow lane and through the small island cemetery, then along a narrow, twisting secret path that we have cleared. It zigzags through the towering spruce and around the bright green mossy mounds of deadfall. When we reach the beach, it never fails to stop us in our tracks. We look as far north as the eye can see along the soft gray curve to Cape Ball and, on the clearest days, we can sometimes see beyond to Rosespit, the northernmost point of land. Then we turn and look south to the far-off mountains. In all that distance north or south, our eye will not encounter a single human or a single human's dwelling.

On this beach lie miles and miles of giant barked and salt-bleached logs, escaped long ago from old-fashioned logging companies' towing booms. Most of these have been permanently beached by the action of other violent storms and now form an impressive barrier at the high tide mark between the water and the blue-black protected forests of Naikoon Park.

Here and there a bright spot of color may be seen – lemon yellow, royal blue, or scarlet – marking empty, recorked plastic detergent bottles used as net floats or crab trap markers by Canadian or Alaskan fishermen. These washed-up items stand alone out on this primordial beach to remind us of the modern world beyond the snow-clad mountains to the east or the waters to the north or south.

Out on the long stretch of sand beyond the gravel stripe, one may, with luck, see a large, clear bubble rolling in the tide. When I do, I set out trotting toward it, fearful that Alice will spot it with our binoculars and come dashing along the beach to outrun me and wade out to scoop up the floating treasure. These days, finding a good glass float made on the other side of the Pacific Rim has become an increasingly rare event – a gift from the Orient to brighten our cottage window, where it will catch the light.

20

Totem Poles

The old Indian villages on Haida Gwaii have now all but disappeared. They were once scattered along the coastlines of the islands that make up this long volcanic spine – Ninstints, Tanu, Skidegate, Skedans, Cumshewa, Chaatl, Yan, and more than a hundred other so-called towns – each occupied in their heyday by as many as four hundred inhabitants, before the white man's diseases wiped them out last century. These small island communities were distinguished by their tall cedar totem poles and wide-planked houses half hidden in inlets to protect them from violent winter storms. Behind the poles and houses loomed dark majestic forests.

Today, barely a score of the old poles remain standing. They edge village beaches as mysterious silver-gray presences whose original colors have been worn away by rain, sun, and salt sea spray. Most of the poles that have not already been taken off to major museums around the world have fallen into the wet moss of the forest floor or have been split asunder by new tree growth. The totem poles of the Haida, like their houses, rarely lasted a century.

Totem poles served many purposes and were a traditional sign of a chief's wealth. Commissioned by persons of rank and shaped by skilled artisans, they were often raised to celebrate a coming of age, a marriage alliance, the ascension of a chief, the building of a house, or simply to honor the dead. It was customary that any family totem pole show only those figures – animal, human, or supernatural – which the household had a recognized right to display. Any misuse of a crest was considered tantamount to tampering with another family's history and identity, and was enough to cause a battle. In a world without written records, where rank and title were jealously guarded, the raising of a totem pole was invariably accompanied by a gathering of witnesses and a costly potlatch feast that might last two or three weeks.

There were several types of poles. Tall commemorative ones were created with a single figure at the bottom and a simple pot-latch ring cut above it to symbolize each potlatch feast the owner had given. Family frontal poles displayed the combined crests of husband and wife. Inside the houses were roof support poles, carved and painted to decorate the interiors. Mortuary poles, adorned with one or two figures, held a burial box on top that contained the remains of an important person, and they exhibited a carved board emblazoned with the crest of the deceased. Regardless of type, all of these wooden giants, standing against the dark green of the forests, gave the old towns a look of ominous grandeur, as is still evident at Ninstints.

Totem poles should generally be "read" vertically, starting with the bottom figure and proceeding upward. The carefully interwo-ven figures represent individual and clan crests. Eagle, Raven, Wolf, and Bear are intertwined with Hawk, Killer Whale, Sea Wolf, Rainbow Man, Moon Woman, Thunderbird, and myriad other mythical creatures. Frog, Beaver, Otter, and Butterfly are figures the Haida believed communicated between the mist-hung beauty of their world and other lands beneath the sea or just above the bowl of sky.

With the exception of mortuary poles, large totems were rarely left fully rounded. A red or yellow cedar tree would be split, and one-third, with its core, would be cut away to reduce its immense weight. A two-thirds round outer shell of red cedar adzed to a thick-ness of about one foot was easier for paddlers to tow and for guests to join in raising. Haida totem poles were less three-dimensional sculptures than deeply carved reliefs, with only one-tenth of their surface wood removed.

The Haida approached their art thoughtfully, aiming always at a strong, if somewhat cold, perfection. Their totem poles – like their house fronts, masks, and painted boxes, and like their ceremonial garb, halibut hooks, even their spoons and food bowls – all bore carefully thought-out crest designs.

The numerous old Haida villages that stood until the end of the nineteenth century are largely gone now. The foreign ship captains, missionaries, and traders brought with them new tools, new ideas, and, fatally, new diseases. But those Haida who survive have not forgotten the vigor of their culture, nor have they forgotten that long generations of their ancestors created works of genius as original as any in the world.

Killer whale helmet

Ninstints, Skung Gwaii, Red Cod Town, Anthony Island – the small Haida strongholds on Anthony Island had many names, because it has been of such importance during its known history, including the arrival there of Captain Dixon in the *Queen Charlotte*. It is a lonely island near the extreme southwest end of the long chain of islands that make up Haida Gwaii. Today, that small south island is like a ghostly cemetery from another world. Its carved memorial posts lean perilously along the edge of a tall fir forest. Ninstints has known the dangers of pre-dawn raids by enemies and the thrills of grand potlatches. Ninstints' houses knew both good and bad times in the island's earlier, wilder days. The two dozen old, square, cedar plank houses, some of which had sheltered up to fifty persons, are all but gone now, their outlines and firepits almost hidden by salal bushes and lush green moss, their giant roof poles now sagged and fallen, rotting in the winter rains. Many of the cedar grave posts still stand like ancient, oversized human statues as large and fully round as English oaks, their tops and carved features now sprouting with salal bushes growing like a troll's green hair. Twenty times the weight of a man, these round poles were carved to honor and support the dead of rank. Their bones, enshrined in decorated, painted wooden boxes on top of the carved poles, could rest high above the dampness of the ground. Placed at the level of the house roofs, these important Haida souls could fly free as soon as they were ready for the journey into the hidden worlds beneath the sea, or in the sky, or in large eggs half buried in the earth.

All of the great totem poles are gone now, stolen or bargained for by the famous museums of the world, or sometimes towed secretly away behind the boats of raiding scoundrels. All of those poles now stand sheltered elsewhere, well dried and preserved. Those were the taller, grander house poles, many of them attached to the front of the seventeen houses of Ninstints, where they formed entrances through the open mouths of important ancestral spirit helpers. These poles displayed the Eagle or Raven house clan crests. Those larger potlatch poles and house poles that remained had been chopped down or had rotted at the base and fallen, or had even, in some cases, been wrapped with kerosene-soaked rags tied at arm's length up the pole, then set on fire to obliterate the carved cedar images. Haida say that this sacrilege was carried out by overzealous missionaries who came in mission vessels to defile the old village site after Tom Price, the last chief, had departed. It's true that early missionaries had always taken these carved clan symbols as devilish, heathen images, but they were, in fact, important family or personal crests with the same proud meanings as the Scottish lion rampant, the Welsh dragon, the American eagle, or the Canadian beaver or maple leaf. Since those destructive days, Ninstints, or Skung Gwaii, has been designated a World Heritage Site and is carefully guarded by Haida watchmen. No one is going to remove those memorial grave poles, the Haida say, that have been left remained on site to mark the ancient ways of the Haida Indian people. They will be left there to rot now, almost the very last of the poles anywhere.

Ninstints remains one of the most fascinating and deeply mysterious places I have ever experienced in my life. Let me recommend that you go wandering alone, although the unseen Haida watch-man who lives with his family in a nearby cove usually has an eye on you. Ninstints' thin, moon-curved beach marks a line between the ocean's mist-hung water and the island's tall, dark forest. If the tide is right, it is easy to land and walk quietly up across the pebbled beach and onto the deep carpet of gray-green moss. I am always overwhelmed at the sight of the last remaining vestiges of this ancient Haida town. I know, of course, as I approach, that the tall totem poles have long since fallen or have been stolen and towed south. The house poles and great ridge poles, like the houses them-selves, have sagged and rotted, so that the squarish outlines of the seventeen houses are now almost buried in salal bushes.

Yet I'm overwhelmed by the grave poles still standing. These are fully round and about the height of two tall men with a depression usually cut at the top of each to hold a large, decorated, bent cedar box, a coffin that once held the body of the important person inside, folded knees to chin. The bent boxes are gone now, collapsed – or looted. These last remaining memorial poles are at various angles, but remain lined up above the edge of the beach like ancient, Oriental guards staring endlessly out to sea. The carved, weather-worn faces suggest a gray and ghostly past cheered somewhat by their bright green crowns of growing vegetation.

What wouldn't I have given to have seen Ninstints alive and thriving, with canoes of many sizes pulled up on the beach like cars and trucks in a parking lot, to watch their fishermen and sealers coming ashore wearing their wide rain hats, the males usually naked or in open cedar bark capes. Women and children would have been helping to draw up the canoes and carry the catch to the houses. There in the gloom of the huge, square dwellings, a central sunken firepit would cast off light among the shadows. In the evening, men of rank would sit, talking, remembering old raids, perhaps, or plan-ning new ones. Women would be a part of all other important deci-sions. Slaves, gathered from their Viking-like raids down the coast, also lived in the same houses, and ate the same food as their captors, and were usually well treated. Watchmen would be out at both ends of each village to watch the forest at their back, ready to sound the alarm and defend its people not just from mainland slave-takers, but also to protect themselves from any vengeful neighboring Haida clan chiefs.

But although there were two towns here – Ninstints and Red Cod Town, one Eagle and the other Raven, always intermarrying – their people largely lived at peace with one another, leading a fine life fed by the rich abundance of the North Pacific Ocean, warmed by the Japan Current.

Watchmen at top of pole

On top of many Haida totem poles sit three small human *tadn-skeel*. These important watchmen are there to guard the powerful houses of the clans against attack. Each watchman is said to be able to watch in three directions, their vision being shaded from the sun by a tall, conical hat and their eyes being wide open, allowing them to stay alert both day and night. These watchmen peer endlessly out to sea, or along the beaches, or deep into the forests that curve behind their seaside strongholds.

21

Potlatching

Be ready, oh, chiefs' sons of the tribes,
I come to make my husband a great chief.
I, mistress of chiefs,
I am seated on many coppers,
I have many names and privileges,
I have many masks and dishes.
Now the marriage feast.
Who shall be my husband?

                 – Old Northwest Coast song

I have mentioned in passing the ancient Haida tradition of potlatching – feasting and gift-giving – that has taken place since long ago. If you were a person of importance among the Haida, Tlingit, Kwakiutl, Tsimshian, Gitksan, Coastal Salish, or other tribes, and you were given a potlatch by some other ambitious house owner and were presented with many gifts, it meant that you were expected one day to give a bigger potlatch, with greater, longer feasting, and much more gift-giving, or you would lose face and have scorn heaped upon your head until you cleared your name.

To have your first proper potlatch, you would need to have your mother give it for you and enlist many relatives and clansmen to help her to provide the gifts and food, plan the entertainment, and invite the presence of important witnesses, enticed by gifts. In the absence of written records, these were the people who kept score, so that all your expensive efforts at hospitality were not forgotten or unfairly diminished by the passage of time.

Potlatches were often huge affairs where the guests ate heartily and remained with the host for half a moon or more. As the potlatching competition among the Haida increased and the gift-giving started to go beyond the giving of masks and handmade gifts to hugely expensive coppers, the chiefs started to add foreign trade goods garnered from the ships by trading sea otter pelts. Soon potlatches featured mounds of washbasins, fancy Chinese piss pots, frying pans, tea and coffee pots, muskets, powder and ball, bayonets, accordions, and great piles of Hudson's Bay Company red or blue wool, two-point blankets, which had become important units of trade. There were even cases where hugely valuable gifts, like war canoes, were given away in a spirit of reckless generosity. If a woman or a man gave a great potlatch, his name was held in the most honored place. But if another chief gave a greater potlatch feast with greater, more abundant gifts, the prior chief's name would fall and his most trustworthy witnesses would sneer at him. These important witnesses were invited like a jury to oversee the event, to precisely count the riches given – how many canoes, how many muskets, how many button blankets and carved food dishes. There seemed to be no end to it.

Haida potlatch

To whites viewing such potlatching, it did seem that a chief was purposely ruining himself as he disposed of all his wealth, sometimes giving away or purposely burning down the house he lived in, and even giving away the wide estuary of a river that he owned where he totally controlled the fishing. In Victoria on Vancouver Island, the whites claimed that potlatching had become madly wasteful and destructive. Canadian government men who witnessed these potlatches considered them a self-inflicted form of native madness, which in some cases utterly impoverished families. In 1921, potlatching in Canada was totally banned by the government.

Almost exactly fifty years later, when Prime Minister Trudeau came out to visit the Queen Charlotte Islands with his wife, rumor has it that one of the chiefs he met said to him, "Too bad we are not allowed to give a true potlatch feast in your honor."

"Why not?" asked Trudeau. When he heard again about the government ban, he said, "I don't support that old idea. From now on, it's all right for you people to potlatch again in Canada."

This was an interesting change. So when young Robert Davidson from the famous Edenshaw line of chiefs created a new totem pole, the first one to rise on the Charlottes in over sixty years, of course that event demanded a potlatch feast. Then other poles were raised elsewhere on the British Columbia coast and other larger potlatches began to occur. At first, the gifts to the many guests were modest, sometimes only a dishtowel and a dollar bill, or a California orange, for every guest. But even that caused excitement, and the old sense of prestige and competition between families, clans, and houses began to build again. And if this seems strange and remote to you, think of fancy weddings, even kids' birthday parties, where the hosts seem determined to out-spend their friends, neighbors and relatives.

Let me tell you of a fairly recent example. A young woman of high standing was going to marry a proud young Haida Islander, also from a prominent family. Certainly, it would be the right occasion for a potlatch feast. As their wedding day approached, relatives phoned over to the mainland and requested a Prince Rupert rental company to ferry over half a dozen limousines to Haida Gwaii – you know the kind, the long, black or white stretch Cadillacs so popular with today's casino gamblers, film folk, and government contractors. No sooner had the limousines arrived at Skidegate than the bride's aunt fell sick. Well, no family would hold a wedding feast with the aunt of the bride ill and on a respirator in the little local hospital. So all this limousine grandeur had to be fully paid for, then ferried back to Prince Rupert.

A few weeks later, the ailing aunt was on her feet again and the wedding day was joyfully reset. The same fleet of long, black and white limousines made the eighty-mile (or 125-kilometer) ferry crossing again. This time, everything went more or less like clockwork and the shiny Cadillacs slowly paraded out of the ferry terminal to meet the bride and bridegroom who waved to everyone as the procession made its way slowly through the reserve.

"Well, nobody's ever going to outdo that," I told Teddy.

"Hell, if I was going against her folks," he whispered, "instead of limousines, I'd hire all eight of those huge Sikorsky helicopters that the logging company leases to airlift out the biggest logs. Each would cost about twenty times the price of one of those cheap stretch limousines. Can't you just see them, hear them thundering up the road? It would take me and my mother's uncles and all our cousins quite a while to pay for a potlatch like that." He held his hands up to his mouth and giggled. "But it would sure as hell be worth it just to drop a raven turd or two on that old bird's parade!"

Paddle

Long ago, Sea Lion Town, Dance Hat Town, Songs of Victory Town, Red Cod Town – and more than a hundred others – were the English translations of the names of the traditional Eagle or Raven communities on the wooded edges of almost all the islands. Most such towns could be reached only by sea. From those beaches in front of the houses came huge dugout canoes that could be paddled by as many as forty warriors almost anywhere to gather slaves. Sometimes they even went as far away as California, incredible though that seems to us now. The other great voyages were in the grease trade, in search of oolichan from the Skeena River region to the east. Having paddled to the mainland, the Haida voyagers and their slaves would trek eastward up the narrow grease trails around the dangerous white water ledges of the mighty Skeena River to Gitksan, so they could load and carry back hundreds of large, bent boxes packed with small oolichan or "candlefish." Each of these fish was so loaded with oil that if dried and lighted they would burn like candles. It was their rendered oil that was such a vital part of the Indian diet, since this would make the smoke-dried winter salmon moist and deliciously rich again.

There was such an abundance of seafood and bird life around the islands that it freed these clever hunters to turn their winter thoughts to art and to the elaborate creations of myths and clan legends. Out of that leisure came some of the best and boldest carvings in the world. At feasts, the chiefs, like Renaissance princes proud of their court artists, displayed the carvings of their artisans to illustrate the elaborate performances of their masked dancers. Some of these chiefs could be overly exacting. One of them proudly proclaimed, to boast of his personal sense of compassion, "I am not like some mainland chiefs. I would not rush out onto the floor of my house with dagger drawn to kill a village dancer because he made just one wrong step."

The practice of potlatching was a truly major event in the lives of the Haida people. Feasting was quite a different matter, meant usually to distribute an abundance of food and at the same time show generosity and goodwill to one's family and friendly neighboring houses, rather like a big dinner party. The purpose of potlatching, in contrast, was to display family or clan superiority. The potlatch, which also included a feast, was in its most rational form the paying back of accumulated debts acquired by a chief in the borrowing of riches in the form of coppers, blankets, canoes, dance blankets, daggers, masks, and often slaves. The chief who was the recipient of all these gifts would then have to ask his relatives, and especially his wife's relatives, to add enough trade wealth to overwhelm his opponent chief, usually of the opposite clan. This became a more modern method of fighting, with wealth instead of raids and bloodshed.

In 1895 at Fort Rupert a native leader summed it up. "When I was young, I saw streams of blood shed in war. But since that time, the white man came and stopped up the streams of blood with wealth. Now we are fighting with our wealth . . . we do not fight with weapons; we fight with property."

The potlatch seemed to remain a manageable system of native banking, involving borrowing and lending, with a rate of interest demanded for each item borrowed in this struggle for self-glorification. Then the foreign captains came to the islands in the eighteenth century to discover and start their madly competitive trade for sea otter skins. The Haida became aware of the easy treasure they possessed in these valuable sea otter that lazed around their islands, enjoying life in the floating beds of kelp. Every item of trade from the ships became new potential potlatch gifts. When the sea otter trade was in full swing from 1790 to 1840, there was great wealth distributed at potlatches. Especially copper. The visiting captains were delighted to discover that copper was important and unusually valuable to the Haida. As it happened, the tall ships' wooden hulls were sheathed in copper as a protection against barnacles that attach themselves below the water line, slowing the progress of the vessel. This copper was thinner than the traditional Haida copper material, but for two otters the captains were very pleased to trade enough to a chief to allow him to create one copper shield.

In the Haida world, copper was considered much more valuable than gold or silver as a symbol of wealth and prestige. Certainly, the rich, lustrous glow that a copper so easily achieves makes it not surprising that it was regarded more highly than gold. Also, since this metal was not native to the Northwest Coast, it was rare. It is believed that copper was traded down from the North in ancient times from free-float chunks of copper found as far away as Coppermine among Canada's Arctic Inuit. Another source may have been the Aleutian Islands.

Copper, a malleable metal, may be pounded into any desired shape even without the application of heat, but pounding copper to be arm's length and roughly a foot wide was a long, laborious task. The reason for the size or shieldlike shape of Northwest Coast coppers is unknown, but these coppers traditionally had a V-shaped spine that rose halfway up the copper until it reached the shoulders. Above that, the space was reserved for a large engraved and blackened pitch painting of a highly stylized animal head often symbolizing the bear. A copper was called *Staget*. The black painted image represented the magical spirit standing between the animals and humans.

The value of these coppers after they had been pounded, shaped, and partially painted can be measured by the worth given to them. One was called "10 slaves." But this number could rise with each giving until it might be called "47 slaves." Another copper had the name "2,000 blankets." Coppers were brought out by a chief during potlatch feasts to display his or her personal wealth and also to be given away to the opposing chief to prove one's own immense wealth and superiority. That very act demanded that the guest chief to whom the gift was given in his turn would have to finance a greater potlatch and give away the copper and piles of other gifts. These might include slaves, canoes, and blankets in great numbers. He might have to feed potlatch guests, perhaps numbering three hundred, who might stay for a week or two. But in the eyes of highborn Haida, the potlatch remained a logical way of settling debts and at the same time aggrandizing yourself and the other extended family members who had helped you.

An ancient myth describes the way it all began. A young Haida man saw a large bird resting on the water. He took his slingshot and, whirling it, struck the bird with a stone. It made a heavy metal pong, the sound of copper. He ran back to the house and told his mother, who said, "Son, that is your father's copper canoe you struck."

They went down to the beach together and waded into the water to the canoe. Soon they began lifting out a number of heavy copper shields, and earrings, bracelets, and a beautiful belt.

After that, the people on the other side of the island could hear the hammering of copper and some of the younger ones laughed and called over, "What's that noise you're making?" No reply came.

The mother and her son went on hammering until finally the

son, now shining and copper colored, said to his mother, "Please take this basket of copper gifts to the Bear chief and tell him I would like to marry his daughter."

The Bear chief went to see this supernatural copper person and had to turn his eyes away because he was too bright and shining to look upon. The Bear chief told the young man's mother that he would welcome her shining son whenever he could come and marry his daughter.

The bright, young copper maker readied himself and went at once to the Bear chief's house and gladly married his daughter. For this, the mother of the shining copper boy gave the old chief a large copper shield with the image of a beaver painted on it.

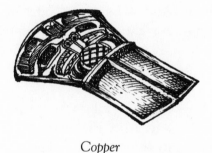

Copper

When we arrived at the potlatch, having traveled south from Tlell – our cottage being forty kilometers north of Skidegate – it was mid-morning. The sparkling blue of the inlet gave every promise of that day being a bright and sunny one. At least a hundred persons had already gathered and were milling around sociably in front of the impressive new Haida Band Council House, which was to be officially opened that day. The two huge, barked poles that would serve as a hoist had the thick rope lines running over them. Both were attached to the cedar totem that already had its cover removed and lay bare, gleaming pinkish white. We gaped at this marvelous creation by the master Haida carver, Bill Reid, and his small team of apprentice helpers. The declared purpose for this Skidegate potlatch was to raise the pole in front of the new house.

What a day for the Haida, such a proud and talented people who had largely rested in the shadows of Canadian progress for a century and more. Now, although non-Indians didn't fully realize it, the Haida were about to come out of their political shell to wave their hands in triumph and to start selling for large prices their splen-did new masks, poles, and ornamented blankets that the North American, and indeed the world's art dealers, would suddenly be more than eager to buy.

An adopted son, Gary Edenshaw, or Guujaaw, as he is now called, is an important Haida man who had formed a young Haida dance group. Guujaaw started the ceremony by tapping on his large tambourine-like drum and dancing slowly, almost shyly, in his elaborate, black button blanket with its scarlet crest and trim out-lined with gleaming, old shell buttons. On his head, Guujaaw wore a traditional spruce root hat. Above its broad brim, big, square, twenty-dollar abalone pieces were sewed around its crown, each one supporting tall sea lion whiskers that waved and clattered as he danced.

After a good deal of speech making and a great deal of grunting or smiling in agreement, with the numbers of mingling guests increasing, the Haida invited everyone to pull along with them on the heavy barge ropes that would raise the pole. What a sight it was, rising and at the same time sliding toward the hole that had been dug for it. In former times, it is said a live slave or two tradi-tionally would be popped down into these totem holes to create real spirits to reside in the pole, but this practice, like the potlatch itself, had long been banned by the government. Now that the ban on potlatching had been lifted, this ceremony (minus the slave part) was being proudly performed once again before the TV cameras of Japan, the U.S., and Canada. Alice and I were encouraged by our local friends to step forward and help in heaving on the ropes as the carved pole skidded slowly and rose in the morning sunshine that made Skidegate Inlet a sparkling paradise, rimmed by its lush green hills and snow-streaked mountains.

Bill Reid was moving excitedly among the guests. He was dressed in a cowboy hat and a South American poncho, which somehow looked just right for a man who had a white American father and a Haida mother. Bill grew up and went to school in the U.S. and later became a well-known radio announcer for the Canadian Broadcasting Corporation in Vancouver and began, as he says, whittling little Haida-like carvings while waiting to go on the air.

It wasn't long, however, before he chucked all that and in 1973 returned to his mother's side of the Eagle Haida family – as any sensible Canadian or American would do if they could claim sufficient Indian status to take advantage of the many free advantages. And, more important, he was able to devote himself full time to the development of his remarkable art, which you will now find in places like Vancouver Airport and the Canadian Embassy in Washington, not to mention museums around the world.

The big pole with the Sand Shark crest on top, its tail projecting high into the air, was almost fully upright now. Everyone who was anyone had had a pull at the ropes, which served to set into their minds forever the pole's importance, as it certainly did in ours. Finally, after some wrapped gifts had been thrown down into the hole and the pole slipped forward, it was firmly implanted in the earth, to become a central part of the front of the Band Council House. Rocks were pummeled into place around the pole and ropes were secured tightly for temporary strength that day. Dancers began moving ceremoniously in front of the pole, Guujaaw drumming encouragement and dancing. All of them sang and stamped their feet with extra force to impact the earth. This pure, unpainted totem was here to stay for perhaps the next one hundred years. With modern telephone pole preservatives, and having been carefully hollowed in the back to prevent rot, this cedar pole takes on an increasing silver grayness of age and, like a modern grandparent, may last much longer than expected.

Inside the new Band Council House, there was around the firepit a square, symbolic ledge of talking seats. The great squared, cedar house beams inside and out gave the small building an immense feeling of strength. The Devonian Foundation in Calgary had financed the cleanup of the beach in front of Skidegate until it looked again like Dr. George Dawson's stunning photographs of

1890, which showed that this beach had once been a Haida wonderland, with over fifty houses and standing totems. Emily Carr memorably painted similar Skidegate scenes. When I first saw it in 1968, all the carved poles were gone save one. It had been created fully round, with a carved Beaver at its base. Only a chief's successive potlatch rings marked the bare pole, except for a handsome Eagle that was flying off its top. They say that wooden eagle blew down in a windstorm and immediately disappeared. Indeed, a white man snatched it away, the Haida say, and God knows where it has flown. Today, even that old Beaver potlatch pole is down.

But that's all history now. There was a second important part to this famous potlatch. Chiefs and whole families from Alaska and all over the Northwest Coast had come here to witness and to share in all this grandeur. All around the Skidegate recreation hall, picnic tables had been placed, and by six o'clock, hundreds were seated there, all dressed in their very best. Smiling Haida girls placed one orange each along the center of every long table. Oranges are expensive on the Charlottes, so everyone quickly put their share away inside their bags, then waited until their handsome, smiling Haida mothers from the Skidegate reserve moved around as efficiently as airline attendants, providing a richness of seafood for every guest.

The chiefs and their wives were heavily ornamented with wide gold and silver engraved bracelets with the wearer's clan crest on them, not just Raven or Eagle crests, but personal or family crests of Frog, Sand Shark, Salmon, Wolf, and Bear. It is a pity that so few of the important oral myths and legends of the Haida are known to their fellow Canadians and Americans today.

In our eyes, Alice and I were given the great honor of being seated next to Florence Davidson, affectionately known as Nonny (meaning grandmother) throughout Haida Gwaii. She was the matriarch of all this, the important aunt to Bill Reid, and the mother of the coming younger carver, Robert Davidson. During the huge feast, our eyes popped at the growing abundance of clams, salmon, halibut, gaaw, venison, octopus, mussels, salal berry pie, blueberry muffins, salal ice cream, coffee, or tea. The hereditary chief, Dempsey Collinson, who owned a modern fishing vessel named

Haida Warrior, was said to have come into Skidegate Landing with seventeen thousand dollars' worth of fresh-caught fish and given them all as his contribution toward this feast.

In the very center of the hall, theatrical spotlights were beaming down. Seated at the main table were Bill Reid and his beautiful blonde Parisian wife, Martine, who wrote her doctoral dissertation on the Kwakiutl cannibal ceremony. Around them sat the hereditary chiefs and the elected chiefs, each, like the Reids, caught in an Academy-Award-like glow. One by one, the chiefs went forward to the stage and made complimentary speeches, blessing Bill Reid and the return of this ancient pole raising and ceremonial life. One speechmaker will stand out in my mind forever, an extremely short, deeply tanned chief, with white hair and wide Haida cheekbones. On his face he wore a curious half smile, and on his forehead a small Moon mask, which only he was privileged to wear. Through the loudspeaker, he whispered that he had never spoken publicly before. Then there was an incredibly long silence while the whole audience sat as in church, waiting for the words of this tiny man wearing his short dance blanket that hung relaxed as ravens' wings from his bent shoulders. Finally, in a cracked voice, he began to speak of his family house at Tanu and of the great Haida past. For some time, I watched that timeless man captured in that single spotlight beam. He did appear to me as someone from another world, a world totally different from my own.

Chief's frontlet

22

Song to the River

Hearing someone's steps on our covered porch, I went and opened the door.

"It's wet out there," I said to a short, dignified Haida woman who was perhaps sixty or seventy years old – age on the islands can be difficult to guess.

"Folks down at Skidegate say your house has the best view of this river, especially when it's raining hard, like now."

"Come in, join us for coffee," Alice called, and we shook hands with her. "Are you alone?" Alice asked.

"No, but I'll be here only a few minutes if you're not too busy for my visit."

"Don't bother about your rubber boots," I said, but too late, for she had drawn them off island-style and stepped inside. She came quietly into the room and headed straight for our large, north window. She opened her hand, revealing a number of blackberries.

"This rain's making them grow great this year," she smiled.

"We love them," Alice told her. "I put some in the pancakes for breakfast this morning. They've got a wonderful flavor."

There was a pause.

"Who are you?" Alice asked. "Should I know you?"

"No, you don't know me," the woman smiled at both of us. "I'm a Kagani Haida. My son and I are down from Alaska just paying a little visit in Skidegate. Do you know Hydaburg on Prince of Wales Island just north of here?" she asked. "It's not Canadian. It's in Alaska, American territory."

"We've never been up to those islands," I told her. "But we plan to go up some time."

"Yeah, it's nice there, all right," she said, then looked back at the long curve of the river. "But this place is my spirit home."

"You mean here in Tlell?"

"Yeah, here in Tlell. Tlell means 'berry patches' in Haida, talking about these berry patches on this river, there, they're ours."

"How do you mean they're yours?" Alice asked her, curious to know.

"I inherited them, all of the berry patches on both sides of the river. My great-great-grandfather was a hereditary chief. He had a big house right near here, big enough to hold a potlatch and sleep maybe more than forty guests, with a real good totem pole out in front, just between the ocean and this salmon berry river. My cousins told me I could still see a big, square, dugout firepit and the dugout holes for the house posts and the pole. That's where I picked these berries. The house and poles have fallen down and rotted or washed away in the river during the high winter tides. But you can still see where they marked the ground."

I pulled out a chair for her.

"No thanks," she felt herself. "I won't sit down. My back side's wet from wading through my salal bushes." She laughed. "Now I just got to do something I promised my grandmother I'd do. That was before she died, she left me a painted cedar bent box with a dance blanket inside. It's all faded now. And there's a woman's wooden mask, a rattle, and a song she taught me that is allowed to be sung by only me straight to this river."

"Well," Alice said, "we'd like to hear you sing it."

"You understand I don't claim this house of yours or anything. I'm just checking on my berries the way I should, and now I'm going to sing my song."

She started singing to the Tlell River with all her berry patches on both sides. "It's too bad you can't understand the Haida words of the song," she said when she was finished. "Lots of the words are so old I can't really understand them myself, and the kids, why they don't know almost any of the words. But now I'm done. I've sung the song for her – and for me. We lost the real Haida words because a lot of outsiders – people with different religions – came here and gathered up the Haida language and hid it away. Others came and gathered almost all the old totem poles, and bought or traded for the masks, the dance blankets, and they took them away and the missionaries traded us back the English language instead of our own, and iron and cloth and church Bingos and victrolas then satellite TVs. That's about all we got from them up there in Alaska or down here."

When the Alaskan Haida woman had finished her song, Alice asked her if she wanted coffee or tea. She looked around, then shook her head and said, "Nice place you got here, all white inside, just right to look at the river. Those rods and hip boots hanging on the porch must mean you two like fishing. So do I. So come visit us sometime up in Hydaburg. That's my son out there in the car. He's kind of shy and wouldn't come in. The troubles at Tow Hill up on North Beach, they happened between some Haida families a long, long time ago, some say more than two hundred years ago. But that's all over now, and the grandchildren of those same families are starting to get friendly again. I hope you have good fishing and lots of berries this year," she said as we shook hands.

She stepped into her rubber boots and started down the mossy path toward our gate and a little rental car that held the ghostly shadow of some young Haida warrior from those times long past, or in the future.

The time I've spent with Inuit and North American Indians has given me a strong link with the past, and knowing them has helped me to imagine and thus shape my future. These early people have been keenly aware of theatrics and were conducting meaningful performances and singing songs to accompany them thousands of years before the written word existed.

Theater, it seems to me, is the most total of all art experiences. Theater alone combines the art of storytelling with fanciful cos-tumes, masks, singing, dancing, face painting, musical instruments, the play of light and dark, laughter and fear, delight and weeping, all the drama and excitement necessary to preserve the dreams, the myths, and the legends for future generations. When I lived with Inuit, I came to know their songs and dances. Over time, I also learned a little about those of the Dene, the Nascopi, and the Cree, who danced in the North, the Zuni and Hopi dancing in the South, and the Haida, Kwakiutl, Gitksan, and Tlingit on the Northwest Coast. Each group has different songs and deities and art styles of their own that seem to have grown naturally out of their environment, their own special way of life.

When I heard their singing and the telling of their myths and legends, and watched their masks, their costumes, and other art objects moving in the northern firelight or the desert sun, I had an unshakable feeling that we were all of us everywhere celebrating that same someone, though he or she may have a thousand different forms and may wear a different mask for each of us.

Haida mask

As I think of Haida and Inuit, it makes me wish that I could be a computer expert today. I would try to use that skill to gather together the anthropological information revealed in a thousand studies around the world. Many cultures are still in their native state, or nearly so. This is the last chance before television homogenizes and cripples them forever.

Many valuable word lists, grammars, and dictionaries were compiled in the eighteenth, nineteenth, and twentieth centuries. Now, time is running out for us to study native languages and carefully record the ones that still exist. There are said to be 6,500 languages used in the world today and more than half of those languages are predicted to disappear during the twenty-first century. Are we moving that fast, too fast? We should carefully record these languages to inform native people and ourselves about their uniquely important position in their lives and our global way of life.

We know a lot about the so-called civilized people of this world. But all too few among us have ever tried to correlate and compare the amazing language and cultural similarities between the native people of, say, eastern Europe and India, or India and the Ainu people of Japan, or they with the Inuit/Eskimo of the Arctic, or they with the Maori of New Zealand. Now, such linguistic and cultural studies are possible with man's ever-developing computer tools. We have the chance to put this to some good use, instead of letting information gather dust in some forgotten doctoral dissertation or master's thesis.

What are we actually giving peoples around the world to modify their customs, to replace their sometimes peaceful, sometimes warlike ways? For one thing, we remain devoted to the idea of imposing our own concept of God to replace their gods, our plastic castings instead of their wood-carved gods, our often childish songs for theirs. I saw this in the Arctic, and I didn't like it. But it is no longer just a question of imposed religions. Satellite television is the instrument to destroy languages and cultures, satellite TV pouring down on people around the world and inundating them with our own and other folktales in tightly edited moving color. True or false, it seduces them into abandoning their old faith and songs, chants, and myths in favor of ours. Most people today disapprove of this, when they stop to think about it, but nevertheless they leave the whole subject to others.

Don't be shy, you younger, on-line computer generation! You could win a Nobel Prize for a solution to such important, global studies. Think of all the knowledge that could be gained and the general peace of mind that you might help to spread around the world! To give just one example, women have been at various times very powerful throughout the world, and in many areas they still are. We should study ancient matrilineal societies such as they have here among the Haida, what caused them to become so strong, and what caused them to disappear in other areas. Who knows what we might learn?

23

The Shipping Agent

One Sunday afternoon about four o'clock, a heavyset man came up onto our front porch. I got up from my drawing board beside the front window and opened the door, expecting this stranger to ask me for directions. Instead, he said, "Nice house, you got here, *señor*. Do you want to sell it to me . . . now?"

He was several inches taller than me, handsome and deeply tanned, with a mass of black wavy hair. He wore yellow socks and Gucci shoes, light gray slacks, a green double-worsted blazer, and a white shirt, with a not too thin, gold chain around his neck. This was a costume that on the Queen Charlottes was rarer than hens' teeth.

"No," I answered, "we're not thinking of selling this place. We like the fishing here too much."

"You don't even want to know how much money I'm offering you for your place?" he asked, reaching toward his breast pocket.

I saw another man standing beside their car, watching us and listening to our conversation.

"Well," I laughed, "I'm not planning to sell it."

"That's too bad," he said, and smiled thinly. "You're making a big mistake. *Buenos dias*. You could buy a helluva lot of fish for the money that I'm offering."

He looked at me in disgust, then turned and strutted down our mossy path and out the gate. The other man was back inside their airport-rental car and had the motor running.

"What do you suppose that was all about?" asked Alice, who had heard our conversation from the fish room.

"I don't know," I said. "He seemed to be dead serious about wanting to buy this cottage – I mean, right away!"

"Why would that be?" she said. "Does he think we're sitting on an oil deposit?"

It has been my habit since army days and Arctic nights to rise early. I have a homemade drawing desk inside the cottage, a long, two-inch-thick single plank of yellow cedar that I sometimes use in the silence of the early mornings, usually after coffee, about 5:30 to 7:30 a.m. The largish window in front of the desk faces east on the gravel road with a thick fir forest one long deer-jump from the window. If coho salmon have arrived in the estuary of the river, I'm used to seeing the odd set of truck headlights turn and head down toward the road's end before dawn, with some kind of a square-sterned boat in back.

Probably two or three weeks had passed since our visit from the Latin American man who had offered to buy the cottage, when I saw several headlight beams cutting through the early dawn. But the strange part was they were going the wrong way, they were coming from the coast, heading inland. As I sat there watching, I could see that it was not just two vehicles. I counted fourteen cars, and not a one of them carried a boat. Almost all of them were tail-gating each other and they were all going way too fast for the gravel road. A few of these vehicles I thought I recognized, but with most I was unsure. Not one of the drivers turned to look at me sitting in my bright square of lighted window, nor did they wave at me, which was in itself unusual. The cars all turned onto our one and only main road on the island and sped south. It was like watching a fast railroad train of cars without a locomotive.

I checked my watch. It was 5:40 a.m. *Was there anything I should do*, I wondered. *Oh, forget it*, I told myself. *You'll hear some logical, local explanation for this impossibly well-organized pre-dawn event.* But, you know, we never did, although we asked. The whole thing remained a mystery. I will say, however, that it was just at the time when the CBC radio news was starting to speak of whole shiploads of drugs coming up into the Northwest Coast of Canada from Colombia in South America, or maybe southeast Asia, then being smuggled south again for distribution on both sides of the border.

That was quite a few years ago and I'm sure by now all such systems have changed. But, still, in the quiet life here on the Charlottes, that was an exciting event for me. I wonder now what might that Latin-American stranger have paid for this simple, green-shingled observation post of mine, even if I had admitted to him that we have carpenter ants?

24

The Mushroom Eaters

The Vietnam War taught most people in North America a lot about themselves. It seems to me now that it changed almost all of us more than we realized at the time. The Vietnam War thrust television into enormous prominence. Click it on in the morning and you'd watch young American men wounded, bloody, and dying in the fresh, uncensored pictures that were moving before your eyes. This war unseated a president and polarized wild political differences in the United States. It also changed the face of the remote Queen Charlotte Islands, for it sent increasing numbers of America's draft evaders tumbling into this wild Canadian paradise, this perfect hideaway.

First, it should be remembered that the draft evaders, like the wide variety of characters in any people's army, represented almost every different kind of human being. Some young Americans were desperately on the run from being drafted into an army that demanded they risk their lives in an uncertain, undeclared war in the rice paddies or the jungle. Others who – along with their parents in some cases – held serious political objections to the war, decided that the enemy was the U.S. Government. Coming to these islands was not like dodging into Canadian cities like Vancouver, Toronto, Montreal, or Halifax – which draft dodgers did aplenty – for in these cities whole underground organizations had begun to form.

On the Queen Charlottes, the newcomers were largely on their own. Sometimes they met a chilly reception from the local inhabitants, Indian or white, who didn't like the look or sound of some of these new people and wanted them to dodge the hell away to somewhere else. But there were girls here, or other girls who migrated here because of them. Some were adapting to the hippie life and enjoyed their truly different style.

To feed and house themselves and flourish on these islands, the hippies had to do a lot of sharing. Some of them, the rich ones, received substantial checks from their families and shared the money around for those essentials that only money would buy. Some of them, as I've said, took up with young Haida women or other locals. Through the knowledge of the fathers and brothers, and from those girls themselves, they began to learn how to survive. They could hunt and fish successfully, if illegally, and raise rough and ready vegetable gardens protected with the aid of tall fish nets from the endless deer that could provide meat on their table every day of the year. Even some hippies disapproved of those among them who would net a river tight and try to take a whole night's run of salmon. But on the Tlell, it was obviously sometimes done. A few of the Haida girls learned from their mothers and grandmothers how to smoke the salmon and pack them into jars and cans and old-fashioned cedar boxes, to preserve the fish through the winter, when the salmon run was over.

The hippies, in my opinion, built some of the most imaginative housing ever seen in Canada. The crudest habitations were romantic, Robinson Crusoe efforts, just driftwood logs and planks roughly hammered or tied together into something that looked like a tumbled woodpile, with old sailcloth covering an entrance to an outdoor cooking place. Almost all these weary wanderers were in their twenties. They gathered together only rarely, and most lived a wild, half-secret life, scattered like some primitive tribe in original-looking dwellings hidden just beyond the forested edges or among the log piles half buried in the lonely beaches along the Hecate Strait.

God knows the best house-building timber in the world lay right here waiting for them – free cedar that was easily split to produce any size of planks. Beautiful-smelling shakes of wood that would last as shingles on your house roof for nearly thirty years were ready for the making, and if you owned a shake splitter, you could replace your roof for absolutely nothing or trade your shakes to others for something that you lacked. With an endless abundance of salmon, halibut, and black-tailed deer, wild geese eggs, and shellfish, it was a place where, as one of their head-scarved women reckoned, "You could watch the tide go out, and see the table set with more wholesome food than you could eat, and it didn't cost a penny."

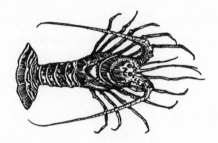

Pacific lobster

The hippies' lives as hunters and as gatherers were probably a good deal more exciting than the lives they had been living in the cities and suburbs of the United States. Of course, none of their houses were built on property they owned, and eventually a government bulldozer came along and leveled their crude shelters. But that first taste of building made the hippies more thoughtful, more home-oriented, and definitely more creative.

The second time around, they helped each other. Some, especially those from California, seemed to have studied architecture and to have real building skills. Others were close to a degree in engineering. Still others had only worked on stage sets, for their constructions were anything but lasting. Still, they built with thick, rich-smelling cedar, usually cut on what is called an Alaskan mill – a large, hand-transported chainsaw with guiding bars – so the wood they needed could be felled and milled deep in the forest and the planks floated by water to their building sites.

Now the old-time islanders, Haida and white, began to look around and see fairy story houses rising almost hidden behind a curtain of trees. These had wide shake roofs and quaintly trembling towers that served as lookouts. For what? Schools of salmon or deer, or government men. Who knows? To the old-timers, it seemed as though a strange, nomadic tribe had moved onto the islands. It was almost as though the newcomers spoke a guarded language, that they were a secret society of anti-warriors who grew the pot they wished to smoke and brewed the liquor they desired to drink.

Their ways and styles became increasingly attractive to the locals. Many of them adopted the long hairstyle, wore beards, wide leather belts, slouch hats, and beads. Their women wore long, colorless, shapeless dresses, brass bangles, and loggers' boots, and Gypsy-like bandanas to more or less hide their hair. Theirs was an extreme example of loose co-operative living in a counterculture. They built and shared what they secretly called "the glass house," hidden in the depths of the forest not so very far from our place. Ultimately, it would take a helicopter to find the glass house long after the Vietnam War was over, when all but a few of the hippies on the run had been forgiven and decided to stay, or drift back home.

More interesting to the islanders is the story of those who stayed. Many of them were well educated and had married young Canadian women, or had American girlfriends who had joined them and had finally decided to apply for citizenship. Many of them, male and female, had become welcome schoolteachers in the Canadian education system, taking hard-to-fill positions in remote schools of northern British Columbia, the Yukon, the Northwest Territories, and Labrador. Now with their spouses and teenaged children, I think they've added a very worthy new dimension to our Canadian society, just as others did after the American Revolution of 1776 when some did not wish to embrace the new republic. Long ago, that group, in itself, represented more than one-third of the graduates of Harvard, Yale, and Princeton who remained Loyalists (or Royalists, as the Americans like to call them). Some of them went back to England. But many of them trekked north to become Canadians in New Brunswick and Nova Scotia and even Ontario. Their offspring are still here.

The Vietnam-era hippies who came here in the early 1970s often bought old school buses down on the mainland and had them ferried over to Vancouver Island. They drove these buses up to Port Hardy and paid to have them shipped by Rivtow Freight over to the Queen Charlotte Islands. To celebrate this odyssey and their euphoria upon being free from registration in the U.S. military, they burned their draft cards, bought cans of paint, and, sometimes using their fingers as brushes, painted their Gypsy-like caravans with soaring doves, sunflowers, and other peace signs. Using the buses as both transportation and housing, they explored the islands' possibilities.

One mechanical genius among them was credited with having kept the whole, quaky-looking fleet of vehicles running. You can still find faint archeological traces of these crumbling, rusted hulks hidden in the forest. They have found their resting place, like the ancient, half-carved Haida canoes that suffered a similar fate when they split or just fell out of style because of the world too-quickly changing. Gradually, an increased number of used Volkswagens and small, battered trucks began to appear, traveling Graham Island's seventy miles of now paved road with its long, straight stretches closely flanked by stands of timber, then by undulating, mossy boglands, then without a human dwelling in sight.

This became the hitchhiker's favorite run. The earlier islanders had become sociable, first out of necessity, and then because of habit. They always stopped to give a person on foot a lift. Some hikers said they usually wouldn't talk to the driver because they knew they wouldn't share his political views. But lots of these older drivers who occupied the northern islands had come here because they, too, wanted to live in this relative wilderness far away from European or North American government meddling. Canadians who had perhaps rejected their own society in Europe or the eastern provinces were here. For any number of reasons, they, too, mistrusted Canadian or U.S. rules and taxes. The hippie newcomers found that they had much in common with other islanders, many of whom had long shared their anti-government sentiments.

One might easily see eighty deer out browsing on the roadside grasses during a rough drive from Skidegate to Haida Village in the north. This was a hippie paradise, with native food abundant everywhere, and for free. By taking several steps backward into the heavy forest, a man could disappear. The hippies, whether they liked it or not, had initially made themselves a tribe apart. But, suddenly, almost overnight, they began to add new life to these islands with their guitars, harmonicas, and summers of casual nude sunbathing with their newfound girlfriends. While the war was raging on in Vietnam, Cambodia, and Thailand, and the colleges and cities of North America were in serious ferment, the Queen Charlottes remained such a bountiful haven that some of those wild young people settled down and never went home. They just stayed here, found jobs, built or bought houses, became teachers, sent their own kids to school, and took on what you might call varying degrees of respectability.

In every season when one studies the Tlell River, it is apparent that a lot of different things are happening at the same time. A black bear boldly crosses the ford near the old Nelson log cabin. Day by day, kingfishers laugh, then dive as straight as arrows to snatch up salmon fry. Deer delicately wade, then swim across the river, and eagles wait, then swoop down to snatch at half-grown fish.

Not far beyond the ford near our cottage, when summer warms the river, two nude female swimmers busily kick up the water, then stand knee deep waving at passersby on the bridge. The girls come down from their tiny, homemade shack on the riverbank when the weather is right to frolic in the shallows between the salmon pools. Or so it was twenty years ago. These girls used to shock the hell out of some of our guests, but that was probably the point.

I think the disappearance of our nude swimmers marked the end of the old-fashioned hippie days, but so many unusual things that used to happen fairly regularly on these islands seem to be fading away. One of those lithe and beautiful bare bathers became one of our many postmistresses. She long continued to hand us our mail, somberly sell us stamps, and firmly frank our letters. That's how the world has turned. "You should enjoy life to the full," she said to us, "while your eyesight's still good enough to appreciate beauty!"

Mushrooms, oh, those little button mushrooms! Finding them and picking them should be considered one of the most dangerous of outdoor sports. Environmentalists have not yet discovered a reason why humans should not pick them. Naturally, this makes the authorities feel sad. Mushrooms have no roots. They refurbish themselves by scattering airborne spores. They fly. The wild ones, the great delicious mushrooms called boletus, chanterelles, shaggymanes, and meadow mushrooms, are all good to eat, and there are others, too.

But there are also toadstools that can look like mushrooms. You should be damned careful and know how to identify them. Scientists say that some people can get a bad reaction from just touching a deadly amanita or a fly agaric. The *Amanita virosa* is aptly called the "angel of death." These big toadstools are, thank goodness, very showy, having bright red-orange caps with large white or yellow spots. Amanitas can be eight inches across, with undergills and stems that are dead-white. Before picking wild mushrooms, you should get a very good book and study it, and them, with care. Then, when you're almost certain you've found something eatable, go and show it to a local expert. Ask them if they'd care to eat a batch of them with you.

Don't expect any real mushroom hunters to tell you where they find their treasures, such as on the edge of a forest or along some mossy, sunlit path. Mushroomers are a very secretive lot. You'll understand why when you realize that Canadian pine mushrooms were selling in the Japanese good times at fine Tokyo restaurants for a hundred U.S. dollars a portion.

The *Boletus edulis*, the King Boletus, grandest mushroom of them all, looks almost like a puffball growing out of the thick moss. But reach down carefully beneath it with your fingers and raise this treasure very gently. It has a rich, almost meatlike taste when sliced and pan-seared in butter. Young French lovers sometimes come here hoping to pay for their return airfare to Paris by picking the King Boletus for sale to France's most gourmet restaurants. We like to hear them billing and cooing in their colorful little French pup tents in the woods when we go down the other side of the river to fish.

The grounds around the edges of our property are famous for King Boletus mushrooms. We prefer them to all other mushrooms, by far. The light that sifts through the tall coniferous trees might not be right for Alice's gardening, but it seems perfect for boletus mushrooms. One of us looks the whole place over each September and October morning, especially one day after a rain. When we find a boletus and it is still small, not quite golf ball size, we usually decide against taking it, but let it increase to baseball size the following day. But we have real competition. I believe those handsomely spotted leopard slugs that grow longer than your pointing finger smell these delicious growths from some distance away and start moving at a snail's pace toward them. Alice, working on the good advice of Benita Sanders, has developed her own slug fence made out of a small piece of fine, expandable screen wire cut three or four inches high. This may or may not outwit the determined gourmet slug, but it's worth trying, for a generous portion of sautéed boletus mushrooms, sliced with a fillet of local venison and a glass of Chilean red wine, is good enough to make you sob for joy.

But be careful they're not toadstools! I've been told that in the old days, Russian peasants on the edges of a similarly damp Siberian forest used to carefully break off parts of some of those most deadly fungi and knowingly eat a portion of the cap. This would, they say, cause wild outbreaks of laughing and whirling Cossack dances in the moonlight. Not so very different, I imagine, than those done on Tlell's bridge in the early 1970s. Almost worse, along our roadsides in the proper season, we have psilocybin, a small, fingernail-sized white fungi that grows in patches almost hidden by the grass. I'll give them no better description. But, let me warn you, they'll jazz you up at first, then turn your brains to mush!

They are wildly hallucinogenic, and overdosing on them can kill you. It is now illegal to pick them or possess them, but in those bold, old, hippie days, these "magic mushrooms" helped to shape that culture. It was said that the true human connoisseurs among them would kneel down in imitation of the long-horned Highland cattle and graze on these little fungi, nipping them off at the stem with their teeth. Long ago, we used to hear some feminine shrieks and deep, bull-like bellows piercing the moonlit air perhaps half a mile along the roadside. Alice would roll over in our bed and say, "They've just found some! I hope they'll go off home to eat the rest."

King Boletus mushroom

25

In Praise of Wood

I have always liked the shape and feel and smell of wood, especially wood that is just beginning to be shaved and shaped by man. I know that I received these feelings from my father when I was young. I loved to walk with him along the beaches of Lake Simcoe and find strange, worn shapes of driftwood, which he would carry up to our woodshed behind the cottage. I can clearly remember him as he sat thoughtfully contemplating each collected piece, turning it over in his hands, feeling it, viewing it from many different angles. "What do you see in this piece of wood, Jimmy? Can you imagine anything hiding in here?" He would perhaps snap off a little branch here and there to clarify the shape of a head, then carve an eye with his pocketknife, then ask again, "Can you see something now?"

"Is it a dog?" I'd ask.

"No," he'd say. "But maybe it's a beaver. Let's try it out."

My father was definitely not working on these natural-found forms for my enlightenment. He was doing them for himself, or I guess for both of us. And if a few of them turned out well enough, he might use them to decorate our family cedar hedges, which stood to the east of the small apple orchard at the cottage. All of our property was surrounded by a tall, thick cedar hedge, with ever-changing wooden animals peering out. I thought of it then as the edge of a magic forest.

My father would have been overjoyed if he had had the luck to live as I do on the banks of the Tlell. Each high tide brings up and distributes armloads of treasures – bark-stripped roots of fir and won-drously twisted shapes of yew and mountain alder, red and yellow cedar, and old pieces of hand-hewn boards. Some still may have old, square, rusted nails made, I like to think, on the forges of the German settlers, the Lutheran families that came early this century. These were hard workers, hewers of wood, planters of potatoes, cabbage, and beets, keepers of bees, chickens, geese, and other livestock – differ-ent in so many ways from those later, laid-back characters who raised as their crop marijuana under glass so the dampness from the winter rains would not weaken the plants' growth.

A variety of eagle, duck, gull, and raven feathers float up lightly on the tide to be stranded on the water's edge. You need only wash away the clay, then steam them over your kettle and they'll unfurl and look as good as new again.

My friend, Teddy, from across the river, said he believed that some of the old arts created on these islands, especially the totem poles, may have been inspired by dead and broken trees that naturally took on the look of ravens' heads, or of bears, or eagles. Haida chiefs of long ago may have wished to declare these mystical images their own, for it was always the chief who could afford to commission a grand house pole and interior house posts. It was he or she who hired the most talented carver and told him exactly what was required, sometimes ordering the carver to make an arm's-length model of the pole to make sure he had the sequence of the chiefly family crests in order and would create the work exactly as the nobleman and his wife demanded it be done.

One of the great privileges of living on the Charlottes is the smell of fresh-cut cedar, and the abundance of that fragrant wood. The kinds of misty weather and mild winters along with the right type of soil join together to produce perhaps the greatest tall-growth forests in the world.

There used to be a small, active lumber operation up the road a few miles north of the Tlell. The Abbots ran it across from their farm. You can still see the graying piles of wood cut into strange, interesting sizes, some of them two inches thick, in lengths and widths of board that house builders have rarely used in the east since the eighteenth century.

In repairing our newly purchased old cottage, which definitely needed work, I used to go up and poke around that lumberyard, which was still occasionally in operation at the time. It was worth it just to smell the fresh-cut cedar, which has an effect on me that's greater than morning coffee. I came to know the owner slightly, but not well. He told me that he was almost never there. This made things difficult, especially since I had hired a carpenter who was doing nothing but counting salmon rises while he sat and waited to have me supply him with wood to work. I went to see old Mr. Abbott at his home and ask him what I should do.

"Go back and take whatever wood you need," he said. "You can pay me for it some time later."

"Shall I tell you what I'm going to need?" I asked him.

"No, no, don't bother," he said, "that's probably hard to do. Why don't you just put an honest amount of money, whatever you think you owe me, into a little plastic bag. Stick it between those two square-looking stones where you turn to get the three by twelves in the nine-foot lengths. They're for the Japanese, that's the lengths they like."

"Are you sure that's okay?" I asked. "If I just take the wood and guess about the money?"

"Sure," he said. "I know you. You live in the green cottage by the bridge. Don't worry. I'll pick up the money from under the rock later on."

That was the way so many early dealings on the Charlottes worked. It told me a lot more about the people here than any words could convey!

26

Royal Flush

The main problem for us in times of crisis was that there was no real, honest-to-God plumber on the islands. Finally, one arrived, and swore he was going to stay. I met him for the first time when I hailed his white van on the road. It had the words "Royal Flush" shakily scrawled on its side.

"Our toilet's jammed," I groaned. "We're in a terrible fix. When can you come and save us? You are a plumbing company?"

"Yeah, we're plumbers, all right, just me and my dad," he told me proudly. "We call our company the Royal Flush. Do you get it?"

We both laughed.

"I just bought this van in Prince Rupert, but I haven't found anyone to paint a royal flush in cards on its side."

"I'm your man," I said. "I'll paint your name and a royal flush poker hand on your truck if you'll get right over to our cottage and fix our plumbing tomorrow morning."

"It's a deal," he said. "Someone told me you're a fancy painter. We'll be there. Have you got the right paint and a small brush?" he asked.

"You bet I have," I told him, "paint and brushes good enough to paint the Sistine Chapel."

"No kidding," he said. "Is that where the Pope lives?"

True to his word, he pulled up early next morning in front of our place in his secondhand white truck that I think used to belong to the Dutch baker in his four-grain bread days. He and an older, more reliable-looking man got out of the truck.

"This is my dad. You can start painting any time," he said, pointing at the truck's panel. "Your wife can show me to the can."

I shook hands with his father. "You got a mighty nice place here right beside the river."

"Come and take a look at this, Dad," the plumber called from our front porch where he stood with Alice.

His father walked stiff-legged up our mossy path, following him. I opened my box of oil paints, linseed oil, and brushes.

Later, when I peeked into the bathroom, they were both squatting in front of our toilet with the back open and its parts lying around. The old man tried to flush it and said, "Hell, still no luck. The boy here's going to have to order you new inside parts from Prince Rupert or Vancouver. They should get up here in a week or maybe two."

"What are we going to do in the meantime?" Alice asked.

They both pointed outside toward the bush.

"That may be okay for us," I told them, "but what about our fancy friends? We're expecting them early next week."

"They'll be dead-afraid of bears out there," said Alice.

"Oh, if you're willing to pay to fly in the parts, I guess we could have them here in a couple of days," the father said. "Is your telephone working? If it is, I'll call off island and order them right now."

We both admired the quick way in which the old man got right to the heart of the problem. He phoned Prince Rupert and sealed the deal. Alice gave us all some coffee and hot buns while I finished the royal flush, in spades, of course, with their name beside it in red.

"We'll have it fixed for sure on Friday morning," said the son.

I looked at the father. The way he nodded gave me a lot more confidence.

Friday, Saturday, and Sunday morning passed before I finally caught up with the son by phone. His voice sounded shaky. "Where the hell have you been?" I demanded. "Did the parts come in?" I asked.

"Yeah, Mr. Houston, they're safe and sound. We got 'em a few days ago."

"Well, why didn't you get up here?"

"We had a kind of party here, Mr. Houston, to celebrate, you know, your new paint job on the truck and, with one thing and another, the party lasted all weekend. And now, honest to God, Mr. Houston, I got too terrible a hangover to even think about a toilet. I can't fix yours today."

"Well, how about your father? He looks like he knows a lot. What about him coming and doing the job?"

"I don't think he can get there today, either, Mr. Houston. Remember, my dad knows how to drink, too. Can you hear him singing behind me? I think he's going to love the Charlottes. Don't you?"

27

Gassing Up

We had a grand old secondhand Chrysler station wagon. It was a kind of a washed-out garnet color that had faded fast in the spring sun and the rains. But it had that wonderful virtue of being long enough to lay a pair of fly rods out full length and carry a pile of groceries, those being its main uses for us. Unfortunately, the Chrysler had a huge tank and drank gas like a camel just in off the desert. This was about the time when the Saudis in Arabia had their grandest moment driving gasoline prices through the ceiling and causing North American drivers everywhere to line up at the pump. You'll notice I didn't say "pumps" because there were only four on the 130-mile (or 210-kilometer) length of the Charlottes, then.

That same year, some wealthy visitor decided to send our nearest neighbors down the road three moped bikes so their kids could romp and play on them. These kids were cute, healthy-looking little cherubs with pink cheeks and curly golden hair. The problem with the exciting new bikes was that the whole of the Charlottes is kind of soft and spongy – mushy, you might call it – because of the rains and the beautiful Chinese scroll-like mists that raise a five-inch layer of moss over almost every bit of ground. The rest of the island is trees – cedar, fir, and alder – or rough gravel beaches completely unsuitable for unescorted young daredevils with brand-new moped bikes.

The way they solved the problem was to have the children come and play around the new hard-surfaced turnabout that the Department of Highways had placed not far from our cottage the year before, and all too close to my hideaway. I put in earplugs and counted the days on my calendar until that Monday in September when the yellow school bus would stop five days a week and haul these impish speedsters far away to school, and I would be spared the sound of their whining around and around the old station wagon on those noisy, high-pitched little bikes. When I asked the kids, quite politely, one day why they didn't just ride up and down in front of their own place instead of our place, they said it was because their mom and dad had said, and I quote, "they couldn't stand the noise."

About this time, I received a very exciting letter asking me to attend an important film meeting, with everybody coming half way to the Seattle airport. The other people planning to attend the meeting would be there on that special September day at 4:00 p.m. This was a meeting not to be missed, so we totally changed our plans, along with all our airline tickets, and got our bags half packed. We drove north and filled our enormous gas tank full. We were ready to go. But all the next day, the little mopeds were screaming around our car again. No more annoying, than, say, three determined mosquitoes buzzing close beside your ear just as you plan to go to sleep.

Next morning, mindful of the drive to Skidegate to catch the bus to catch the ferry to catch the plane, I lugged our baggage out in lots of time and made sure the old station wagon was alive and eager to go. Well, alive, but perhaps not eager. After a few long, wet groans and coughs, she started. I looked out over the beautiful gray-green stillness of the river, knowing that there were many more salmon planning yet to come our way. And here we were, forced to leave the islands early.

"We're off!" Alice called as she flung her bag in the back and hopped in the seat beside me.

With the engine roaring, the Chrysler moved out then down the main road. We had not gone very far before the engine began to falter, then sigh, then make a little chug, before she died. I rolled off onto the soft shoulder of the road. "Oh, God, we can't be out of gas," I said.

"You're right. We can't be out of gas," said Alice, "we just filled the tank. Look under the car. Can you see a leak?"

I looked and saw nothing dripping, but my watch told me that time was running out on us. The early morning ferry that would take us to the airport at Sandspit always left on time. We both stood by the road, desperate, but in no way surprised that no car passed us. Hell, seeing early morning cars on the Charlottes was almost as rare as seeing flying saucers.

Finally, a little yellow Volkswagen bug came rolling toward us going in the opposite direction. "What's wrong?" Cindy asked as she stopped and stepped out beside us.

"We don't know," said Alice. "It's got to do with the gas. Jim stuck a stick in the tank and the damn thing's empty. But it can't be."

"I'll give you some if you've got a siphon or maybe a douche bag in your suitcase," she said to Alice. "They work fine."

"Lord," I said, "we're going to miss that ferry and there's only one plane out a day."

"Jump in the car," said Cindy. "I'll drive you to Doug's. He's got a tractor there. He must have gas for it."

We drove to Doug's and he quickly lent me a pail, a funnel, and about three gallons of gas. What a break. But he looked at his watch and said, "Gas or no gas, I don't believe there's any way you're going to catch that ferry."

"You've got a phone?" I asked him.

"Sure, in there." He pointed to his house.

I found the number in the book and called the Sandspit airport. "Is the plane in yet?"

"Not quite," the woman said, "but she's right on time and the weather's good. She'll get in and out of here today for sure."

"Oh, God," I said. "Is there a small plane around there?"

"Yeah, the pilot's in here talking to my girlfriend."

"Will you put him on?" When he answered, I said, "Can you fly over to the floatplane landing at Skidegate and pick us up? We've had gas trouble and we're afraid we'll miss the ferry."

"I'll be there," he said, "but, Houston, you'll have to pay the shot for the trip whether you catch your flight or not."

"Oh, sure," I said. "Just meet us at the floatplane landing."

Cindy drove me back and I poured in the gas.

"You're a life saver," we yelled to Cindy, and after a little trouble starting, we roared down the highway, seeing only one truck on the half-hour journey. We stopped at Kendall's and picked up Jack, the garage man, who looked like last night's outing had been almost too much for him. Frankie Kendall had agreed to store our car by their side fence, in the winter rains.

The small floatplane was waiting for us at the landing and we quickly slung our bags inside.

"The plane from Vancouver is on the runway and the passengers are boarding," the pilot told us. "Christ, I don't think you're going to make it, but we'll try."

He zinged out onto Skidegate Inlet and took off in a deafening hail of spray. The trip over to the airport took us less than five minutes, but we had to land. I could see the last of the passengers climbing the ladder, and the flight attendant looking up while clutching the door handle. I hoped to God she would wait for us.

Luckily, our charter plane was a wheeled-float model and the pilot put down the wheels and landed close to the larger plane. The passenger agent was standing waiting for us on the runway by the ladder. She gave us our tickets. I gave the pilot my scribbled check and he helped transfer our baggage. The flight attendant slammed the door behind us and we staggered into the nearest seats.

Much later when we called Teddy to tell him we'd be back next spring, he told us that even during the early winter after school, they could hear those little mopeds screaming as they slowly drank up the last of our large Chrysler tankful of gas. Today, those little cherubs and their parents have drifted away, I hope forever, and are probably driving their little mopeds around using somebody else's tank of gas, and dreaming of their first, much noisier motorcycles, with the mufflers removed, of course.

Cutthroat trout

28

Hibby and the River

Not long after we bought the small green cottage on the east bank of the Tlell, I rose early and made coffee, which steamed the windows as the cold, gray dawn began to rise. I stepped out on the front porch, intending to watch the river for signs of salmon. There, to my shock, lay a human figure crumpled in the corner. Beneath a navy pea jacket, his knees were drawn up to his chin. He was ominously still. My God, was this a corpse, a dead man on our veranda?

I went over and squatted down beside it. "Hello!" I called.

The figure shuddered.

"Who are you?" I asked him. A bony hand reached out of the tattered navy pea jacket sleeve and rolled the woolen navy cap up off the face. It was someone I had never seen before.

"Do you mind my sleepin' on your porch, mate? I was only doing it because it rained the whole goddamned night and no car or truck passed over the bridge going either way to give me a lift. Your fir trees by the road, they leak!" he said accusingly.

"Let me help you up," I said. "You look like you could use a cup of coffee."

"Bloody right, I could, friend," he answered with a slight accent. "If you've got a slug of rum to go with it, that would suit me even better!"

It was still dark out on the porch and I was a little doubtful about bringing this man inside, but in we went. He took off his hat and looked around. "I've been inside this house of yours aplenty. Most of the owners and borrowers before you used to leave the door unlocked in winter just in case I passed along the road at night. I tried yours. It was locked and it was late. I don't know you, and I didn't want to wake you in case you're a nervous type that's handy with a shotgun."

He wrapped both trembling hands around the mug of coffee the way a person does when they're really cold and wet. Our house at that hour was not much warmer inside than out, but it was dry. I started up the heat and gave him a belt of rum.

"Would you like something to eat?"

"No, no, thanks," he said. "My stomach just doesn't welcome food at this hour of morning. When I was in the merchant marine during the war, they used to put a good, big double shot of rum in the coffee." He kind of held out his cup toward me. "That used to put a better face on life."

I did not respond this time and we finished up our coffee in silence, until he said, "My name's Hibby. Everybody knows me on the Charlottes. I'm a poet."

He looked around at the stuff in the cottage, mainly two large posters from the Metropolitan Museum of Art, each one part of an eighteenth-century Hokusai woodcut of a Japanese wave and a carving of a fish and some glass net floats. "I gotta go," he said.

"Good," I told him. "I'm going out to have a look at the river to see if the salmon are coming up on this tide."

I put on my rain jacket and held open the door for him. As we started off the porch, Hibby said, "Because you and the wife are kind of new out here, I guess you've never seen my artwork."

"No, what kind of artwork do you do?" I asked.

He dove his hand into his jacket pocket and drew out three smallish dried avocado pits with faces carved on them.

"Well, they're different," I admitted.

"Five dollars each is what I get for them." He paused. "But you being a new customer, could have them for two dollars and fifty cents apiece."

I studied the nuts and thought about this proposition.

He bent sideways as he reached into his other pocket and drew out a number of smaller dried walnut shells. These, too, had faces carved in them.

"These are only a dollar apiece," he said. "That price might better suit your pocketbook."

"I'll take one of each," I said, "and give them as a present to my wife when she wakes up." I picked through my wallet for the money.

"Oh, she'll like them." Hibby laughed. "The women always like them better than the men. You can have all three for three dollars as a special bargain, since you've got the money right there."

"Thanks a lot," I said, looking at him more carefully in the rising morning light. I had placed his accent now as Scandinavian, maybe Danish.

Hibby appeared to be a hard-worn man maybe somewhere around seventy. Protruding down from his navy pea jacket, his legs in blue jeans looked damp and painfully thin. Once a tallish man, he was bent now and had a crooked way of walking. His face below his cheekbones sagged, and his pale blue Scandinavian eyes were red-rimmed and watery. Hibby had a nose that had been broken and lots of facial scars. Well, hell, he'd been a sailor, and probably a bare-knuckles barroom fighter during his tougher years of rum and war. Who knows what he had been through? Whatever it was, time seemed to have treated him badly. He had a lot of random tattered sheets of penciled poetry that he carried folded in his pockets. I learned in due course that Hibby had come north as a deckhand on the troller, *Orca*, in 1929, had fallen in love with the Queen Charlottes, and never got over it.

Sometime after our encounter, life turned on Hibby and laid him low. Here's an example of a last part of a poem he showed me:

> . . . *here in hospital I lie in bed*
> *weak of knees and doddery of head.*
> *One has a feeling of despair,*
> *VER-TI-GO — un how to get 'der.*

"Well, I'll soon be on the road again," said Hibby, as we parted. "I'll go down beside the bridge by your house and wait. It's only misting now, not really raining. I'll have my thumb in the air. I'm sure to catch a ride sometime. If anyone is driving on the road, they all know me. They always stop and give me a lift."

"Which way are you going?" I asked him.

"Oh, I don't care a damn which way, up north to Masset or down south to Skidegate Landing." He laughed painfully. "It doesn't matter. I'll just go across the road to one side or the other and thumb whichever way the truck is going. I like one village just as much as the other. I'd kind of like to settle down someday, maybe right here, somewhere near the middle of the island here at Tlell."

And that's exactly what Hibby did. He didn't exactly settle in the housing sense, but he did choose to be buried here in the small, almost hidden cemetery at Tlell. That's about thirty deer leaps from the writing room in my hideaway, looking east toward the Hecate Strait. One of the former islanders, a decent, public-spirited young woman, generously bought a proper tombstone to mark Hibby's grave. He lies right beside my best friend, Teddy Bellis, whom Hibby liked to call the great romancer. Hibby's stone near the cemetery fence reads:

HILBERT SEVERIN GREN
HIBBY
1913–1982

In that same year, a small book of Hibby's poems appeared, a limited edition of three hundred copies sponsored by the wonderfully warm-hearted Celia Duthie of Duthie Books in Vancouver. She knew Hibby well, and his art and poetry and her kindness would surely have delighted his soul. Her own story is interesting, another case of a visitor falling hopelessly in love with these islands.

Celia had taken a year away from her Vancouver life and had come up to the Charlottes to do something positive. She lived in a tent down near the estuary on the left bank of the river and helped a family living there to take care of their younger children and home-teach the older ones, since there was no way they could continue in their chosen lifestyle and get their children to school.

After Celia had finished her year of good work and gone back to do more good work with her father's Vancouver bookstores, I also had an encounter with a family squatted down there. I had driven on the narrow gravel road to a pool halfway down between the river's mouth and our house. This pool long ago had been unromantically called "the meat hole" back in the days when the salmon fishermen fished to feed their families and not for the sport. The very sight of a much later catch and release program actually made these meat fishermen mad as hell.

I was fishing along the path from our parked Chrysler when I saw an old rowboat crossing the river closer to the mouth. A man and woman were in the boat and they seemed excited and in an awful hurry. They jumped out on my side of the Tlell and started running up the river, towing the boat against the outflowing tide. When they drew near, the woman shrieked at me. I laid aside my rod and ran toward her. I was shocked when I saw a young boy lying in the bottom of the leaking boat. His face and hands were bluish white.

"What happened?" I asked as I took the tow rope from the parents' hands.

"He tried to hang himself," the woman gasped. "My husband cut him down. Oh, dear Jesus, I hope he got him down in time!"

I couldn't feel his pulse. I started pulling, running, staggering in the large, loose gravel, and the two of them, sobbing and gasping, ran after me, the father holding the stern out from the shallows.

When we got close enough, we took a good grip on the unconscious boy, carried him up to the car, and laid his limp body in the back. The boy's mother got in beside him, carefully supporting her son's head. The father crawled into the seat beside me, and I drove as fast as I safely could around the potholes on the slithery gravel road. We drove until we met the ambulance coming up from the hospital to take over. By the time the three arrived at the small hospital in Queen Charlotte City, the boy's mother told me, his eyelids were fluttering and he was gasping hard for breath. The boy survived that terrible event.

A year or so later, I'd sometimes see him standing near the bridge, waiting for the school bus. That family had been forced to change their remote lifestyle and had come up to live closer to the road.

So, in a way, one might say that the quiet and remote beauty of life on the river could sometimes be as wild and hazardous as life in the big cities. Indeed, in the spring, some fishermen tie a bell to a strap around one of their hip boots – not just because of the pleasant sound it makes, but also to warn the bears that man is stalking down the river, with all his own animalistic ideas only temporarily held in check.

Octopus

29

A Hideaway for Any Weather

Before power was distributed on the Queen Charlotte Islands, our cottage had been served by a crude and very noisy gasoline generator. It stood next to an old-fashioned outhouse, a double-holer, down at the end of the garden. In more modern times, after we had purchased the place, I decided to remove the old outhouse and generator shed, even though I thought they had a certain amount of romantic and historical charm.

Smack in the middle of the generator shed there was a major problem, a knee-high, poured concrete block that had once steadied the light generator itself. When Teddy, Noel, and I tried with all our might to remove it, we took turns applying two sledgehammers, but with almost no effect.

"Maybe we'll have to leave the whole shed up," I told Alice, "or it will look like a battered enemy concrete gun emplacement."

Could it make a small writing room, I started wondering, *free from radios, tourists, symphony recordings, unexpected visitors, and the telephone?* I grew excited by that idea. "I'm going to rebuild that generator shed into a hideaway," I told Alice, "and I'll fill in the old outhouse, give it a floor, and use it as a woodshed." I started making drawings of exactly how it should look, including a weathervane in the shape of a cedar salmon, and a deer horn handle on the shed door.

I asked my friends, Noel Wotten and Lon Sharp, to make it work. We bought the necessary planks and a bucket of nails and the cedar shingles that we would need. I realize now how lucky I was to have help from these two talented, woodworking friends of mine. When we looked together at the terrible problem of the concrete block looming in the center of the single room, Lon said, "You'll drink coffee in here, won't you, Jim? This looks like a perfect place for a coffee table to me."

With sighs of admiration and relief, we put away the sledgehammers and began to look for a coffee table top. Our goal was to find a single slab of yellow cedar, several inches thick, for which the Northwest Coast is justly famous. But after building our dining table, we had nothing left but one short piece of wood with a curious, deeply indented shape on one side. On closer inspection, however, Lon and I decided that the natural grain made it look very *wabi*, "beautiful" in Japanese. The curving edge gave the feeling of flowing water. Lon attached it to the top of the concrete block. That disguise turned out perfectly. It is now not only a coffee table, it's the support on which to drop the wooden double bed with its hidden foam mattress that we hinged against one wall.

Inside, we also built a long, deep cedar plank stretching across the entire far end of the shed to act as a writing desk. Above it is a window of the same length, looking out along the river. On the opposite end, beside the entrance, we built a cupboard under a second, much smaller window. Inside the cupboard, I tucked away my electric kettle, coffeepot, and cups beside the pop-up toaster.

Outside, we built a square uncovered front porch surrounded by plank seats and a railing all around. This is the perfect place to eat clam chowder and salmon sandwiches, drink, and have good conversations in anything but rainy weather. (No matter what some people say about the Misty Isles, sunshine often breaks through, just in time.) The wall shingles are stained green to match the cottage, and the rough roof shakes have weathered gray as wolves. When the wind gusts and the rain squalls dash steadily against the west wall of the hideaway, they cause the big fir branches to scrape their evergreen fingers across my sturdy little roof of cedar shakes. Near the porch is a unique sculpture of an Eskimo, a gift carved by Teddy. As a life-sized *iqqaipaa*, "a remembrance" in Inuktitut, of my earlier Arctic days, Teddy carved out of a cedar log an Inuk hunter holding his harpoon. He also fashioned a large lifelike eagle to guard our garden path.

Tlell makes the perfect hideaway for a semi-hermit who wants to have a long, clear view of the river. From the window just above my desk in the hideaway, I can often see a female merganser swimming toward the bridge, followed by her brood of thirteen young. As I watch, she'll frequently stop and gather her offspring close around her while she instructs them all on the rules of safety. First, how to quickly break apart and scatter really fast, then how to dive in order to hide or to start to learn to fish for themselves. A year-old mule deer doe comes nervously out of the forest, looks both ways as though for traffic, then wades in delicately before she swims across the river.

Hooded merganser

From the wire above the bridge, I see a flash of blue as a pair of kingfishers, one after the other, make their separate dives to snap up trout fingerlings, then fly off swift as lightning to their nests to feed their young. I watch glaucous-winged gulls strutting up and down along the river's shore, not far from a new pair of land otters that have come to do their daily fishing. It's rare this far upriver, but we do see the occasional seal, watching us gravely with its large, luminous eyes. And always the eagles and the ravens circling or perching on each side of the bridge, carefully studying us as we study them. Oh, they drop the odd shit splatter on the roof of the cottage and the hideaway if they see that I am sketching them, but when you think of it, what comment of theirs could be more expressive or fair?

Often, the thought of rising salmon is just too much for any man, eagle, bear, or fisherperson to bear. (I write the word *fisherperson* to pacify Alice because she went to Smith College with Gloria Steinem, among other feminists, which implies that she thinks it better to be called a *fisherwoman*. Alice is not, thank God, a rabid feminist, but her awareness is increasing, as it perhaps should.)

One day, with the help of a legendary local character, I set about trying to repair the wire fence that stands around the border of our small property by jerking here and pushing there to straighten out the bulges in the wire. We painted white our front slat gate that leads into the cottage, and the smaller gate that leads down to the river we painted white as well. It is the most exciting one to use, since beyond that gate the bank plunges almost straight down to the river and the trout and salmon.

Looking north from the bridge, after your eyes have been trained and quickened, you can often watch salmon come up on the surging tide. They will lie in pools upstream until the tide turns, and they'll usually swim back down past our white gate again. They'll school once more in or near the estuary, working up their nerve to make their last long, great run upriver, usually marked by the moment when the full moon makes its final, irresistible call to them. Upstream the females will deposit eggs in trenchlike rudds pre-dug for them by their husbands. Afterwards, these males will cover the eggs with their thick white sperm called milt, which will later melt and allow the eggs to roll free and hatch. Then these adult coho, or silver salmon, having completed the demands of their four-year lifecycle, will start turning purple as they grow thin and die.

Kingfisher

One day, we were driving on a logging road near Juskatla, to the camp at the base of Masset Inlet, a half-hour's drive away from Port Clements. There I saw my dream house – a large, dead, twisted cedar stump that had been uprooted and was lying sadly on its side. I stopped the car and climbed through the slash to reach it. Yes, it was surely the stump of my earlier dreams. It was almost hollowed out from rot, but its curving, armlike roots were long and perfect. My father would have started dancing if he had laid his eyes on such a prize.

On the way back to our cottage in Tlell, I fantasized to Alice about that stump. We talked about how it could be moved and how I would ask Noel Wotten and Lon Sharp to help create the finest details, such as fishtail shingles and shutters around the windows. I suggested that maybe Evert Carlson, the ironsmith working at Juskatla, could hammer out romantic-looking hinges and a bold iron door pull.

I made an elaborate colored drawing of a new, old-fashioned, tree stump house the very moment I got to the cottage. I gazed out at the space deep at the back of our property. I thought, *wouldn't it be great to have a small tree house?* I was remembering the wonderful colored drawings of Arthur Rackham, a Victorian English illustrator, and Edmund Dulac, the Frenchman famous for his children's illustrations. He had drawn his tree houses with small, half-hidden doorways and chairlike toadstools and small, leaded, diamond windows usually lit inside by soft orange candlelight. I sat there dreaming until the stars came out, and I thought I heard an owl hoot, and I continued drifting happily backwards into my second childhood.

Living on a north Pacific island, you can expect rainstorms, followed by bright sunshine, to come sweeping daily over you. Neither of them usually last for more than half a day before they blow away to allow another weather system to come in. With the change in weather often comes a change in mood.

Next morning, the need for new tree house planning had drifted away from me. I rose and went fishing instead, and caught and played and released a big one, not because it was the law but because of our rule that allows only one salmon in the house at any time. And the tree house? We'll just have to wait and see.

30

Gaaw Fortunes

It's a strange thing to admit that the best place to fish for those big, beautiful spring salmon during certain seasons is off a small point of land in Skidegate Inlet. The Haida told me the only way to get at that point (this was a few years ago), however, was to knock on the front door of the Queen Charlotte Museum and wait for Trish, the director, to let you in. Rod in hand, you and a friend could tiptoe in your hip boots through the main hall of the small museum and slip out the back door, past the two tall and recently stripped and restored Haida totem poles. Once outside, you could start to think fish.

Also, you could try for the big spring salmon on a fly. One Sunday morning, Teddy, Don, and I were doing just that. It was gaaw gathering time and we just dropped our anchor and sat watching the surprising sights. We weren't used to seeing two good-looking Haida girls all dressed up for Sunday brunch. The one in the white dress was rowing very awkwardly while the one in the pink dress remained kneeling in the bow, staring into the water as their boat neared the rocks on shore. Both were talking and laughing about something that had happened the night before.

"Here's the gaaw," the young woman in the bow called to her friend, the rower. Then, reaching into the water with her paddle, she started hauling in long, bright greenish-brown skeins of seaweed. It had a glistening, silverish look, like decorated Christmas branches.

"Those two are gathering gaaw," Teddy told us, pointing out the girl doing the rowing. He waved and she waved back. "Only the Haida are allowed to gather the gaaw."

"What's gaaw?" Don asked Teddy.

"It's the eggs of herring that cling to seaweed and sometimes to spruce branches if they are hanging down into the water."

"You're not allowed to harvest gaaw." Teddy smiled at us. "Only the Skidegate Haida can take this gaaw."

The kneeling girl in the bow had the knife out now. She had kicked off her high heels and asked her friend at the oars to ease closer to the rocks as she cut the seaweed free. They started to fill up the boat with the long, heavy skeins of shining, wet seaweed.

"It's a good year," said Teddy. "Those fronds of seaweed are just packed with herring spawn. Did you ever eat them?"

"No," said Don.

"They're damn good," he told us. "These people living on the reserve, they'll dry that gaaw on the seaweed out on their clothes-lines, across house screens or hanging from their porch railings. The Japanese are crazy about gaaw and they'll pay a helluva lot of money for it. They use it in those little round sushi cakes they make. They'll be waiting to buy this over at the Skidegate dock. They're always in a hurry to fly it over to Japan."

The good-looking girl who was rowing let out a little shriek and waved her hands. "George, George, we're over here. Come and get us. We've got a whole boatful."

We watched as a brand new blue Ford pickup truck moved along the road, then turned at a boat launching slip that ran down to the water and began to ease down the slope in reverse. The two girls stood in the fully loaded rowboat as one of them started paddling with the oar toward the truck. George, the girls' brother, held the door open to lean out as he started backing farther down. To our shock and surprise, he kept on going until the back wheels, then half the body of his new truck, had disappeared beneath the water, until it touched the level of the door he was holding open. He rolled up his hip boots and got out and waded to the rowboat, caught his sisters' hands, and pulled the boat in close beside the truck. His two sisters, still laughing, told him jokingly about what had happened to them the night before as they helped him unload the piles of wet gaaw into the bed of his new blue truck.

"Those two have ruined their fancy Sunday dresses," Teddy said, "but they can buy new ones sent in from Vancouver on the money they've earned today."

"I've never seen anything like that." Don shook his head as the brother tied the boat to a piling and they all three climbed into the front seat of the truck. "Hey, you, driving that truck," Don called, "do you realize that the rear axle end of that new Ford of yours is going to seize up on you? After that dose of salt water, you've ruined it. It's going to be useless."

"Forget it." Teddy laughed. "He doesn't give a damn. The Japanese will pay one Godawful pile of money for all that gaaw and the next few loads they take. The Japanese will fly it over to Tokyo and I've heard they charge about ten bucks for a little two-inch square of it. That gaaw they're taking today and tomorrow will pay for a new truck, along with a helluva lot left over for a pair of nice dresses, and high heels, and new wristwatches if theirs got wet."

The two girls waved and called "Hello" to Teddy and to us, his friends, as they wiggled seductively ashore in their wet dresses and put on their high heels again. It was getting late and they were in a hurry to get to the little local café during the fashionable hour for having brunch. Life can be prosperous on these islands, as much as in cities like Vancouver or New York or Tokyo.

Sun mask

31

So Sings the Wolf

Calgary's Devonian Foundation, encouraged perhaps by the natural abundance of Alberta oil, wanted to assist worthwhile cultural film projects in Canada. Devonian's vice-president wrote and asked if I would care to present some ideas on possible documentary film portraits for the Glenbow Museum of some of Canada's older native people. Donald Harvie, a Devonian board member, was particularly interested in a well-known coastal Salish Indian named George Clutesi, an artist and a poet of some note. Encouraged by this, I was eager to undertake a half-hour documentary film about him.

I had met George in 1968 during my first art survey of the Northwest Coast, the one that brought me to the Queen Charlottes. At that time, most Indians met us very unenthusiastically, for they had experienced various surveys before and expected nothing of this one. George Clutesi was entirely different. When I met him for the second time, six years later, he was nearly seventy, but he leapt from his fishing trawler and ran toward me along the dock. He was a Sheshant Indian, a man surprisingly full of joy and hope, in spite of an incredibly hard life that had never managed to beat him down. Clutesi had a lean, brown, hawklike face with burning black eyes and the tight, strong body of a lightweight boxer that showed nothing of his years.

We went back to his boat and sat on its deck while he reminisced about the fact that when he was young, fishermen used to be paid five cents for each salmon by the fish buyers, no matter how much that fish weighed. Ten pounds or up to a hundred pounds, they paid just five cents each. How's that for raw exploitation?

George eventually left fishing and remained a painter and a poet until the end, still sleeping on top of Emily Carr's gifts of her paint box and blank canvasses, which he kept beneath his bed. We decided together to entitle this Devonian film *So Sings the Wolf* because George is part of the Salish Wolf clan and was a walking repository of local Indian history. Though he had taken a battering through his life, one can tell by his stories, his poems, and his paintings that he managed to remain a cheerful man, full of hope for the joint future of the Salish people and all other Canadians.

George Clutesi, it seems to me, could best represent his own ideas, for he was a philosopher of a kind not often heard. He spoke directly to you in English, so no interpreter was needed. As an old man he talked to me in these words. In part, he spoke about his own life, which began on the small Indian reservation of Sheshant, near Port Alberni, on the West Coast of Vancouver Island.

"They said then that I had to go away to a mission school. But I had lost my mother and I was afraid to leave my father. I can remember him forcing me, hauling me down onto the beach toward a mission boat. 'Don't make me go,' I cried, and saw that he was crying, too.

"The mission house was frightening. It seemed to me that I had been moved to the other side of the earth, with children who shared fear with me and had lost their families. It was the saddest time that I have ever known. I tried hard, but I was never a good student. I used to draw a lot, making pictures of everything I would remember about my home – the animals, the forest, and my friends along the Somass River. One day the school's master told me drawing was bad, that all artists and musicians were bad, that it would be an evil way to make a living, that I should be a minister of the gospel, a carpenter, or a garbage collector, something useful. I didn't believe him then or now.

"When I left school, I went fishing. It was a better life. I was living out on the sea in the open air again. Everyone had to work hard in those days to make a living – a young man, old man, and woman, too. Working with white men could be tough. They always had to have their own way. They used to pay us five cents for a spring salmon weighing maybe ten, twenty, thirty, sixty pounds or more. The price was always the same, five cents a fish.

"I went pile driving as a young man on the docks. It was harder work than salmon fishing. But it was steady. I had to earn money to support my family, which was growing fast. That went fine until one day I fell off the pile driver and landed on my back. I broke my spine and it fused together wrong. I was eight months in hospital. Most people thought that I would never walk again. For seven-and-a-half years, I could not work. But I knew I had to walk and wanted to more than anything else in the world, so I got crutches and a walking stick and I made myself walk again. When I was getting better, Emily Carr, the famous Canadian painter of our West Coast, helped me learn to paint, and when she died, she left me her big paint box and her brushes, which I will show you. I keep them safe here under my bed. She meant a lot to me. I had really liked her, respected her. Because of her, I decided to do something about nature painting, and I did.

"When I could walk again, I was broke. I went to Mount Curry painting houses. I was up on a ladder with a bucket of paint and I hurt, but I had to have money to support my family.

"When I used to go home through Vancouver, I would look up at the Vancouver Hotel and think, *its green top looks like one of our chief's hats.* None of the new buildings have good hats anymore. Most have their heads cut off square on top. They have gone and lost their human look.

"When I got home after being gone so long, I could see that lots of our Indian children had lost their human ways. I would ask them about the forest, the mountains, the fish, the animals. They didn't care. I could see that our Indian children were becoming weak carbon copies of white children. I could see how wrong that was. I wanted to try and help them find a strong, new way that would maybe take the best from both societies. So I showed them my grandfather's dance hat. An old lady I know taught them dancing. Then I painted a Wolf clan house front and they started learning the songs and the dances. It was good helping them because they had never done anything like that. But you could see by the excited way they sang and danced that they wanted to do it. You could feel the spirit of their ancestors start to move inside of them, dancing toward the light. Three other old ladies who remembered the songs and dances helped us, so that the link between our Salish past, our present, and the future was not really broken.

"I want my children to look at the sea, the land, the mountains, the forests, and feel that we are all a part of it together, a part of creation. And that the river and the forest and its wild creatures are a part of them. Many of the whites look at a forest and they say, 'All this could be lawns, houses, and city streets. It could make money for me.' Then they cut down the forest and fill in the streams and say, 'This land is mine. Mine.' They don't even pause to remember the land the way it was, the way that the Creator made it to enjoy. And after the winter, the spring rains come and buckle their streets and wash away their lawns and fill their basements with water. But still they don't understand. They only curse the weather. As the rivers turn yellow and the trees disappear, we drift further and further away from humanity. Our children rush into your cities and start grabbing, never asking themselves, 'Where are these white people going? Am I going with them? How will it end?' I am sure now that as they move away from nature, they will surely lose themselves.

"Emily Carr strongly painted the Indian village of Ucluelet many years ago when she was still a young girl. She said that she always felt safe among those people whom many would have called savage. Emily was lucky. I myself would be afraid to let my growing daughter far from my sight in any of the modern cities that have sprung up across North America during my lifetime. How can this be? I see people drunk, spoiling their lives, losing their money, and I ask myself, 'Why, why do they waste themselves?' Look at the animals. They are much smarter than that. Animals know how to live in the world and enjoy life. They know how to care for themselves and bring up their young. I often go back to the sea. I love to hear its voice, for I have had a life of storms. But always a sense of calm returns to me. Painting is like entering a world of dreams, and there, I get my best ideas. Only late in my life did I lift up the drum and begin to speak my heart."

For his remarkable work with young people, George Clutesi was given an honorary doctorate at the University of British Columbia and was awarded the Order of Canada by Her Majesty, Queen Elizabeth II. *So Sings the Wolf*, a half-hour documentary film, may be obtained through the Glenbow Museum, Calgary, Alberta, Canada.

Shaman's spirit catcher

32
Gold!

After the major gold rush on the West Coast of the Charlottes in 1851, there would often be as many as eight three-masted ships waiting in what came to be called Gold Harbour. This was new and exciting, but very disruptive to Haida life and no good at all to the gold seekers. That pocket of gold ran out too soon and nobody made anything except the Hudson's Bay Company fur traders who, as usual, became the suppliers of food and tools and blankets to the miners. But rumors, along with the odd attempt to re-mine gold, have lingered on until today.

One attempt made early in the twentieth century has always interested me. It surely stands as one of the greatest Haida legends. That is to say, it is based on true people and true locations, but it may or may not be a genuine story, although it is widely accepted here on the islands as the truth. The old account was given to me by Teddy, my reliable Haida friend.

A young fisherman came in to Chief Albert Edenshaw's large

house at Kiusta, a cove on the North Coast of the Charlottes, well known for its three linked mortuary poles that once carried a bentwood coffin. This Haida youth showed the already famous Edenshaw a thumb-sized piece of gold. Edenshaw turned it in the firelight, then took it outdoors and with a knife point scratched it. Yes, it was soft and heavy. It was the kind of gold that the Hudson's Bay trader wanted.

"Where did you find this?" Chief Edenshaw asked the young fisherman.

"On a rock ledge not far south along the West Coast of this island," he answered. "It was just lying there by itself."

Edenshaw hid the gold beneath his blanket, saying, "Speak to no one about your finding this. I'll keep it for you for a year. Then you can give it to your mother to excite the traders in Masset. They are not nearly smart enough to cheat your mother, but still you tell her to be careful. They can be very deceitful. Now wait, lad, describe to me exactly where you found this piece of gold."

The boy did so in great detail. When he left, Chief Edenshaw sat by the firepit thinking before he summoned his nephew. "I believe this gold that that boy found must have fallen off the cliff above it. You get our family's canoe ready and we will go there. Make it seem that we are going halibut jigging to teach my young son, Cowhoe, how to fish. His mother will come with us to take care of Cowhoe while we two climb to look for gold. Bring these two new trade axes, the heavy hammer, and some sharp iron chisels."

Next day the summer seas were calm and the Edenshaw family set out with their elaborately carved halibut hooks for fishing. They had to paddle from Kiusta without help from their small sail. It took them several days to pass Langara Island and travel down the West Coast to Susk, in the place called Kloisy Drums. Now it's important to understand that while Hecate Strait to the east of the Charlottes is fairly shallow, the islands sit on the edge of the continental shelf. To the west, where the open Pacific lies, the drop-off in most places is many thousands of feet to the ocean floor, so the cliffs tend to be sheer. When they reached the appropriate spot, the climb they chose was not too high, but it was steep. When Edenshaw and his nephew reached the ledge, they found the little pile of stones that marked the place where the young fisherman had found the gold.

"It must be just above this place," Edenshaw told his nephew. "You're young. Climb up and try to find it."

His nephew found a series of holds and narrow ledges, hauled himself nimbly up, then stopped and called down to his uncle. "Some of the rocks are white and shiny here. They're cracked. Could this be where the gold came from?"

From the ledge, Edenshaw called down to his wife in the canoe below, "Stay where you are. Hold onto the cliff. It's too deep below you to put out the anchor. Tie the tools to the rope my nephew lowers down to you and we'll haul them up."

With that, Edenshaw followed the difficult path his nephew had taken and finally reached the upper ledge beside him. They both hauled up the tools and soon they were hammering and chipping at the rocks. Edenshaw looked at the thick yellow vein and said, "We've found it." He chipped out a piece of gold, then they pried more and more out of this precious vein. "You hold the canvas sack open," said Edenshaw, "and I'll fill it. Then you can carry it down."

Edenshaw turned and looked out at the ocean lying calm beneath them as it stretched away to the far horizon. "We must hurry," said the chief. "The sun is falling and this West Coast calm is strange. It will not be the same tomorrow. We must rush to get all the gold we can. I wish I had brought more than these two sacks. Be careful going down and ask my wife to try to find a place to tie the canoe to the ledge so that she can come up herself and help us carry the gold down."

Edenshaw's nephew hurried cautiously down the cliff and emptied the sacks into the canoe. The chief's wife and he went back up with the sacks, calling to the chief that they had managed to tie the canoe to the cliff face and were coming up to help him carry the gold down before dark. The wind was changing.

The nephew duly carried the second bag of gold down and

emptied it into the canoe beside young Cowhoe. It was becoming a good-sized pile, he said, with more to come. Cowhoe's mother once again followed the nephew up the cliff. She was still young and strong, good at barefoot climbing.

Watching them come, Edenshaw was grinning with delight. What a potlatch, what a witnessing he could give after he traded all this gold in Victoria. He could buy piles of gifts to bring back and give away at a feasting. In Victoria they would all cost far less than half the price they would from the Hudson's Bay Company at their little fort at Masset. Into his largest freight canoes Edenshaw planned to pile gramophones, sewing machines, rolling pins, teapots, pisspots, even double-barreled scatterguns – everything his Haida neighbors yearned for!

When the two arrived, Edenshaw was ready to fill their sacks. The nephew went down first and piled more gold in the canoe, then climbed back up, passing the chief's wife as she carried her load down. The gold was running out now. The vein showed no more of the precious metal.

"You take this bit down and I'll follow you," said Edenshaw. "The sun's cooling in the water for the night and I can see wind rifts blowing up out there."

At that moment, they both heard a woman's scream. "Wife, are you all right?" Edenshaw hollered down the cliff face.

"Yes, but I'm going to be sick."

They could hear the anguish in her voice.

"Come down, come down," she cried.

When they reached the canoe, young Cowhoe was sitting proudly in the bow, like a chief's son should, and his mother sat in the stern, shaking and weeping.

"What's wrong, woman?" Edenshaw yelled.

"The gold, the gold," she answered in a choked voice, "all the gold is gone!"

"How could that happen?" the nephew demanded.

"As I started up again, I saw Cowhoe making a game of it. He was throwing the gold out of the canoe into the very deep water."

Edenshaw let out a curse. "You mean he threw all of that gold down there?" The chief gazed at the steep, rocky slope as it plunged straight down into the water below them.

"He's just a small boy," said the mother. "He was only playing."

Cowhoe started to cry, realizing perhaps that he'd done something wrong.

"Yes," Edenshaw admitted, "it wasn't Cowhoe's fault or yours. I should have left you in the canoe to mind him. We've got only a little bit, the last of it, only enough for me to go south to Victoria. Don't tell anyone that all this happened. Don't cry, Cowhoe. Be a chief," his father said. "They rarely cry."

But secrets never hold for long in Haida Gwaii, and this event soon turned into a famous legend.

At the end of the story, Teddy shook his head, in shared sympathy with the frustrated Haida chief, and with parents everywhere.

Pacific oyster

33
Legend vs. Myth

Both *Webster's* and the *Oxford* dictionary give similar definitions. A legend speaks of historical persons and events that have been carried down through history in story form in a way that cannot be proven – King Arthur, Tarzan, or Johnny Appleseed.

A myth is a story possessing elements of dreams and dragons

that are seen as being beyond all realms of possibility – St. George, Aladdin, Little Red Riding Hood, Jack and the Beanstalk, or Rapunzel.

Here is a myth of the Haida people: That wonderful, mythical little person, Mouse Woman, whose name is Ksem wed-zin, she saw a good man who was out searching for his son. "Have you any moun-tain goat fat?" she called to him.

He saw Mouse Woman looking out of her hole in the pole. "Yes, I have some fat," he told her. "My wife wants to use it to make her face smooth and beautiful."

"If you give me some of that fat," said Mouse Woman, "I will help you find your son."

Mouse Woman was well known for helping animals and humans find their young, so the good man gladly gave her the small amount of fat she wanted.

Mouse Woman then led him along the beach to the house of a fisherman who was sitting looking grim before his fire. The fisherman had not caught any fish for several days and he was hungry.

Inside the house, a young boy wearing a salmon mask was dancing and singing around his fire. The hungry man, his temper raw, took up a salmon club and struck the child, who cried in fear and vanished into the smoke. In the place where he had danced lay a large, wet, wriggling salmon. The hungry man dropped his salmon club, then eagerly baked and ate the fish.

Followed by the searching father, Mouse Woman scurried up and stood before him. "Fisherman," she called, "it was wrong of you to strike that child. Can you not hear him crying out in fear? Quickly, quickly take this goat fat and gather every scrap of that salmon's head and tail and bones you left when you were finished eating, and lay them carefully back into the fire."

When the fisherman had followed Mouse Woman's advice, the fire flared up from the burning fat, and the child he had struck instantly reappeared through the smoke and continued dancing and singing around the fire. When the boy pulled off his salmon mask, the father let out a shout of joy, for he had found his own true son.

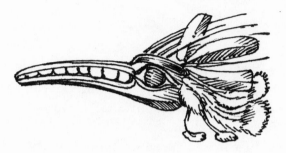

Mosquito mask

And another myth: Beaver is a hard worker and a strong peace-maker. He sits high on many totems between Eagle and Raven, for these two supernatural birds do not always get on well together.

Once Beaver heard Eagle and Raven arguing about which one would snatch Beaver's chew stick from him. Beaver saved his chew stick by flinging it down under the water where they, not being water birds, dared not dive after it.

Then, with a whistle and a slap of his wide, flat tail, Beaver dived off the pole and swam around his pond. He called up to both the Eagle and the Raven who were sitting on their pole, "This is the pond of the giant Beaver. It is a far bigger, deeper, better dam than the biggest nests you two could ever build."

The two supernatural birds laughed and cawed and screamed when they heard the Beaver's story.

"Watch this," called Beaver, and he dived down off his pole into the deepest part of the dam. Then, with the help of his wife and chil-dren, Beaver began pulling away the small logs, the mud, and the delicious alder chew sticks that held the water behind the dam. It flooded out, and when the pond was empty, Eagle and Raven looked down in surprise, for there at the bottom of the pond crouched the largest, most enormous Beaver that anyone had ever seen.

"Look!" called Beaver as he pointed upward proudly with his chew stick. "This giant relative of mine has faces all over his body, carved faces of the beavers that have dammed and watered all these forests. My relatives have made the ponds that caused the sweet, clear water to spread and grow our fresh new alders." Beaver shook his chew stick at the birds, "Come, wife and Beaver kits of mine, it's time to repair our dam. This giant Beaver of ours needs more good, clean river water for his home."

34
Argillite Secrets

Argillite is an evenly grained gray stone that is relatively soft when first mined, but turns hard about a year after it has been carved. It will take a beautiful luster if the carver applies seal grease or black shoe polish. The Haida say that they did not use argillite at all until about 1821. Then it was discovered that the pipe-smoking sailors who arrived during the sea otter trade were always anxious to bargain for any kind of lasting, useful souvenir to take away as gifts and mementos of their voyages. The Haida did not smoke but raised tobacco and ground it with a pestle into a stone dish, then chewed it, as we used to do. When they first saw foreign seamen smoking pipes, they thought their heads had caught on fire, and that they had to use a small clay chimney to let the fumes get out. Some Haida craftsman had the wit to make a pipe and drill it into a mouthpiece made from traded walrus ivory or a sperm whale's tooth, thus presenting a whole new art that would begin a trade.

Over the years, hundreds of elaborate argillite pipes were made, which were soon thought too valuable for sea-going crewmen to smoke. Then other larger argillite items began to appear: hand-length replicas of large but meaningless totem poles, black stone dishes with Haida fish patterns carved into them, and countless other items. At first argillite carvings were all artistic souvenirs for the square-rigged sailing trade. Later, these stone carvings were made to trade during sales ventures to Victoria and Seattle, much as Haida do today.

This art depends totally on the argillite source on Slatechuck Mountain near Slatechuck Creek not far from Skidegate. This site was believed to be the only place on earth where argillite is found, though on a recent trip I learned that it is abundant in New Zealand. Argillite was created by fire within the earth that boiled and shot up hot steam, which softened the normally iron-hard slate rock. This very ancient steaming makes the slate carvable when first quarried, but in time it dries and hardens. On Slatechuck Mountain the stone on this rare reserve is restricted for Haida use alone. Imagine having a rare, steam-heated geological miracle like that on the very island on which we live!

One northern Haida, Chief Charlie Edenshaw of Masset, who lived from around 1840 till 1920, became known as the finest argillite carver of them all. He made boxes with low reliefs portraying details of important Haida myths and legends, a wonderful way for a people having only an oral language to keep alive their old religious beliefs. Many museums and art galleries, including the Art Gallery of Ontario, (where I took art lessons from Arthur Lismer a considerable time ago), display carvings by Edenshaw, and *The Canadian Encyclopedia* notes that "Art historians and anthropologists continue to study his vast corpus of works." Equally impressive is his Haida name, "They Gave Ten Potlatches For Him."

He learned Haida traditions from his uncle, Albert Edward Edenshaw of Masset, a chief who once, during three nights of oration, spoke of the Yehl, the young white raven, and of the eagle thunderbird that came up from the south and enriched his nephew's fingers so that the younger Edenshaw became a famous slate carver.

Argillite carving reached its zenith in the 1890s and then almost disappeared until it was reborn again in the Great Depression. It was further encouraged by visiting soldiers in World War II and now benefits from an increasing art interest in western Canada. The small argillite totem has become the favorite of the average souvenir buyer, and so most of the earlier, more imaginative items made have fallen by the wayside as airport totem imitations increase.

Today, some Haida carvers still carry on the art of argillite. One of these, of course, is Rufus Moody of the Skidegate Reserve, the taciturn, physically powerful man whom I first met more than thirty years ago, as soon as I set foot on the islands. At that time, I was told, he had a very large, strong dog that used to climb Slatechuck Mountain with him. After sawing out the soft gray stone that he required, Rufus would load his dog with stone distributed evenly in two large canvas packs that hung down on either side of the dog's strong back. Then Rufus would load another heavy pack, hoist it on his own back, and carry it down jammed full of stone, accompanied by his faithful dog.

Today on Haida Gwaii, not much argillite trading goes on for Haida carvings. Most of the present-day carvers will do anything to avoid any kind of middleman, so they much prefer to go and live and carve right in Vancouver or Victoria and sell directly to their dealers, or better still, directly to wealthy collectors who come up to see them from the west coast U.S.A. Most of the artists cling to the many privileges of reserve status, but many live away from Haida Gwaii, preferring the excitement and facilities of Vancouver or Victoria.

Newly created traditional Northwest Coast Indian wooden masks have also found a ready demand. The carvers have studied the old-style masks in photographs and in museums, and have slavishly recreated them, giving them an old, authentic look through the use of painted face designs and human hair, horse hair, bear hair, and abalone shells. Whether any of this can be equated with their genuine old art and with some significant ritualistic meaning to the tribes is unlikely. These newly carved masks, like the argillite curios and poles, are artfully recreated for the tourist trade.

Inuit art, on the other hand, is newly made but original. There is usually nothing copied (unless the carver copies himself, as in the case of Edward Hicks's *Peaceable Kingdom* or Pauta's *Dancing Bears*). A cascade of original Inuit ideas is created for the same reason, to prove saleable to the market that has once again appeared outside. Artists everywhere have been doing just this – creating art – to earn their living, unless in some rare cases they have inherited wealth or have decided to earn their livelihood by teaching art to students.

In the 1875-1895 period, Chief Charles Edenshaw and others were creating museum quality argillite carvings on the Charlottes. Their opposite numbers at that time were the best impressionist painters in France. Edenshaw, in fact, might have been allowed to show his argillite in some of the important salons in Paris where Cézanne, Van Gogh, and Gauguin were then having their paintings scornfully turned away. Right now, the active Northwest Coast contemporary carvers, like recent Inuit carvers, are producing art that can be considered as fair competition with anything our Euro-American artists have created in the last fifty years.

Hand sign

35

Highlanders Abroad

Until recent years one of the unusual features of the Queen Charlottes was the herd of Highland cattle that wandered freely on the roadsides. Then the local farmer who owned these wondrous beasts over the quarter century while we were there simply decided not to have them any more. We were saddened to lose one of the great sights of the island.

Scottish Highland cattle really do look like some ancient mammal painted eons ago on the wall of some cave in the Dordogne region in central France or in Altamira in northern Spain. Their huge horns are arm's length and only slightly curved, with threatening-looking points. They have long, lank, slightly curled red hair colored like an Irish setter's, and they're built short-legged and squat as a musk ox. At first sight, they invariably made our civilized friends a little shy about going outside our fence, especially since that was a fence these primitives loved to rub against. It was all too easy for a fisherman to become convinced that the heavy, hairy-looking throwbacks must certainly be wild and dangerous. So far as I know, these Highland cattle have always been gentle, except in breeding season when they let out challenging mating roars. All this was very picturesque and would give anyone the false impression that they were fishing on the rivers of the western Highlands. The flesh from these Highland treasures I judge to be superior to any other beef that I have ever tasted, including the kobi beef of Japan.

But now, alas, the local herd is gone and I can no longer prove my point to guests at dinner or enjoy the appearance of such pre-historic-looking animals. A new local bylaw has been passed. It states that all cattle owners have to fence their livestock and can no longer allow them to graze in the lush green grass along the roads – another bit of the island's romantic past lost to progress. No longer will we hear the echoing clatter of their heavy hooves as those great auburn-haired beasts nervously crossed the wooden bridge at Tlell. Instead, we must learn to be satisfied with the odd group of skinny dippers, or French, Swiss or German cyclists with their packs behind them on their racing bikes, dressed in brilliant spandex – red, yellow, and green rear ends held elegantly high as they, too, now cross the bridge, unaware of the prehistoric, long-haired, long-horned red beauties that just a year or so ago had pre-ceded them. Since that time, I've missed the roadside horses and the cattle, though I do admit night driving is safer. One of these sturdy, Jeep-sized cattle might stand in the middle of the road looking like a red brick wall in your headlights. Hitting one of them on an ice-glazed road could certainly ruin your evening, and the fol-lowing morning as well.

Thus, time here marches slowly on, sometimes for the better. The timber industry has learned to be more careful now about re-planting, much more thoughtful than in earlier buccaneering days. At that time, great floating hosts of escaped logs (escaped from the huge booms that were towed to the mainland when the strait was calm), used to parade like seahorses up the river, urged on by the big moon tides, to batter against the rusted iron armor nailed by the contractor to the four lower pilings of our all-wood bridge. It used to be great to awaken in the middle of the night and hear the sound, like huge battering rams thundering against some castle's doors.

Those cyclists heading north over the bridge might once have been hurrying toward the old, now-filled-in dump that possessed the most beautiful view in all of the Charlottes. Were they looking for the big black bears that loved to gather and taste the choicest morsels so carelessly flung there? Or had someone told the cyclists of the mystical white raven that we have all seen and that the Haida believe forewarns some special message to mankind? I, like many others, used to go and watch the white raven, a rare, pink-eyed albino bird that lives, they say, for forty years. But I wouldn't know where to look and find her these days, now that they've covered up that beautifully located, awful, smelly dump northwest of us.

Not far from the dump was the site of the incredible, almost magical, Golden Spruce. This was a giant of a tree that scientists said had somehow gone genetically wrong, with the delightful result that instead of growing green, every needle on its branches was a yellow gold. Glorious to see in the early morning or the evening light.

In one of the most monstrous acts that I've ever heard of, someone – and his identity is widely known – went in at night with a chain saw and felled this unbelievable Island treasure. Hell, it was a unique North American treasure. The man who cut it disap-peared, and later his upturned kayak, pack and lots of identification were found on the Alaskan shore. Most Charlotte people sneer at that and say it was just a trick of his to throw the law off his track. Many attempts are now being made to graft branches and replicate the Golden Spruce, but it is far too soon to know the results. Maybe some day we'll see the white raven and the Golden Spruce on this island again.

36
Joys and Horrors

One of our favorite things to do on the Charlottes each year when we return to the cottage is to choose a good day, pack a lunch, and drive on the only road north, all the way to North Beach. We might not meet any traffic until, perhaps, we reach the long, deep fjord on Masset's left-hand side. Here, we pass dozens of small fishing vessels crowded into the harbor. By crowded, I mean close enough to step from deck to deck.

We stop and try to buy fresh fish, always being on the lookout for a white spring salmon. It occurs sometimes, a lot more often than a pure-white raven! A spring salmon's flesh is supposed to be an enticing deep rose-red, but for some unknown reason the flesh of a few of these fish is pure white. They taste wonderful, but because of the color difference, they are totally undesirable in the fish trade. So they are consumed by the fishermen themselves, or sold to locals like us at half or, with luck, quarter price.

After saying hello to friends, we drive on through Masset, where there are still some Canadian military personnel wandering around town or to and fro from their own private PX store. We drive on through Old Masset, the northern Haida Indian reserve whose houses in general usually need a new coat of paint. Then we bounce along the unbelievably terrible, corrugated, gravel-topped, former logging road that skirts North Beach, drive over the little bridge that crosses the Sangan River, and enter into the dark mysteries of what is perhaps Canada's most impressive rain forest. Dark clumps of furry green moss cling like animals to the tree limbs and make rounded elephant- and hippopotamus-sized backs on the mossy ground beneath that is interlaced with shining rivulets and pools of water. On the other side of this forest the light returns to view again and the land turns sandy.

We twist our necks and duck our heads, trying to catch a better glimpse of a little colony of post–hippie squatters' houses. North Beach legal owners seem still hidden, like the former nervous Vietnam War dodgers and flower children, but they have themselves built improved, sturdy, imaginative quarters. In the 60s and 70s, the houses were protected, by this, the roughest of the islands' deeply rutted corduroy roads, its condition probably keeping government land inspectors well away from those houses built on someone else's land. I don't much approve of this kind of civil disobedience. On the other hand, these tricky, often inspired-looking houses are none of my business, and they are more than an hour's drive from our own not-nearly-so-interesting-looking cottage.

Looking outward on a huge and beautiful beachfront, these houses of thick, unpainted cedar stand weathering, with handsome gray planking and fish-scale, cedar shake roofs that the builders split themselves. These small, communally built structures often have concealed entrances, hidden escape routes, and tall observation towers built on top of the houses. Who are those hermit-like dwellers that thirty years after the Vietnam War continue to dwell in these curious little fortresses, whose charm challenges the best of ultramodern North American architecture? That's all part of the riddle of the still secret, still isolated Charlottes.

Our car is halted by a giant, long-fallen tree that blocks the end of the road. Through the forest, we can see the waters of Dixon Entrance. We hurry out onto the wide sandy flats of North Beach, a huge expanse cut short in the west by a wooded point projecting into the water, the historical Haida fortress of Tow Hill. To the north and east, the beach curves away to the far, treeless reaches of Rosespit – an almost mythical place where few humans have ever ventured. It is dangerous to try it in a low four-wheel drive because if you are stuck even for a short time, the fast-moving tide will catch up with you, mire in your tires, then cover your vehicle so that it's not worth trying to recover it again. Looking along the vast flat beach, you may still see some low sunken objects that give evidence of this.

Far out on the wet flats – if the moon is full or nearly full and the tides have their biggest separation between very high and very, very low – you may also see several Haida families out clamming. They search for the big, long-necked clams that are so delicious – and also so adept at sensing the first touch of the amateur's digging spade, then darting away beyond your grasp. It's discouraging to cross paths with your small, almost empty clam bucket near a group of hearty Haida – men, women, and children – who are smiling, with their bulging sacks jammed with clams slung atop their shoulders.

One of the keenest clam and crab fishermen I've known was the Dutch baker. He was from Holland, where I would suppose many men engage in the catching and eating of seafood. The Dutch baker had arrived on the Queen Charlotte Islands both to make the finest bread and pies and buns, and to fish. He was a strong-looking, ruddy-faced man and a cheerful one, but the memorable thing about him was the new and worthwhile recipes that he carried packed inside his head. He chose a humble, concrete block build-ing for his bakery on a side street in Masset where he commenced to make the islands' first astonishingly good, dark, four-grain bread. This sort of honest, eatable bread was at that time almost nowhere to be found in Canada – hell, in all of North America. (Of course, some good European woman somewhere in the provinces or states was surely making such delicious bread for her own family.) This unique Dutch treat suddenly arrived on the Queen Charlottes, and to our delight he also started baking muffins, pies, and cookies, thoroughly supported by his neat little wife. His baked goods stood on child-like erector sets, with aluminum shelves right in front of the door. As you stepped inside his shop, the smell of freshly baking four-grain bread would make you want to lean against his doorjamb and just stay there breathing deeply forever.

The Dutch baker himself was big, a chubby man with an over-whelming passion for seafood. When the full moon tides dragged back the tidal waters to expose the vastness of North Beach, he could be found at dawn digging on the flat, wet stretches of sand, searching for razor clams or gathering mussels. Sometimes, in season, he would be waddling deep along the water's edge in his patched chest waders, dipping for the mating Dungeness crabs that make love on the water's surface. Some Haida suggest they do so because it gives them the hots having such a clear view of the rising moon.

In his enthusiasm the baker bought a secondhand trap boat, because he heard that crabbing could be more successful that way, and like many island folk, he preferred the delicate flavor of crab-meat to all other seafood. One day when he heard from Haida friends that the crabs were plentiful, he went out looking for action in his boat. Sure enough he found crabs, scores of them, basking in the sunshine on the surface of the water, the males moving their claws to entice the ready females. He started to scoop them in, unable to believe his good luck.

All too soon, he felt obliged to hurry, for he could see a cloud-bank to the north that had blotted out the mountains of Alaska. Small whitecaps were rising. But he kept on scooping up the hand-sized Dungeness crabs that were floating all around him.

The Haida crabbers, who knew the baker well, were all starting to pass close by him on their way back to shore, their boats rising then spanking sharply as the waves increased and the sky to the north turned blue-black and the wind blew cold.

"Come on, breadman," they yelled, "get your ass in off this water." They ran their fingers along the northwest horizon.

"Forget the crabs. It's going to be bad out here." The Dutchman waved his agreement, but still he went on eagerly dipping his crab net, determined to catch as many breeders as he could before he stopped.

As the wind increased, the seas grew higher and foam started tearing off the white wave heads, blowing like large cottonballs that went bouncing across the waters, then flying across the wet sands of North Beach. The Haida gathered on the dock and just inside the edge of the forest. They waited for him in their trucks. They turned on their headlights to guide him in the ensuing dark-ness, but he did not come ashore that night.

Next day at dawn, they went out to look for him, but there was no trap boat wreckage, nothing on the whole length of North Beach. When the storm settled, a clam digger found his boat turned upside down on Rosespit, not too badly wrecked. But a hundred yards away lay the much loved Dutch baker, the lower half of his body buried in the sand, his pale blue eyes stared upward at the clearing morning sky. Who knows? Perhaps those same crabs that he had gathered were the ones who, in the end, had fed so vengefully off him, stripping the flesh from his strong right arm, the one he used to slip his baking paddle underneath his famous bread.

His grieving wife finally left the islands and moved over to the mainland. For a long time, that was the end of good, four-grain bread and delicious pies on the islands.

The Queen Charlottes can be like that, still ruled by the whims of nature. With so few people here and lots of time to mull over the good and the bad of life, the good are often well remembered. In fact, I believe the baker himself has become a legend caught in island time. When all the printed words, along with the films, computer chips, and voice tapes have washed away, for the human survivors oral myths and legends will once more rule the shadowy winter shelters built around the firepits of the future.

Large Dungeness crab

37
Crooks and the Bandit

Bob Crooks is a newspaperman on the Charlottes' only weekly, *The Observer*. Bob's a type composer for that paper, which sticks oh so close to the islands' news. Its base is in Queen Charlotte City, that small town forty kilometers south of Tlell, on Skidegate Inlet. Now Bob is a devoted fly fisherman, one of the best I've known anywhere. He came over to the Charlottes in 1973 from Kitimat, a town on the mainland, to work at Half Moon Bay in a logging job. Almost immediately, he told me, he was overcome by the possibilities of fishing the various rivers, so he just decided never to go back. He stopped right here – sent a letter home to the mainland, told his friends to box up and send his clothing, his hip boots, and his spare rod and reels to him by mail, said that he'd be staying here near the Tlell River forever.

Bob is widely viewed here as a salmon master, a kindly resident expert. Once I saw him hook a large and very active salmon. At that same moment, the old English reel that he was using came apart, its spool falling into the river. Crooks carefully bent and fished around elbow-deep until he retrieved the parts, while at the same time he kept a hand tension on his fish. I reeled in to give his fish the space to run the whole pool and down past me. Crooks stood calmly enjoying the battle, thumbing tight his line and adjusting his glasses. Then, drawing the fish in by hand, he thoughtfully got a small screwdriver out of his pocket and started to repair the reel. I thought from time to time that he had lost or would soon lose the salmon. But no, his reel being fixed, he continued to play the fish, and in due course brought it ashore.

It was Bob's style never to move after he had a hooked a salmon. Like a bullfighter, he would stand and fairly win or lose, and grass or release his fish without assistance from anything like a net. No one knows more about the movement of the coho or the cutthroat trout on the islands' rivers, or how and where to fish them. Bob has always been a lover of the cutthroat trout that grow very large in the rivers of the Charlottes.

When air fares were much more reasonable, cutthroats were once bountiful enough here to cause Alice and me to make two cross-Canada trips a year – in spring for trout and in autumn for the salmon. But for a number of years, the cutthroats have been in alarming decline. Mercifully, it can be reported that they are coming back in this river. This year, it will be catch and release on the Tlell for trout, and salmon will be restricted to a barbless hook. When it comes to taking and releasing wild coho salmon, that separates the men from the boys.

Bob is a strong, heavyset man, usually with a well-trimmed beard and a balding head. He wears small, round, steel-rimmed spectacles and appropriate earth-colored clothing so he won't spook the fish as he cautiously wades the river. He used to be easy to recognize a long way off along the river because of his dog, Bandit. Bandit was a sort of mid-sized mostly black, white-spotted dog, with a perfect, natural black bandit's mask that stretched across his eyes. I believe that Bandit was just as keen as Bob about the fishing. He liked to wade out chest-deep and look back to admire his master's high skill with a light fly rod.

In the early days when I scarcely knew them and was working my way along the river to fish, I never saw Crooks or the Bandit standing fishing in any one place the way Noel Wotten used to do with his Irish setter, Rose, until she died at the age of seventeen. It seemed to me that Bob was always on the move. But as I discovered later, he and his dog had seen me coming and didn't want to reveal their favorite fishing spot to anyone. Sometimes a large rock lies on the bottom of a tidal river, usually not far beneath the surface. Cutthroats are fond of gathering behind such a rock and feeding off the nymphs and insects that are drawn into the swirl. Slowly, as we became friends, Bob stopped moving, until we could stand a respectable distance from each other and cast out onto the river and sometimes talk about the run of fish that spring.

Bob, a true country man, is mad for meadow mushrooms and for shaggymanes, and he pickled in vinegar the local glass wort sprouts that grew along the dunes near the water. He labeled this "Tlell Asparagus," and is it good! But, unfortunately, the storms one summer, combined with the rising tides, all but wiped out the beach house where he lived, and he had to move. He built a new house on the other side of the road. His friend, Claire, a French schoolteacher who used to teach here on the islands, helped him, and they decorated the house with her weaving.

The miracle of the Tlell River was that in mid-week, even in the best part of the season, Alice and I could usually fish together in the early mornings and see no one up or down the beautiful reaches of the river, except maybe our friends, Noel Wotten and his dog Rose or Crooks and his dog Bandit. Crooks is a great advocate of the Brown Muddler fly, a small, wet fly, dull brown to look at, but one that deserves all the respect it gets in the rivers of British Columbia's Northwest Coast, in New Zealand, Scotland, and on the Maritime rivers of Canada.

Zigzagging around the world is fine, but it is comforting to think of the friends that we have on Haida Gwaii who, like Noel and Bob, have found a place they truly love and live there almost all the time. Noel calls Bob the best salmon fisherman on the river and Bob says Noel's got it way over him when it comes to winter steelhead fishing on the Yakoun River, another long twisting tidal river like the Tlell. It's hard to tell between them. I think I've been wonderfully fortunate to have two such skillful and good-natured fishermen as friends.

Highlander salmon fly

38

The Doctors

At our first annual meeting on the river that year, my old doctor friend Hamish appeared dramatically, plunging down and bursting out of the salal berry bushes behind me straight onto the beach. His face was flushed and his old regimental beret had been knocked askew. You could tell he was excited, and just off the Vancouver-Sandspit flight.

"What's the trouble, Houston?" he called out to me. "Are you hooked up on the bottom? Did you catch a log?"

Bottom, I thought, *Hamish, you must be kidding. I've got hold of one of the biggest salmon I've ever hooked!* "This fish is sulking," I told him. "My leader's too light and I'm afraid I'm going to lose this beauty right before our eyes."

A fisherman across the river, whom I scarcely knew, had properly taken his fly line out of the river to give me full room for the fight.

"Well, what sort of a season have you had so far?" Hamish asked me, paying no attention to my circumstance.

I looked back frantically and saw Hamish settling himself comfortably on a log as he took his fly box from his vest. Was he joking? Couldn't he see that I had hold of a glorious big fish? How could I conduct a polite conversation with him when it was absolutely touch or go whether I'd keep or lose this salmon?

"A surgeon I know in Seattle," Hamish continued, "gave me a few good-looking Blue Wing flies he tied last winter. I'm very eager to try them."

"Can't talk to you right now," I told him, with admirable politeness. "Can't you see this?" I nodded toward my arched rod and the line that was starting to cut ominously through the water as though I had hold of Peter Benchley's giant shark in *Jaws*.

"Still hung up, are you?" said Hamish. "Try moving upstream and shake your line. Your fly will probably come free." He paused. "Have you seen any rises here this morning?"

I've often awakened at night and thought about that conversation. Sometimes I believe Hamish was kidding me, sometimes not.

Across the river the Vancouver lawyer named Craig called out, "Doctor, your friend's got a helluva big fish on. I saw it jump!"

Hamish chuckled, then tested the strength of his leader's knot and tightened it with his teeth before he put away his fly box and stood up, ready to fish.

The salmon turned and ran upriver now and set my reel ascreaming.

"By George, have you hooked a fish, Houston?" Hamish called to me. "My being on this river always seems to bring you luck. Did you happen to see that motion picture *A River Runs Through It?*"

"No, I didn't," I answered as I started to hand haul in the slack line as fast as I could, for the salmon had turned and was running straight back toward me.

"Don't bother with that movie," Hamish said. "It must have been about something, but it certainly wasn't fly fishing."

"Tough luck," the lawyer called across to me, for he could see and I could feel that my big fish had broken free and was gone, after feeling like the best fish of the year.

Farther down the river on the opposite bank, I could hear a lot of laughing, the sound of good friends bantering with each other.

"They're back," Alice called down to me. "The doctors are all back. And Graham and Doug and Am."

Alice had come down to the upper end of the pool and a good-sized salmon had just risen between us. The big moon tides would be at work for the next few days, drawing whole schools of salmon into the river on the rising tides, singing sexy songs to them too subtle for the human ear, and wooing them upriver to their spawning grounds.

Like us, the doctors had long been eyeing their autumn calendars, possibly pushing some operations forward and holding others back. They planned this trip, a get-together, where they rigged themselves out in their oldest, dearest, and most tattered fishing costumes or, some years, in the brand-new fishing hats, chest waders, and latest-style fishing vests that their wives or children had bought for them. They had all met in the Vancouver airport, having journeyed from wherever they practiced medicine, and joined to catch the flight north to fish together for four days in their rollicking fishing club.

"That must be you, Alice?" I heard a voice shouting from across the river. When Alice laughed, the voice called, "I didn't really recognize you, dear, but I did recognize the long, flat length of your fly cast. Not many can lay out a line like that."

"Good to see you again. We're counting on all of you to come for drinks and dinner tonight," she called back across the water.

There were various shouts of agreement from along the other side and the doctor wearing the Australian bushman's hat answered, "You're damn right, we'll be there, Alice. Everyone is coming. Tell Jim to set out the glasses and fill the ice bucket full. We'll bring the rest."

I saw the doctor cast again, then heard him whoop, "I'm onto the first salmon!"

"I'm going to take my fish back to the house," Alice told me, "and make him into a salmon mousse."

"If it's a 'him,' save the milt for breakfast, fried with bacon and Barbara's green hen's eggs."

"Can you see Robin fishing up at the long pool with Hamish?" she asked. "Isn't it lovely having all of them back again?"

Alice left and I wandered downriver to greet them. Robin had taken one bright salmon and released another larger, darker fish. He was such a consummate fisherman that he fully expected to catch and release more, though the daily limit then was two salmon in fresh water and two more a little farther down beyond the meat hole at the tidal river's boundary. None of the doctors thought it was proper to keep more than one salmon a day.

Sharp at 6:00 p.m., we heard their two van doors slide open, then slam shut. The doctors came laughing up the path dressed in all those older cocktail costumes that one would no longer be allowed to wear in civilization. They wore violent red or green plaid pants, thick British Columbia Indian sweaters, fancy fishing vests with colorful flies stuck onto them, dangling surgical scissors, and strangely angled rain hats that made them look a little like John – or was it Lionel – Barrymore. Some guests were already holding out wine – or other, stronger – bottles, fearful that their friends might beat them to our tiny bar. After a good deal of greetings, kisses, gasping, and handshaking, we all poured ourselves what was said to be the first drink of the day. Alice passed the hors d'oeuvres, while others re-examined our wonderful view downriver.

"*Scots wha hae wi' Wallace bled*," called Hamish. "Let's drink to the fact that every one has made it safely here again this year."

"Did you get a chance to read that article on DNA in the *Journal?*" one doctor asked another.

"To hell with shoptalk. Did you get a chance to try that Blue Angel fly I gave you?"

"I'm saving it for tomorrow," said Graham, before the laughter drowned their voices out.

"Now this is the kind of party I love," Douglas said.

"Can I help you in the kitchen, Alice?" This was from a fisherman who was always helpful, a successful banker who probably never did a touch of kitchen work at home. Alice would remind me later of what a grand and truly helpful person that man was. I sat talking and staring out at the river, pretending I couldn't hear the noisy rattle of the dishes! Then I could see Teddy making his way across the span, accompanied by Sassy, his one-eyed Labrador.

"Do we know him?" asked the heart surgeon beside me.

"Sure, we know him," I said. "He'll be right in and we'll have a better party for it."

"Hello, folks!" said Teddy as he opened the door. "Glad to see you're all back fishing again this year."

When Teddy came inside, we could hear Sassy flop down on the front porch, sounding like someone had dropped one bag of cement and then another. Teddy found his favorite chair and hunkered down, all smiles, with a drink in hand. Although the house had purposely been left cold for ourselves and the doctors, who were wearing wool shirts and heavy sweaters, Teddy wore a thin, short-sleeved, nylon shirt unbuttoned almost to his navel, exposing his tanned, hairless, barrel-shaped chest.

"Did you have any luck today?" he asked the doctors.

"Sure," they told him, each eager to describe the catching of their fish in finest surgical detail.

"Alice, let me help you with that food," Teddy shouted above the noisy conversations. "What are we having tonight?"

"Beef," said Alice. "One of the doctors brought up a beautiful red roast and left it here this morning."

"Great!" said Teddy. "I'll sharpen the knives and stay to help you with the carving."

Teddy could edge a carving knife to razor sharpness. Soon, he was standing at my place at the head of the table with someone else pouring the wine.

"I wish I'd had the good sense to become a surgeon," he said as he cut into the redder portions of the inside meat. "But I was just too busy doing other things to take it up when I was young." He filled another plate and passed it. "I hope you guys keep coming up here fishing forever, with your best single-malt whisky and your prime roast ribs of beef."

The doctors laughed and toasted Teddy. They were proud to know him and, believe me, so were we. After he died so suddenly of that heart attack, when just sixty-two, the fishing parties seemed to lose a lot of their original vibrant life. Teddy somehow made every meal a potlatch feast. I know that Alice and I, like many others, will miss Teddy forever.

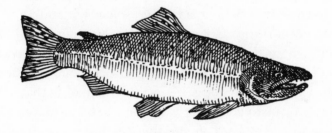

Coho salmon

39
The Cutoff

During our riotous evenings with the doctors the talk often turned to stories of the war. I had one or two to contribute. In 1940, as soon as my age allowed it, I volunteered into the Toronto Scottish Regiment. As training to go overseas, the army sent me to Trois-Rivières, Quebec. There I drilled in heavy machine gun. I took to the old gun, as the saying went, and much to my surprise was promoted in rank and became an instructor with my regiment and other machine gun regiments, the Cameron Highlanders, the Saskatoon Light Infantry, *Le Régiment de Maisonneuve*, and the Royal Montreal Regiment. We were all studying the deadly art of laying down a cone of fire at various ranges from the heavy, old-fashioned, water-cooled Vickers machine gun.

In our regiment was a handsome, outgoing young soldier with a natural talent for amusing people – not only girls, but all the troops that served with him. And yes, most girls seemed hypnotized by Regan. (I've changed his name for reasons that you'll come to understand.) In time, we both received another promotion. This was a great shock to both of us. Well, that was war for you. Weird stuff happened all the time.

In the opinion of the press, the theater of war was about to shift from Europe to the Pacific. Regan and I were delighted to be re-posted to the Battle School, a famous, somewhat remote and secret place inland in British Columbia, a training ground for instructors from throughout the British Empire to gather together sociably to learn to teach murderous commando tricks. Believe it or not, we were all dead-eager to get going, for rumor had it that a military action was about to get under way against the Japanese, who were busy spreading eastward along the Aleutian Islands. Canadian forces were certain to take part. So on the station platform at night in Trois-Rivières, we said a choked farewell to our local girlfriends. Regan's girl said she was broken-hearted, but told me that her father, a high-ranking officer in the military, had cruelly suggested to her that he was in no way sorry to see Regan get out of town because he had the reputation of "overheating" girls.

Regan and I boarded the night train that shunted us away from Trois-Rivières through Montreal and westward to our secret desti-nation. For a wartime train, there were relatively few military per-sonnel aboard, with less than half of the passengers soldiers, sailors, or airmen. But, surprisingly to us, there was a handful of civilian women, and others in military uniform. We had been warned against telling anyone at any time where we had come from or where we were going on our vital wartime posting. The enemy has ears, the posters told us.

Regan and I excitedly flung our ditty bags into our berths, then cruised the whole length of the long passenger train. We had worried about the prospect of the four wearisome days and lonely nights that we'd have to spend aboard as we crossed the country. We felt a whole lot better after discovering that there were lively looking girls aboard.

We cut the cards and Regan won the lower bunk of our sleeper berth, numbers 7 and 8 in car 12, as I remember. We met two eligible girls next day and gave up two of our military dining chits for them, and laughed and joked together until after dinner. We were becoming almost over confident when they suddenly admitted that they were both newly married, with young husbands in the air force waiting for them.

Hell, what could we do in a situation like that? We couldn't get our meal chits back from them. They assured us that it shouldn't make any difference to our new platonic friendship, but, alas, it did. Young soldiers during those five years of war were always in a hurry – a hurry to leave, to fight, then a helluva hurry to get back home. Troop ships were blown up, friends were killed. Who could even guess one's future? We all felt sure we were running out of time. I, for one, wanted desperately to experience as much of life as could be packed into any one night, and that was not always an easy thing to do.

Next evening, we arrived in time to seat ourselves at a table for four. These dining cars on trains were intimate and small, with glistening silver, fresh white linen tablecloths, and small shaded lamps that gave off a soft, enticing light, one of the last reminders of pre-war style. Along came a pretty girl that we'd seen only once before, when she got on at Montreal. We both rose, smiling gallantly, introduced ourselves to Linda, and offered her the choice of seats beside us. My heart leapt when she chose the one next to me, but only, as I soon discovered, so she could stare deep into the eyes of the unreasonably handsome Regan. I knew by the alert look on his face and on hers that the game was over for me.

Slowly, I grew used to that, and we three had a joyful dinner together. Regan gave the headwaiter two of his military meal chits to cover the dining costs of this newfound love of his. As we finished our coffee, I noticed that this beauty was still gazing into Regan's eyes. She confided to us that her grandmother had saved her monthly liquor ration and presented it to Linda as a going-away present, a full, twenty-eight-ounce bottle of dry gin.

Regan smiled and said politely, "Well, my dear, what is your address on this endless train of ours?"

"Car 16, lower berth D," she smiled at him before we rose and shook hands. She said goodnight to me, then nodded at Regan.

Regan quickly led the way back to our sleeping car and I was glad that I could scarcely hear his singing over the rumbling of the iron wheels on the iron rails. There was a so-called ablution section for men at the end of every other sleeping car. Once inside, we pulled off our jackets and undershirts, washed our faces and upper bodies, then brushed our teeth. But the reprehensible Regan went further, carefully lathering his face and shaving for the second time that day, putting talcum powder underneath his arms, and slapping Aqua Velva on his face. Then he carefully brushed and combed his hair. Laughing wildly, Regan rushed into the little toilet, slammed the door, removed his trousers, and reappeared wearing only a green silk dressing gown which he said, bless his mother's Irish heart, she had bought for him as a gift because he, "poor dear, was going off to war."

"You going somewhere now?" I asked.

"Damn right, I am." He grinned. "Mind you, I'm only going to say goodnight to that dear girl and possibly pause for a minute or two to drink half that bottle of gin. Goodnight, Houston," he said, "sleep tight," then started to hustle toward the rear end of the train.

"You're not going dressed like that!"

"Why not?" He laughed. "Almost everyone aboard this train's asleep."

I sat and sulked a little on the worn-out plush of the washroom's long settee, staring out at the flat, endless prairie bathed in moonlight. Finally, I went forward, climbed up into my berth, and fell asleep.

I felt cheerier in the morning. At least I told myself I'd escaped a hangover. I shaved and dressed quietly to the delicious smell of bacon frying with eggs. I was eager to ask Regan what kind of night he'd had, so I paused beside the heavy drapery of his berth and called his name. No answer. A wild night, I guessed, but he wouldn't want to miss breakfast.

I shook his draperies, but nothing happened. I drew them back a little, then flung them wide open. He wasn't there. His uniform with his kilt and his battle dress hung on the rack above his unused bed.

God, I thought, *everybody's up now. He'll look crazy as hell parading through the cars in those slippers and that Irish green silk dressing gown.*

I turned back toward the cars at the end of the train and made my way through the next sleeper, then stopped in horror as I saw the bright rectangle of daylight through the window ahead. The string of cars that had trailed behind us had disappeared. I now vaguely remembered feeling the train stop in the middle of the night and do some violent shunting and grunting, but we had grown used to all of that.

When I turned, I saw the porter and pointed back. "Where are all the cars?"

"Oh, they cut off at Regina, sir, you know. That's the terminal before Moose Jaw. The back cars have hooked up with another train and they're headed north to Saskatoon and Prince Albert, Saskatchewan, just the way they always do."

I didn't know whether to laugh or cry or shout as it all dawned on me. Regan, in his green bathrobe, and Linda and the dry gin had all gone north. The only things of his left on this train were his uniforms, boots, ditty bag, and kit bag – all of his possessions.

When I finally changed trains and arrived at the Battle School deep in the mountains, I threw off Regan's kit with mine, glad to be among other heavy machine gun friends of mine again. All of them knew and liked Regan.

"Where is that dizzy bastard?" they demanded.

When I convinced them of his awful plight, they were delighted. "But don't let the Adjutant or the old man hear about it," they said, referring to our much admired commanding officer, Brigadier Milton Gregg, VC, DSO and Bar. "We'll all try to cover for Regan until maybe he finds a way to get here somehow."

"Where did you say his train was going?"

"Prince Albert."

"I never heard of that," said Inman. "Is it in Canada?"

Most long travel in those days was by train, and it was slow, smoky, noisy, and majestic. Each evening as the one and only daily train whistled, we would leap into a jeep, and three or four of us would drive down to the tiny railroad station on the edge of town.

Regan failed to arrive on the first or second night. After that, we brought a bugler with us, expecting him on the third or fourth night for sure, and planning some fun at his dressing-gowned expense. At Battle School, it was getting harder and harder to cover for him. The major was getting restless and I was getting worried. Had Linda perhaps killed Regan with her grandmother's home-made gin?

On the fifth night, a brakeman got off the short train at the far end of the platform. "All aboard," he shouted, and started swinging a lantern in the fading, evening light, then handed it back into the train.

The engineer leaned out with others in the crew and shouted, "Good luck, chum. You look really good in that hat and uniform. They damn near fit you."

It could only be Regan. Who else could have talked himself into a bottle of gin and a romance, then got cut off, and finally wound up here in a train conductor's uniform that almost fit him? We chased him the length of the platform as the train departed, caught him finally, and threw him into the jeep.

"Hey, you buggers, be damned careful of this hat and uniform. I had plenty of trouble borrowing them, and I've promised to send them back. But, believe me, Houston," he laughed, "that dear girl was more than worth it!"

He drew his green silk robe halfway out of a crumpled paper bag. "I thought of giving her this for the loan of her father's uniform. But how could I have explained that to my mom?"

40

The Twenty-Five Pounder

The Battle School in the Okanagan Valley was my first taste of British Columbia. The camp itself was nothing but a collection of ancient, tar-papered barracks left over from World War I. But they built them well in those days and the place had developed spirit in the way of personnel who arrived there almost daily. The Okanagan Valley is in B.C. but it might as well be a million miles from the Queen Charlottes. It is a high, dry valley surrounded by beautiful, protective mountains, so the climate, hot and dry in the summer, is easy on such buildings, which all had a good, gray weathered look. Soldiers of many ranks from many countries were gathered there to train and to coordinate commonwealth military plans and actions. They would, in turn, go back to where they'd come from and advise their own troops.

All manner of stuff was practiced there, from unarmed combat to commando raiding tactics, the use of new small arms, and new machine gun rates of fire. We used tanks and weapon carriers, and the Brits taught us how to bowl a hand grenade like a cricket player. The largest of the infantry weapons we used was a twenty-five-pound gun, so named because of the weight of shell it fired. It was considered a fairly light artillery piece, and we towed ours around behind a small, fifteen-hundred-weight truck. Our range area for firing the twenty-five-pounder was across toward the high cliffs on the other side of Kalmalka Lake.

I'm pleased to say that a jolly, very wily, Permanent Force Major from the King's African Rifles was in charge of these artillery pieces. One morning, he hopped into his jeep, ostensibly to whiz back for some binoculars he'd forgotten. "Take charge of the guns, Houston," he yelled to me, and waved as he raced off.

I had never liked the sight or sound of these big gray mechanical brutes. Infantry meant armed men to me. In my mind, these monsters were artillery.

I turned my attention away from them and concentrated on the art of teaching marksmen. Twenty minutes later, something strange caught my eye. Those practicing the hurling of grenades had taken a ten-minute break and were wandering about or lying around in the sunshine. Perhaps it's a human instinct, but I didn't like the look of one officer cadet. He had wandered off from the cloud of cigarette smoke that hung above his group of grenade-throwers and was approaching our four twenty-five-pound guns. Each one was attached to the back of its truck and pointed safely down the hill and out over the deep blue waters of the lake. *That man is probably going to have a leak beside that tree*, I thought. But no. He kept on going right up to the wheeled gun. He stopped and stood, staring at the heavy weapon's breech block, then turned his attention to the steel pin that attached the gun to the vehicle.

When I saw him reach out his hand, I bellowed, army-style, "Hey, you, keep away from that fuckin' gun!"

He jumped back, but with the linchpin clutched nervously in his hand.

As in a dream I saw the gun detach and start to sway and shudder on its rubber wheels as it began its slow and gentle run downhill. The military boob who had pulled the linchpin ran after the gun, grabbing at it as though he could somehow stop its rolling tonnage. Every man of every rank was standing now, watching in horror as the gun gained speed on the increasing slope toward the lake.

I clutched my face, but could not hide my eyes as that new and impossibly costly piece of ordinance hurtled itself over the cliff face and disappeared. A long moment or so later, we all heard the splash. When I got up my nerve and looked down the cliff where the gun had disappeared, I found myself gazing down at God knows how many fathoms in the blue-black waters of the lake.

I was in a panic when I saw the jeep returning.

"Bloody cold up here in the mornings," said the South African Major, shivering and smelling of Scotch, but still in a very good humor.

"We've lost one of your guns," I fearfully admitted.

He looked at the nearest fifteen-hundred-pound truck and saw that its gun was gone. He eyed the wheel marks in the light snow that led to the cliff face. "Good Lord, Houston, how the bloody hell did you manage to do that?"

"I didn't do it, sir," I said. "Some goddamned bonehead left grenade practice, wandered over here, and just pulled the friggin' pin."

"Do you have any idea what one of those big buggers costs?" the Major asked me, and when I had no answer, thinking how many years of pay I would be losing, he laughed in that larcenous British-type accent of the King's African Rifles. "Houston, we've got to requisition a new barrel for that bloody gun. It was pretty well worn out, don't you think?"

"I don't know artillery, sir," I said foolishly. "I'm not in artillery. It looked like a new gun to me."

"Well, for God's sake, forget that! If I tell you it's old, Houston, it's old. We'll have our ordinance Quarter Master send off a requisition to Ottawa for a new barrel *tout de suite*. Got it? Then we'll wait a month," he continued, "and request a breech block, a new gun carriage, and the bloody wheels."

"We might borrow a crane from town, sir," I suggested. "Get one of our Aussie divers here to go down with a cable and hook onto the gun and haul it up."

"Forget that, my boy. That would set off tinkling fuckin' memory bells in too many people's heads. Pacific Command would start yelling that it's our fault that we two allowed some unsupervised boob to go and pull that linchpin out of that gun and let it roll off the goddamn cliff. No, no, requisitioning a whole new artillery piece is just so much simpler and safer. If you'd been with the Permanent Force of the King's African Rifles as long as I have, you'd know that by now, my lad. Jump in the jeep. I'm hungry and thirsty and it's damn near time for lunch. But first, tell all those boobs of yours not to talk this up when they get back to barracks or we'll send them swimming down in a daisy chain to haul that bloody gun straight up that bloody cliff. And if they argue that, we'll have them up for insu-fuckin'-bordination!"

Those on the twenty-five-pounder course didn't say a word, and in a few months we had reassembled a brand new gun. So in the proper military manner, all was forgotten by all. And even the boob who pulled that linchpin that set the gun arolling to its watery grave was able to go on and help to win the war with the rest of us. And that included the old Major, who could swear as well as any soldier I'd ever known.

41

Quite Unsuitable

It has never seemed right to me to just go on fishing one river, no matter how good that river may be. One should go out and make comparisons and see what other people are talking about. We've salmon fished the Grand River in Gaspé, Quebec, and the Miramichi in New Brunswick, and enjoyed both. But as everyone knows, those fine, old, traditional rivers are short of Atlantic salmon these days. So with two good friends of ours, we decided to fish the Garrynahine in the Outer Hebrides, on the Isle of Lewis, in Scotland. Being Scots, we were dead-eager to try this river of our heritage, our homeland. Knowing that Scottish fishing guides – gillies, as they are called – are often sardonic, memorable characters, we looked forward to meeting a grizzled veteran full of grand stories.

Early on the morning after we had made the ferry crossing, we met our gillie, a young man who looked at us with utter suspicion, apparently judging us to be Americans, and disapproving of what he saw. What could be worse for him? He might have gotten some sociable New Zealanders or even Swiss, but here we were.

"What fly do you recommend?" I asked him.

"Let me see your fly box . . . sir," he demanded in a very Cambridge, upper class English accent. He held them to the window light and sighed. "Quite unsuitable," he said. "No fish here would dream of taking anything like *that*." Of the other fly boxes, he declared the same, then tied onto each of our leaders a fly of his own choice.

We followed this guide dejectedly along the beautifully barren riverbank of the Garrynahine and each took the pool that he suggested. We all watched carefully for rises, but saw not a one.

"We expected you to be a Scot, you being the gillie on this river," I ventured.

"Oh, I'm not the gillie," he said, "I'm just doing this to scratch together a bit of cash. The real gillie's upstream with an Austrian gentleman. I'm just, well, you might say, escorting you out, while I learn the trade."

We enjoyed a cheering lunch packed in a hamper with two splendid bottles of French wine and a plaid rug that we could spread to sit on. Lunch was the best part of the day, and the young gillie was of no help in finding any fish. Back at the fishing lodge in the salmon day book, we could see that a lot of good fish had been taken when the local laird up from London had been there. While we were there, however, the place, though picturesque, was largely free of salmon.

The best thing we got out of our lovely visit to the Hebrides was a true Scottish tale (confirmed by a newspaper account) of a famous salmon poacher. This is a much-admired profession in the Scottish Highlands, and these men become legendary in their communities. In fact, people swear it takes at least three generations to become a serious poacher, one truly worthy of that ancient title.

Finally, at long last, this man of renown was caught by the laird's fish wardens near the river with a large salmon hidden in his pack. The day of court was set. There seemed to be no escape this time. The laird himself came all the way up from London to lay the charge, and all three of his fish wardens who guarded the river were present to support him.

To everyone's surprise, the poacher's wee wife appeared on his behalf and stood humbly before the justice, then blurted out, "He's guilty as the devil, your Honor," she said.

There was consternation in the court.

"He's a poor man, mind you, with the bairns to look after, but he told me he was guilty and to ask you how many shillings he must pay to the laird."

The judge (in Scotland they call them sheriffs) mumbled with the prosecutor for a while before he pronounced a five-pound fine, a hefty fine for a poor family, one certain to make the poacher think twice about straying again. The wee wife fumbled through her purse and counted out five crumpled one-pound notes.

As she was leaving the court, a wee boy ran up the stone stairs and whispered to her, "Dad just came in with four big ones and now he's going over to Ullapool to sell them. They're heavy, maybe twenty pounds apiece," he said, "easy to take with the laird and all those damn wardens in court. Dad says he'll get four quid a pound for them. I figured when I was coming here that's more than three hundred pounds."

"Well worth a fiver!" The boy's mother giggled. "It will take this laird and his schoolboy gillies a good while yet to outwit your father. He's a grand man from a long and famous line. You pay attention to your old dad, Angus. You've got a lot to learn from him about the salmon poaching trade."

Trout creel

42

Down Under

Fishing, of course, was one of mankind's earliest acquired skills. Throughout history, it had to be done with great seriousness, to fill empty bellies and keep families alive. Stone weirs were built to last for hundreds of years, and nets were woven by old men and women who had the skill to make the mesh just the right size for the fish the humans wished to take as they drew their nets across the river. Even when the importance of catching them has gone far beyond the question of preventing your family from starving, the instinct to fish has remained strong in some humans, male and female.

Of course, a little fishing trip that meant crossing the vastness of America, then taking a 747 over the Pacific for an eighteen-hour flight might, to some, seem just a bit ridiculous. However, there are still those among us who will manage to do it somehow. New Zealand, you see, is world famous for its enormous brown trout and rainbow trout that may weigh ten, twenty, or even thirty pounds. Now just the thought of a trout that size will keep a fly fisherman up all night, then send him scurrying to his tourist agent to gather travel pamphlets. Twenty-pound brown trout? Well, our salmon and steelhead have weights like that, but a brown trout that size? What a diet those fine, fighting fish must have.

"Oh, let's go," said Alice. "I've never been down under. They've asked you to give two museum lectures there. Let's do it. What other excuse could we possibly need?"

Alice is always wild to see faraway places and meet the people there. After our life on the Rhode Island rocky sheep farm, she loves sheep. Staring at the pamphlets she received from New Zealand, she gasped, "They've got three-and-a-half million people living on their North and South Islands and eighty-six million sheep. Oh, dear, let's go! Let's go!"

We did go. The way is a wee bit long and somewhat wearisome, that's agreed by all who make the journey. But when we finally arrived in Aukland on the North Island, we went straight to bed and slept. There was no sense worrying about losing time, for our week had two Mondays or two Tuesdays or whatever. In fact, we lost all sense of time, and instead of leaving winter and going into spring, which was about to burst forth in Canada, we woke up down under and just slipped into autumn. In the first bed and breakfast, we flushed the toilet bowl and watched to see if the water does swing the wrong way down the bowl, and, by golly, it does!

When I awoke in a comfortable New Zealand bed I eyed our long, green fly rod cases – one for Alice, one for me, and one to replace either that might get broken. We had been told by our own North American experts exactly where to fish on the North Island at that season. They say to buy your flies down there, and they mention towns and shops they favor. The fishing's good, they say, but different. It's not like fishing in Canada. It's highly technical. They do everything a bit different down there.

We fished first the Mohaka River on an enormous Maori sheep station of forty thousand animals. We started out with a guide, a young New Zealander of Scottish origins, and drove in a four-wheel drive across rough country through many sheep gates to a new eucalyptus forest with a very pleasant smell, which reminded me instantly of my youth and getting over a head cold in Canada.

Now a guide can be very important when you're fishing waters you don't know, for reasons more than just "Where are the fish?" The New Zealand guides are really big on this aspect of New Zealand fishing. After you've heard all the stories of New Zealand, seen monstrous taxidermist masterpieces of huge trout, and endless walls of color photographs of fishermen from everywhere, clutching outsized examples of local trout, you're ready to take one on the first or second cast. But wait up, mate, not so fast. These *fuush*, to quote the guide, are different from our trout, damned difficult for a North American to take. I suggest they won't be especially hard to catch.

"Do you lay out a line or two and let your fly drift to them?" I ask.

"Oh, no," our guide laughs. "Our fishing here is technical, highly technical." He looks dubiously at us. "I'll take you two along to an easier place."

We walk along beside the riverbank against the current.

"See just up there?" he cautiously nods.

I point. "You mean up there?"

"Oh, God, man, never point at one. They'll know you've seen them and they'll go. I told you, our fishing down here is technical."

We move along, not seeing another fish.

"There's another one," the guide whispers in Alice's ear. "That's a really big *fuush*."

"Where is he?" Alice asks.

"Dear Lord, don't speak aloud when you're near a *fuush* down here. They can hear you and they'll flash away. See that?"

We both saw the next fish lying, feeding, head upstream.

"Is that a Canadian fly you've got on there?" he asks.

"Yes," I whisper. "It's an Umpqua."

"Probably no good down here, but go ahead and try it if you want."

I make one false cast and the fish is gone.

"Too bad," says our young guide. "You seem to spook them all. Did either of you have onions in your sandwiches? You know, that's a smell that will chase away a big *fuush* any time. But doubtless, in a day, or two or three, if you pay attention, you'll start to get it right. Our fishing is not at all like yours. Our fishing down here is very technical." He tried Alice's rod, but it even proved too technical for him.

When the other, older, Maori guide came down the river in a small blown-up raft, he suggested, "Maybe you're not used to fishing."

"Oh, we're used to it," we said. "We fish salmon and trout in northern British Columbia."

They both laughed and repeated, "British Columbia! We've heard you folks just walk across a river on the backs of your giant *fuush*. Haven't you heard that our fishing here is very, very technical?"

"Yes, we have heard that. We'll move along tomorrow morning to fish in the South Island. But we promise to try and become more and more technical every day."

Steelhead's Fancy

43

Lions, Whales, and Women

Dale Chihuly, one of the world's most brilliant glassmakers, whom I had got to know during my days at Steuben, came up to the Charlottes to visit us. When he had asked John Hauberg, the important Northwest Coast art collector, about the very best places to visit on the Charlottes, he had suggested Ninstints on the southern tip of the islands, and I fully agreed with him on that.

I got in touch with the helicopter people at Sandspit Airport and asked for a half-price flight on a Sunday, when there are no demands upon them from the logging companies. We set out early and picked up our licenses to visit from the Haida Band Council, then drove to the morning ferry on time – without gas problems – and crossed to Sandspit where we took off in a small helicopter just large enough to accommodate us.

It was a clear, still, autumn day and the view on the way down was spectacular. We flew slowly along the snow-laden Mosquito mountain range with its lower slopes richly clad in tall Sitka spruce and cedar trees, none of which will ever see another logger's clear-cut, after being recently turned into a national park. We saw an eagle flying to our west, and I tried to forget hearing about the one that came crashing through a helicopter windshield with devastating – or it could have been vengeful – effects.

At Ninstints our pilot landed his helicopter on the beach that curves before the long-abandoned site of Red Cod Town, as it was once called. When he shut the motor off, we were awestruck by the utter silence of the ghost town. Probably fewer than two hundred Haida people lived here in the old days in the dozen large, square houses strung along the beach, all of them with totem poles now fallen, and their houses long rain-rotted and disappearing into the ground, with only their outlines remaining. Even their terraced firepits are now almost hidden beneath a thick layer of bright green rain forest moss.

We walked up among the more recent mortuary poles still standing after perhaps ninety years. Most of these grave posts, which were twice as tall as a man, remained standing. They had turned silver-gray with age, but their splendid carvings of ravens, eagles, bears, and other supernatural characters were still bravely standing up to the filtered summer sunshine or the heavy winter rains. Their mortuary boxes that had once held bodies, and their elaborately carved and painted fronts, were gone, fallen, or perhaps stolen.

If your party goes along to Ninstints, it's a great temptation either not to speak, or to lower your voice, because there is such a ghostly aura about the place. One thinks of all the people in their canoes who have arrived and departed, all the feasts and the fighting, all the clever carvings of the dance masks and the poles now gone. We sat in astonished admiration at this Haida site, abandoned during the smallpox epidemic. We frowned as we gazed at two of the poles still standing, their family crest figures having been burned off with kerosene-soaked rags tied around them by the zealous missionaries who came down by boat and climbed them long ago.

We ate sandwiches, drank a good bottle of wine that Dale had brought from somewhere in his worldwide travels, and once more boarded the helicopter, literally stepping across the centuries. As we flew north along the West Coast, the pilot swooped down low over a large rock where a herd of sea lions had gathered, pressing tight together.

"Yes, we see them," we called to the pilot, as he circled then hovered over the rock for us.

"Do you see those three killer whales?" he asked.

Suddenly, we saw them rise, their tall fins and elegant black and white shapes cruising close around the rock, waiting for a sea lion to panic and leap off the rock to a disappearing bite.

"The lions have been up there for days," the pilot said. "We saw them earlier in the week, with those same whales waiting below."

When we got back home, our neighbor, Teddy, came over to visit us. We told him about the sea lions caught so long on top of the big rock. Teddy knew killer whales. He told us that he'd seen a picture in a magazine of a pretty girl in a skimpy bathing suit kissing a killer whale that had risen up out of his big pool to greet her. He snorted. "But you noticed that those smart sea lions wouldn't jump in the water with those killer whales. No, not for all the tea in China."

Don't tell me our killer whales aren't smart, too. They know exactly when it's right to kiss and when to kill. That's why some Haida here have them for their family crests.

"By the way," said Teddy, "that foreign wine you took down with you for lunch, was it any good?"

"I think it was," said Dale. "We've got another bottle in the basket. Alice, let's all try it."

Teddy smiled and nodded in his most agreeable way and his big black Labrador, Sassy, hearing and fully understanding her master's question, sighed heavily and collapsed once more on our porch. She may have been as sensitive as a female killer whale.

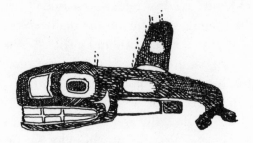

Killer whale design

There is a Northwest Coast myth about a man who healed a sea lion's flipper. While he was doing this, he was abandoned on a low, flat rock by his brother-in-law who was jealous of his kindliness and his skills as a fisherman and hunter.

Before a storm could come and drown him, this kindly man was rescued by Teeben, the Sea Lion, and taken to the sea lions' strange, glittering home in a cave, where they fed him fish. Then, in gratitude for his healing of their chief, they gave this man supernatural powers. These powers helped him become a carver, and he made eight large, high-finned, wooden killer whales. Thereafter, beneath that family's Raven, the crest of Sea Lion went on the pole, and beneath him Frog. That was because a woman of this clan had once insulted a frog, and for this she had been taken by the Frog People to their watery green home as a punishment. A small Frog crest is often seen on many poles to prevent this misfortune from happening to humans again.

As for the killer whales, their fame increased after it became well known that these sharp-toothed, fast-swimming supernatural whales can easily tell a swimming man from an upset canoe, and have never harmed a single one. But when it comes to feeding to stay alive, killer whales soon know the difference between a plump sea lion and a pretty girl.

Teddy told us that was more than understandable to him. You could easily see that Teddy was proud of these distant, swimming relatives of his, the highly intelligent killer whales, who enjoy a tasty school of salmon just as much as we do.

44

Bears with Cubs

Grizzly bears, *Ursus arctos* or *horribilis*, can be a serious menace to man when they are determined to compete and fish on the same stretch of river with you. Fortunately, we have no grizzlies on the

Charlottes, only black bears – although our black bears have been biologically charted as the largest black bears on the North American continent. The rich flesh of the salmon and the abundance of berries must account for their size and blustery good health. In turn, recent scientific studies have shown the huge role bears play in spreading – one way or another – the nutrients from the salmon they catch back to the forest floor.

Our handsome blue-black bears very often produce twin cubs in the spring. If you surprise a mother black bear with cubs, be damn careful. To avoid such a surprise, blow a whistle if you hear a noise near you in the woods. Or better still, wear a bell on your boot so that as you wander it will twinkle and ring and warn the bear who will wish to protect her cubs, and is probably even less eager to meet you than you are to encounter her.

Almost every day we see a black bear crossing the ford at Tlell, the one that we ourselves use. Some years, you can almost set your watch by the sight of that bear crossing into Naikoon Park. It's useful to remember when fishing that a black bear, like a grizzly, wants to do her salmon fishing exactly where you'd like to fish. Leave her alone, let her do it, I'd say, and if you don't know anything about the fishing in a river, you might watch the bear and go where he or she goes later. But never try to fish the same pool together. Bears are serious fishermen, too. You don't want to make them mad at you.

Fishing in real grizzly country on the British Columbia mainland should cause you to carry a heavy-caliber firearm with you, where it's permitted. If you're fishing with an unarmed wife or friend, don't let them wander out of sight. It's said that if a bear overtakes you, it's safest to lie down and play absolutely dead. This often works, I'm told, but I'm not eager to test out the theory.

Bears cause me some anguish when I sleep out in a tent at night. I've had just enough experience in the Arctic with polar bears to be permanently wary. Don't leave any food uncovered near bears. Anything like the smell of bacon, and especially coffee, is known to attract a bear. I read an account once of an Alaskan bear that continued to attack a human for over six hours before it finally ate half its prize. This is perhaps an overcautious note to end on. Remember, black bears are shy and elusive. They're wily fishermen and make reasonable neighbors, usually.

Black bear

You can hear what the Haida think of bears in this well-known myth of theirs:

Rhpisunt was a young Haida woman. She went out to pick salal berries with two of her sisters. Rhpisunt gathered so many berries that her basket strap broke and spilled the berries. She sat down to repair it while her sisters continued down the mountain path to the canoe.

After a while, a mother bear came to Rhpisunt and said that she would like Rhpisunt to meet her two sons, saying, "You'll like the honey they gathered."

These young bears, the girl soon discovered, were not just ordinary bear cubs but were supernaturals who could easily turn themselves into strong young men. The twins, who wore bear skins over their shoulders, said, "Come up the mountain with our bear mother and we will show you the grand house in which we live."

When they reached the house and went inside, it was full of gloomy shadows. The cruel-looking house post carvings frightened the girl and she began to think of running away. That night, one of the bear twins came and said to her, "If you marry me, you'll live. If you refuse, you'll die."

The bear mother woke, and warned away her son. After that, she only allowed Rhpisunt to go out and do her natural duties and to bring in the water and the firewood for the house as well.

When Rhpisunt went outside and stepped in some soft bear droppings, she was disgusted, and wiped her foot hard to clean it in the mountain moss. "I am different from those two brutes," she said, and from then on her own droppings fell only as purest copper, which the bears, like the Haida, valued more than gold.

When the bear twins found these pieces of pure copper, they were surprised. "She does this because she wants to show us she is better than we are. We'll share her between us tonight while our mother sleeps."

Rhpisunt had befriended Mouse Woman, who gave her some warning of this, so she escaped by running outside the ugly house and down the mountainside. But instead of running straight when she heard them coming after her, she turned off and hid in the forest until the angry bear twins had run growling past her.

Some time later, the bear mother came down the path and found Rhpisunt and told her that her two cubs, who were supernaturals, had tricked her while they were in human form and had stolen all her magic copper droppings, which they had hammered into valuable copper shields. But now, the bear mother said, her cubs had once more become proper bears, and she sat down and held up her two front paws to show Rhpisunt the faces of her twin cubs. If you look carefully at a bear's front paws, you will see the facial images of these two cubs on them.

Rhpisunt started running again, and didn't stop until she was safely back in her home.

45

Jack

Jack McClelland has long been a very special person on the Canadian publishing scene. He took over from his father, who was head of McClelland & Stewart of Toronto, one of Canada's oldest and most respected publishing firms. Jack built it into the largest and most successful publishing house in the country. He was able to do this because of his down-to-earth character and a natural, untamed quality that appealed to many Canadians of that period. Jack had a wonderful list of authors when I first came to his firm, and he was able to keep most of them, in spite of the legendary fickleness of authors and their agents.

I once complained to Jack about some problem that McClelland & Stewart had had in the printing of my first book with them. Jack laughed. "Hell, Houston, you think you've got bloody problems? How about my best female author? We got the title on the dust jacket of her new book right, but then somehow things got mixed up and we printed another author's name on the jacket of her book! She got ripping mad at me when she saw it sitting in the bookstores. Finally, I talked her into going over to the Park Plaza and we had a few martinis together to calm her down. After that, I was able to convince her during dinner that the whole thing was pretty damned funny, and we laughed so much together that if I hadn't been a friend of the headwaiter, they'd have thrown us out. You know how it is, Houston. You were born around here. These damn Toronto people and their hotels, some of them can be awfully stuffy."

Jack had been in the Royal Canadian Navy, in command of a PT boat that went sub chasing off Newfoundland's coast. That was where the German wolf pack of submarines regularly gathered to torpedo troop ships and supply ships before they had a chance to gather into convoys to cross the North Atlantic with destroyers to defend them.

When you gave Jack a manuscript, he'd be back to you himself in a day or two after having carefully read every word of it, and would give you his well-considered comments. Not many publishers are like that in Canada or any other country these days.

There are hundreds of stories of Jack's wild escapades with his favorite list of authors. Without speaking of our mutual friend, Farley Mowat, I will only give you one other good example. About a dozen years ago, when the practice of having drinks to celebrate an event was much more common than it is today, Jack and his beautifully elegant wife, Elizabeth, came out to stay with us at our cottage on the Queen Charlottes. At that same time, British Columbia's would-be Premier, William Vander Zalm, was running with the Social Credit party and had chosen that same weekend to come to our islands to solicit votes from Indians, commercial fishermen, and loggers. Vander Zalm arrived in a rented helicopter just across the bridge from us at Teddy's place. As luck would have it, Vander Zalm arrived on the same day that Jack and Elizabeth appeared. That evening, we all walked across the bridge to Teddy's lodge to join in one of those slambam northern B.C. political feasts, and Jack celebrated that evening – perhaps a touch more than some – with a Russian commandant-like flurry of toasts to Vander Zalm.

Next morning when I looked out our window, I spotted Jack standing in the very center of the Tlell bridge in his white pajamas, leather slippers, and blue silk dressing gown. He was always a strikingly handsome man with his military erectness and his longish, snow-white hair above a face that was a ruddy, healthy red, as though it had been burnished by the sun. He stood there, his hair blowing wildly in the wind, clutching his hand-blown glass, grandly lighting one cigarette off the other. He was nodding or waving to all the huge logging trucks that passed, then to the children on the schoolbus, then to other citizens going to a pancake breakfast given in Vander Zalm's honor by Teddy and Dorothy. That caused a great flurry at Tlell, especially the blue silk dressing gown.

"We saw Vander Zalm standing on the bridge near your place," some told us. "What a sight."

"We swear to Jesus," one of the loggers told me, "Vander Zalm was still in his pajamas and he was wearing a silky-looking blue dress. You could tell it was him by his head of hair."

We encouraged Jack to dress before we all went over and had delicious smoked dog salmon and Saskatoon berry pancakes. This was a special breakfast designed for the soon-to-be B.C. Premier, whom I heard asking Jack if he would publish a new book, his first, which he planned to write as soon as he found the time. "Sure, I will," Jack said, "if it's any damn good," which, I believe, was his standard answer.

Book publishing, it seems to me, became a much more sober and serious business in Canada. When Jack retired and sold the company, he laughed, "Hell, Houston, you just may manage to survive without me. God!" he said. "Remember the fun we had across the river and visiting at Teddy's? I wish we hadn't both been crazy enough to give up drinking!"

I looked over and saw our wives glance at each other slyly, like a pair of female leopards. Yes, Jack's world, my world, the whole world, was wiggling and changing too damned fast. Even if Jack and I were still young, I doubt the two of us could set it really straight again.

Oyster dish

46

Local Scuttlebutt

Sergius De Bucy is a long, lanky man with a classical French profile and a very philosophical and inquisitive turn of mind. He was born on these islands and for many years used to drive the bus from the airport at Sandspit on South Moresby Island across beautiful Skidegate Inlet on the small ferry to the Skidegate Landing. We didn't mind at all if there were delays, for it gave us a chance on that small bus to adjust to the islands and, best of all, to listen to Serge, as he gave us a full account of all that had happened here since our last departure.

One typical time when we arrived, we grabbed our rod cases and bags and hurried out in a rush to get a seat on Serge's one and only small bus, because it would take only seven passengers. Another couple came out after us, and Serge said in his slow-drawn island voice, "Sorry, folks, I'm all filled up. But you can put your packsacks in the back of the bus, then follow me. Freddy," he said, sticking his head in the window of the nearest car, "I see you've got no one in your rear seat. This couple needs a ride across to Skidegate and I've got no more room."

"Oh, sure." The driver grinned, swinging open his car door. "You're welcome to jump in."

Serge walked back and said to us, "There, I got them a free ride over with Freddy. That's a new young guy on the island. I don't know his other name or his wife's name yet. She's the new school-teacher here and he, well, they say he's a kind of poet, whatever that means. Probably he's some kind of impractical dreamer." He grinned suspiciously at me. "The two of them are just married. Maybe he's rich, or she's rich. They say he's not looking for work at all, and they've rented a good house with an expansive view out over the Sound. She could be Johnny's daughter."

"I didn't know he had a daughter," I said.

"Oh, yes, I heard he has. She looks like him all right, a good-looking young woman, and she didn't have a camera or a fishing rod with her, so she's no tourist. I believe it's Johnny's daughter by the way she snuggled up to her new husband."

He readjusted the rearview mirror. All talking ceased, which is one of Serge's rules when he is navigating around a slippery curve in the wet road.

"How's your mother?" I asked as we came safely out of the curve.

"Oh, she's fine. She told me if you two came up this fall for fishing, she and Mrs. Ryan would like to drive up to Tlell and visit Alice, who asked Mother a year or so ago to come to tea. It'll give them both a good chance to revisit the cemetery that's so close by your house."

"That'll be nice," said Alice from the back seat of the van. "How old is your mother now?"

"She's ninety-six," Serge answered, "but I told her she should quit driving. She's having some trouble with her eyes lately."

"What do you think about the new B.C. Premier?" I asked.

Serge looked into his rearview mirror, suspiciously checking the passengers again to see who was aboard and who wasn't – Liberal, New Democrat, Conservative, or even anarchist, perhaps.

"Well, I don't know as it's going to make the least bit of difference at all," he said. "This new man running sounds just about as bad as the one we just got rid of. They're every one of them promising to give one hundred and twenty-five percent of our provinces away to the Indians."

"Away to whom?" my wife calls out to him.

"Well, you've heard of native land claims, Alice. Nobody minded that until the Indians claimed that they own Shaughnessy Golf Course in Vancouver. That got every one of those rich golfers mad as hornets."

Many of the visitors to the largest northern island of the Charlottes come or go with Serge, and over the years he may have had a significant effect on the thinking of the tourists and the islanders. I mean, most days he's open on all subjects – politics, fishing, the weather, and all recent island changes. However, he's always been wisely cautious about his position on the Haida Indians. He knows them well – too well to talk about them loosely.

We once took a tour in North Africa where a frowsy tour guide, with her microphone turned up too high, was so racially biased that it made me consider jumping out the window of the bus. Serge is nothing at all like that. He's a soft-spoken, very low key man. Some days he won't speak at all. But it's more likely that he'll look into the rearview mirror of the minibus and pick out someone that he knows and start up a casual conversation. Everyone in the bus listens, intensely eager to pick up some worthwhile tidbit of local news.

"I saw that friend of yours, the American doctor, up here fishing last week," said Serge.

"Oh, did he catch anything?"

"I didn't ask him, but he and his friend had a box of wine and whisky when they came in, and it was just as heavy when they went out. So I guess those were salmon they were taking home."

There was a long pause before one of the passengers said to Serge, "Did you like the way the vote turned out?"

"No," was Serge's immediate answer. "Write this new Premier, ask him for something, anything. While he's new, he'll probably give it to you. Jim, you tell him you don't want them cutting down any more trees because you want to save them all for drawing pictures. He'll think you're an environmentalist, and he'd give them anything. These politicians, they'll all promise to do everything exactly right if they only vote for them. Then once they do get elected, they build themselves a theme park with big pictures of themselves hanging around, staring at you like those portraits of Mao Zedong."

Some passengers snorted and the others laughed as Serge's bus swept past the line of cars and trucks and arrived in first place to drive up the rumbling iron ramp of the B.C. Ferry. During the ride across, the Sound was mirror-still and beautiful.

The bus eased down the steep front platform of the ferry as it landed, then up the concrete slope beside the battered wooden pilings. Serge turned left, then stopped. The passengers wrestled to open the old-fashioned sliding doors of the van as Serge wandered around to the back and casually helped unload their luggage.

"Thanks a lot for getting us a ride with them," the young girl said as she pulled her backpack out of Serge's van. "They say they just got married and they asked us to come to dinner at their house tonight. We're going!"

"That's good," said Serge, "I thought that maybe you four might hit it off together."

"Yeah," said the girl, "my other half here, he's a poet just starting out."

"That's nice," said Serge. "We used to have a poet here named Hibby. Good fishing, Alice," he said as he passed us our rod cases and our duffle bags. "Teach Jim how to catch one this time, will you? See you when you're coming out again." Serge smiled shyly. "I'm turning eighty this year, but I still feel spry enough" he said, and waved goodbye.

Prawns

47

I Liked Sockeye Sue

I liked Sockeye Sue. She was a Fisheries officer here on the Charlottes for a few years, and she believed in a strict upholding of the law. She was the first female Fisheries officer any of us had ever heard of. We couldn't believe our ears. What could a woman do against a bunch of slightly drunken, rough, tough, cold-eyed Northwest Coast fishermen, sportsmen or commercial?

Well, the answer to that was *plenty*!

You wouldn't call Sockeye Sue tough, but then you wouldn't call her gentle either. She took Canadian fish law very seriously, and was death on violators. Her deputy told me that she would sit near shore in a tin boat all night with her binoculars at the ready, eager to race out at dawn and grab any unlicensed poachers or those who tried to exceed their legal limit and were caught in her pre-dawn raids.

Sue turned the Tlell estuary into a very law-abiding place during the autumn salmon runs of the eighties, and I congratulate her for it. I mean, even the doctors and the artists, the pseudo-nobility, and the fish restaurant owners were all scared to death of Sockeye Sue.

She told me that she had been threatened several times by roughnecks. After that, she took her muscular, bare-chested fish warden with her on those nightly stakeouts to catch the meat hunters whose aim was to supply distant big-city restaurants with a vanload of illegal salmon. They're the ones who trolled through the misty mornings trying to trick her just before the early dawn.

Sad to say, Sockeye Sue saw an ad in the Victoria papers offering much more money and a chance to be head Fisheries officer in the Philippines. Being an adventurous type, Sue applied by mail and got the job. She left her job in Canada and went for bigger pay in the far-off Philippines. When she arrived, the government officials there were shocked. She was a woman! A woman as head of Fisheries? Impossible, they snorted! Never! They wouldn't even allow her to fill out the forms. My wife, Alice, says women will just have to wait a little longer to get some jobs abroad like that. Those other countries will eventually have to have women as presidents, prime ministers, and mayors, before they have female Fisheries officers. But the women will have to keep on trying. I for one hope like hell that Sockeye Sue, or someone with her fortitude, will soon return to Haida Gwaii.

The Tlell bridge, like other wooden bridges beside a rain forest, could use a coat of paint every few years. This highly regarded, all-male chore has been one of the plums of the Provincial Department of Highways for the sixty years of the bridge's existence. We have had the questionable privilege of watching this paint job progress in anything but simple ways for the past twenty years.

First, the work was almost always done exclusively on Saturdays and Sundays; islanders in the know here swear the painters get double pay on Saturdays and triple pay on Sundays. Could that be the reason the painting has always taken place on weekends and, despite a gang of painters being involved, the job has always taken an unbelievable length of time to complete?

Now, it seems, only a few years pass and suddenly it's bridge painting time again. On this most recent painting, to our shock and surprise, only three girls jump off the highway department's truck – one handsome young Haida woman and two ponytailed, blonde islanders. These young women are all dressed in snappy, neatly fitted male highway attire – bright orange sleeveless vests, sun-yellow safety helmets, very tight blue jeans, and large, steel-toed construction workers' leather boots. They quickly pry open their five-gallon pails and, talking cheerfully, fondle their brushes, spin their rollers, and get ready to paint.

I get ready, too. Eager to sketch them while they work. *Surely these women have made a mistake. They've got the wrong day. It's a Monday during the ordinary, no-overtime work week and they're sure to be far worse at painting than those experienced overtime men. But wait, wait! What's happening? These three females are going at the work quickly and neatly, preparing it like a theater set for tonight's play. Their white paint rolls on fast and smooth. They use their brushes for the corners, no dribbles and no places missed. What the hell's going on here? A dribbly paint job on this bridge used to take forever.*

I can't believe my eyes. I call Alice. She says, "Well, of course, those three are girls. Naturally, they're going to make a neat job of the bridge." She says she's going to go out just before it starts to rain and ask them in for coffee and cookies. But Alice doesn't have the chance to do that. The girls finish that side of the bridge *tout de suite*, and suddenly a yellow highway truck appears with its lights flashing red, and a fourth handsome, dark-haired female driver picks them up and whisks them away.

The rain slacks off, but I have scarcely managed to finish my first sketch. Next day, they're back on the job precisely on time. They begin to paint industriously, at the same time talking, laughing, and seemingly enjoying themselves in the mid-morning sunshine.

When Alice goes out with her offer of a coffee break, they chat with her sociably, all the time painting like mad, while explaining to her that they have brought all the food and thermoses of coffee that they need. They thank her, and smilingly say, "Maybe another day."

Watching so much industry by these red-vested women with their ponytails bobbing in time with every roller stroke makes me feel I, too, should be doing some hard work. I take my fly rod and go down to the far end of the long pool, which is out of sight of the bridge. After a while, the tide changes, and covering a rise I get a strike and eventually manage to grass my salmon.

Feeling better after my honest labors, I return to our place, ready to finish my sketch. But to my utter astonishment, the bridge is totally and beautifully painted – every millimeter of it. The handsome truck driver has come and picked up her painting team and disappeared. Good God, this seems incredible! It's only Tuesday and they've already completed the job, packed up, and gone. No cartoon to be made, nothing to bitch about with that crew. This year, with computers doing half man's work and women like those painters doing the other half, I wonder how the hell are we males ever going to fit into the working world again? I'm serious. What in the devil's name has happened to that painters' union? How is the government going to spend all that extra double, triple overtime they've saved? How about a few new female fish wardens to protect the river the way they so neatly preserve our bridges? I'd be all for that.

48

The Goat Man and Others

We have a kitchen window that faces out toward the south end of the Tlell bridge. Alice prepares food there and I taste her work. The cleaning of an already gutted fish is a stand-up job that requires filleting and great care to remove all the bones. Outside it is quiet, with few vehicles passing. It's the unknown human travelers, those that go by on foot as we do, who are the ones that interest us.

There was for a while a habitual passer-by who used to cross the bridge perhaps two or three times a week during the early seventies. He was worth putting down the fish knife and just gazing at his progress in wonder. He was a very, very, old-looking young man, skeletal thin and bent, with a long, long fringe of hair, for he was balding much too early. He took off his hat when it rained, perhaps to bathe the top of his naked head. He wore a huge, unkempt brown

beard, the lank yet curly kind that looked as though it belonged anywhere but on a human's face. I know because I once had a beard in
the Arctic. He wore ancient, pale grayish denim overalls that sagged
down into his knee-high rubber boots. He moved slowly, almost
painfully for a man approaching thirty, and always stared straight
ahead. Almost every other human pauses to glance into our
windows, then mounts the bridge to peer up and down the river for
signs of salmon. Even the big logging trucks usually stop while their
drivers hop out of the cab and pee, then stride back to the bridge to
study the river for fish. But not this man.

He had in tow behind him a female goat, a big, bony one. Alice,
a sometime Rhode Island sheep farmer, told me that it was a
Tannenberg, that it was characteristic of such goats to have an
immense udder. It was probably the basis for much of the family
food. The goat man kept this nanny on a large, worn piece of ship's
hauser, and her hooves made a clattering sound as she crossed the
wooden bridge. Behind this bearded man and the goat came his
other half, a pale, fragile young girl who looked neither right nor
left. She carried a small baby on her back Eskimo-style, but wrapped
in a worn Indian blanket tied around the baby, then over her shoulders and around her waist.

Where did they come from? Where did they live? We never
found that out, for the woods beside the road are dark and deep.
We knew there were other people hidden in the forest. They had
built their strange little wicky ups that didn't even look like houses,
had lived there during the early Vietnam War years, and still clung
to that lifestyle. This man had come north onto these islands of
plenty to live here in hiding. Someone told me that he was fairly
intellectual and very Thoreau-minded. He had come here, probably not unlike me, to find a new "Walden Pond."

Why had he not, like Thoreau, gone back to his other life after
his troubles ended? That was something I later tried to find out from
other islanders who had lived here throughout all those uncertain
times. This man with the goat had surely gone too far beyond
becoming a respectable schoolteacher like some others. He chose
not to find a job among the right wing loggers, nor did he find

someone to teach him commercial fishing. Perhaps he was already
a writer, a painter, or a poet. They dress strangely, and may like
goats. When I asked others about this little hidden family with
their baby and their goat, some people seemed to remember them,
but only vaguely. No one seemed to really know anything about
them. We never found the answer. Some future archeologist may
find their bones mixed in with those of their Tannenberg goat.

In the early nineties, we also knew a young woman – I should call
her a girl, really – who was very shy and lonely. For some reason of
her own, she had lived alone for more than a year in a tiny cabin
she had built herself downriver from the Tlell bridge. Most mornings, I'd hear her walking quietly past the hideaway along the
silence of the narrow gravel path between the fir trees that led to
the bridge. Then again in the evening, we'd see her on another
lonely walk.

What made our jaws drop was that she dressed in the current
fashion of Greenwich Village, or San Francisco, or Toronto's Queen
Street West. She was tall and razor thin, with her hair shaved off
as close as an Iroquois warrior before that was very fashionable,
except for a narrow, bush roach of hair spread out in front and dyed
a brilliant peacock blue. She wore many silver rings on every finger,
and more rings in her ears and nose. To me, these seemed out of
place with her heavy black military-style boots and her bulky leather
bomber jacket. But, hell, all that was just coming into fashion.
Perhaps, I thought, *she's some kind of modern missionary from* Elle *or*
Vogue, *paid to spread style in the wilderness.*

If she saw that she was going to meet me on the bridge when I
crossed to fish the other side of the pool, she would stop and half-
turn, perhaps asking herself whether it was too late to whirl around
and walk or run the other way. But then I could see her stiffen her
resolve and continue on toward me. She'd close her eyes when she
passed, and I could see that they were surrounded by a massive
application of raccoon mascara. Sometimes when I said, "Good
morning," she'd give me a little winsome smile through dead-pale

lips. Then I'd hear her heavy boots echoing on across Tlell's lonely bridge.

I've known and done some wild things in my life, but I could never imagine working up the nerve to appear at dawn rigged up fit to kill in the loneliness of the central Charlottes. But who the hell am I to judge the way young women dress? She was probably trying to get over something in her life.

In early spring when we returned, I looked for her, but she was gone. I wondered where. To tell you the truth, I missed her zingy touch of civilization in this secret world of salmon, deer, emperor geese, tufted puffins, and every now and then a shambling bear. It made me think again. What do women want today?

Emperor goose

49

The Film World

The very thought of writing a novel and having it actually bought by Hollywood filmmakers has always excited me. It has happened to me only once in a long while, and then the screenplays that resulted only sometimes reached the screen. Authors have to be crazy to trust Hollywood to make the kind of film they have in mind. But what the hell? *One could work again sometime*, I say to myself. I always hope. And it's comforting just knowing that someone has actually read my book and wants me to try the screenplay. So I go ahead and do my best, then sell what I consider to be a byproduct of the novel.

Wait, hold on! A blizzard of telephone messages arrives from everywhere asking me to rearrange and rewrite my screenplay for *Eagle Song*, and they're willing to pay me to do that for them. Hell, that's not all bad! I've got the whole original plot imbedded in my head. A novel takes about 350 pages, but a screenplay is only 120 pages long. That represents a page-a-minute screen time, which is considered standard, a two-hour film.

Sounds easy, doesn't it? Well, it's not. I find that the writing of a novel, especially in the beginning, is a deliciously lonely business. There are many chances to read, correct, reread, and quietly reflect, with lots of time for staring out the window, and, of course, wandering off to do whatever I like when the day and hour seem right. Making movies – even planning them – is an altogether different kettle of fish.

I write the screenplay and, if they accept it, my wife goes dancing off to the bank to deposit their check. Later, there's a telephone conference with six of them and one of me, or should I say two of us, with Alice. God knows who is sitting unseen, unknown to me, in some sunny, distant room in California or perhaps New York or Toronto, figuring exactly where my plot went wrong. "You wrote a *book*," they say, and I imagine them curling their lips as they say it. "But hell man, that's not a film."

After this vital replanning phase, when I have given some ground and they much less, I start my rewrite. Then they decide it's absolutely necessary that we all get together – the producer, the director, his assistant, the cinematographer, whoever.

"Okay, I'll come down," I say, "to help get *Eagle Song* just right."

"No, no, we think that might be inconvenient for you. We should all come north and meet at your place on the Charlottes, a place that we have never been," they say. "That will make it easier for you. Hell, this movie's going to be about the North Pacific Coast. All of us need to go up there and gather a little local atmosphere."

"That could be helpful," I admit.

"Fine," they say, and set the date.

The director calls from Paris and announces that he's going to bring his lady with him. Yes, yes, they've heard we have a limited number of beds in our cottage at Tlell, but they assure me they don't care. They'll rough it. His Parisian lady has never been in the wilderness and, *mon Dieu*, she says she'll be delighted to sleep like an enchanted princess out in the dark primeval forest.

"Not when she sees what lives in there, she won't," says Alice. "Not if I show her the size of the deep tracks left yesterday when we saw that bear cross the ford."

My son, John, makes movies and he decided to come with them. And my other son, Sam, who hates to miss anything, came along more or less for the fun of it.

All the participants arrived in their various ways, some by private plane, some by commercial flight, others by ferry, then by rented car up the one and only island road, which passes our small and humble cottage. Alice and I had decided to sleep out in the hideaway in our rarely used, fold-down, homemade double bed. John made plans to use his sleeping bag, and Sam, the downstairs sofa. The famous director and his enchanted forest lady, after having a safely distant look at our dark, brooding forest and at the still-clear bear tracks, requested that I make new last-minute rearrangements. They decided to sleep in a small and pleasant house for rent owned by our neighbors four miles up along the road.

The sky that evening turned bright and clear, as it often does. We hunkered down around our gift from Teddy, a large, outdoor picnic table, scarcely noticing the glorious sunset, so intent were we on getting all our filming details straight during this one last chance together before the cameras started rolling. I asked two Haida friends with high cheekbones and interesting eyes to come over and visit. The film folk were impressed, saying these two must be in the picture. "They're fantastic." The associate producer, a handsome, powerful young woman, was dressed in old-fashioned D.W. Griffith-type whipcord jodhpurs with short brown Wellington boots, a blousy white shirt, and a Barrymore black slouch hat. Instead of brandishing a riding crop, she carried a large pink notepad. The producer, a devoted fisherman, never took his eyes off the river after he saw the first two salmon rise. Soon, he was unscrewing the top of his Sage rod case.

"What time do we go out and cast a few in the morning?" he asked me anxiously as he started setting up his rod. "What kind of fly should I try first?"

The associate producer changed the subject. She was desperately trying to get him to forget the fishing – until we'd settled on the script, the local film locations, and the timing. That night, Alice gave us a great salmon dinner with the finest California wines that the filmfolk had kindly brought with them. We talked of mutual friends and famous films and enjoyed a hilarious dinner, but we still hadn't settled one damned thing.

"Tomorrow, maybe," Alice groaned as we closed the door of the hideaway and wriggled into our rubber-padded, barely double, wall bed.

In the early morning, nothing would do but we go fishing – the producer, John, Sam, and me. The producer caught a good-sized salmon right on cue! *Thank God*, I thought, *that will soften his heart, and loosen his purse strings, and guarantee our use of these islands as our location.* We hurried back, breakfasted, then together drove in two cars up to North Beach, a stunning film location. There we had lunch, a cookout comprised of practically every native island food that one could eat. The food was great, but it was a strange event. Just as northern Canadians usually look awkward and out of place in southern California, so these Californians managed to look like rare pink flamingos or other tropical birds that had been swept violently north by El Niño. They huddled close together on North Beach, shivering and staring listlessly through the windswept mists in hope of catching a glimpse of the mountains of Alaska, forty kilometers to our north.

The famous director there with us had recently achieved a big film success and we hoped he would be the one to undertake the direction of my novel, *Eagle Song*. A lot depended on his enthusiasm. Oh, yes, he was eager to make a picture here, he said. "Let's do it right away." But he was a citizen of France, he explained to me, and he had just started to write a screenplay himself about Jeanne

D'Arc and he knows Isabelle Adjani and would like to have her play the lead. *This is understandable*, I thought, having seen that gorgeous woman in *La Reine Margot* in Paris, but his whole elaborate scenario seemed to me damned unlikely to happen soon.

Here we all are, I thought, *eating, drinking good wine, and fishing on this, the perfect set for* Eagle Song, *and our potential director's got nothing on his mind but writing his first damned screenplay about Jeanne D'Arc. After that, he says, he'd love to do* Eagle Song. *Well, I'm used to all that sort of talk.*

Sometimes the right story, good chemistry, and the essential amounts of money get together and make a film work, but much more often they do not.

When we got to bed that night, Alice listened to all my complaints. "Well, that's why your agent and lawyer made them pay for both the book rights and the screenplay in advance."

"They'll all be gone tomorrow after breakfast," I said, "back to Hollywoodland, Paris, and Toronto. Goodnight."

"Pleasant dreams," she answered, and gave one of her gentle, conversation-ending snores.

That picture has not been made. That is, not yet!

Chief's hat

There is nothing wrong with that smaller, calmer world of documentary filmmaking. Canada's National Film Board has been famous for more than half a century, and it has done some fine short films. For one reason or another – mostly an inability to say no whenever something new came up – I have been deeply involved as director, producer, or technical advisor in half a dozen documentaries. These films actually saw the light of screen or television, won prizes, and were a pleasure to make – a fact that cannot be claimed today for many of the larger films. Although, of course, I'm still proud of the movie Hollywood made of *The White Dawn*.

When I was asked by the Devonian Foundation of Calgary, Alberta, to make a small series of half-hour documentary films about older aboriginal people in Canada, the first film was about George Clutesi. The next was made in the Canadian eastern Arctic and entitled *Art of the Arctic Whalemen*; the third, *Legends of the Salmon People*, on the upper Skeena River in British Columbia; the fourth, *Kalvak*, about an old Inuit woman artist of great distinction; and finally *I Remember Horsemen*, a story related by Augusta, a Shuswap woman at her home on Soda Creek in the B.C. Interior.

When Augusta was ninety-eight or ninety-nine years old – church records said she had been born February 1, 1888 – she had been told by relatives that someone wished to come and make a film of her. She agreed, and when the day arrived, she stopped splitting wood and opened her gate to shake my hand, smiling widely. She was a very small, thin, and bent woman who lived alone in her log cabin. She dressed in a longish, faded black dress, with a sun-bleached blue babushka on her head. She reminded me of an illustration I'd seen, one of the characters out of a Russian fairytale. Her skin was deeply wrinkled and her eyes were softened to the color one sometimes sees in a young girl's eyes. Augusta's wide grin was close-lipped to hide the fact that she wasn't wearing her government-supplied teeth. She had given up wearing them, she said, because they didn't fit good, and perhaps because she lived alone and no longer cared.

Augusta had a kindly female relative who lived on a ranch some twelve kilometers, just under ten miles, away and came to visit Augusta once a week. She told me that she and her husband and the Indian agent had all tried to get Augusta to move to a rest home in town, but she would have none of it. She told them she had been born on the banks of Soda Creek and that, God willing, was where she was going to die.

On the following day, Augusta, moving surprisingly fast, led me to a trail that almost disappeared beneath the overhanging alders. She told me I was looking at a part of the old gold trail where many rough-looking horsemen had come by, some with wagons and supplies, some drunk, and all of them hurrying north to seek their fortune, for a big gold strike had been made on the Horsefly River. Soda Creek, where Augusta lived, ran through high, arid country. The river there was well known for its giant sturgeon, some longer and weighing more than a good-sized man.

Augusta's cabin was gray with age, but it was sturdy. Inside, it had turned a yellowish gray and had the smell of old newspapers. The two windows were very small, but she usually left the door wide-open for air and light. A narrow, old iron bed was pressed against the far wall. Beside it was an unpainted homemade table and two chairs. There was a black barrel stove with a shelf above it and a tin of tobacco with a man's pipe on top of it. A large calendar hanging on the wall showed the wrong month, which didn't really matter, for Augusta's calendar was six years old.

Augusta made us both a mug of tea that we carried outside, where we sat on a half log bench.

"My daughter-in-law says you might want to take some pictures of me. Is that right?"

"She's right," I answered.

"Sure, you can, but why?"

"Not too many women live so long, in the way you do, and all alone."

"Lord, it ain't no trouble being out here at all if a person's got their health. And I still got mine."

"Maybe it's the wood-splitting and carrying water that does it," I offered.

"Nawh, that ain't it. It's the good, fresh air around here. You ever been into one of those agents' offices or the hospital near Hundred Mile House where they want you to sign your name, then poke at you? I can hardly bring myself to breathe those awful smells. I'd a lot rather muck out a horse barn any day, the way I used to do. Them horseball smells are a whole lot better, better for you."

"Is it all right with you, Augusta, if we start filming you tomorrow? Of course, I'll pay you for it."

"Sure, you can make a moving picture about me. Sure. And you're welcome to call me Augusta. That's not my real name. I can't even speak the Shuswap language any more because the nuns wouldn't let us speak a word of it while I was going to school, and I've forgot most of the French my husband taught me." She giggled, holding her hand over her mouth. "Do you want me to sing for you a few verses of O Canada? I can do that in French or English, and play along on my mouth organ that somebody gave me. Sure, go ahead," she chuckled, "make your movie pictures. I got the wood split early today. I got nothing else to do. You come today, tomorrow, anytime."

"Thank you. I'll be here with the crew tomorrow. I've got a photographer, a sound man to record what you've got to say, and Allison, she's the girl who's going to pay you. She keeps everything going right for all of us."

"And you?" she asked. "What do you do?"

"Oh, I stand around and try to look like I know what I'm doing."

"Yeah, you mean kind of like a chief," she snorted. "Chiefs don't do anything either."

Augusta told me she had been married to a Frenchman for a while, but that he had died some years ago. She talked about the legendary hanging judge, Matthew Baillie Begbie, who had once ruled the district. She said he found the criminals guilty and made one of his quick decisions, deciding to use the noose on three bad men. Augusta had sometimes done a little sewing for the judge. This time he gave her the cloth for three small black pillowcases. She said she didn't realize that they were to go over the bad men's heads before the judge ordered the gallows trap to be sprung from under their feet at Soda Creek. What a story! I got excited when I heard it and she assured me it was true. I changed the script that night, which producers and directors love to do, and stayed awake to cram in a version of the hanging. But my quick-change idea turned out badly and had to be dropped on the cutting room floor. I might have been able to turn it into an hour-long film, but there was no market for that. Quick, exciting ideas like that one are prob-ably what caused this film to be the only one in the series that remains unfinished.

I and the crew did manage, however, to finish up the last scenes with Augusta, which she did very naturally, sometimes breaking off abruptly to go and split some wood or make some tea for all of us. I admired Augusta more than I can say. Here was this old lady who had found contentment out there alone in her small log cabin, almost free of all the evils that plague other humans in our world. When the filming was over, the rest of the crew said goodbye to Augusta and drove back into town to pack our gear.

We had, with the help of Augusta's daughter and Allison, opened an account for her in the town bank. I sat sadly looking around her cabin, trying to remember every small detail of its inte-rior and the Spartan life she led. Then, with a flourish, I took out the checkbook and wrote her weekly pay, which she had more than earned for her talent and her time.

"How much money is this?" she asked me, squinting at the check.

I told her, saying she could go down and draw the rest of the money out, bit by bit, as she needed it.

"What are you going to do now?" Augusta asked me. "Where are you going to go?"

"I'm going to drive down into town and pack my bag."

"If you ain't in a big hurry, how'd you like to drive me with you?" She smiled. "I was thinking this money could buy us one of them good-sized bottles of rye and, well, we could sort of sit on a park bench I know and drink it together."

I looked at that best old woman in all of British Columbia and said, "I'd love to do that with you, Augusta, but – the trouble is, our plane is leaving soon, this afternoon."

She shook my hand at the gate. "I thought you looked kind of like a sport to me," she said, "but I guess that I was wrong. You're probably hurrying off to stand around and watch some other old Indian or Eskimo get asked a lot of foolish questions with that camera going and that hairy sound thing in their face. Goodbye, Jimmy," she said.

"Goodbye, Augusta," I mumbled, and got into the old rented car and drove away.

50

Antiquing

A telephone call came from the American Indian Art Center in New York in the early 1970s. They asked me if I would agree to visit a major Indian and Eskimo art show in Alaska to be held at the new University of Fairbanks. I was delighted to hear that Bill Holm, a Northwest Coast Indian art expert from Seattle, was to go as well, and we two would judge the two separate aspects of the work. Prizes would be awarded and we would both have the opportunity of knowing more of the important Eskimo and Tlingit Indian artists.

Driving back to the hotel one evening during the several days of Alaskan events, I found myself in the back seat of a station wagon with Bill Holm. We hadn't seen each other often and had much to talk about. The subject that night was Haida art and Kwakiutl art. I took the view that there was no North American art to beat Haida and Tsimshian art, certainly nothing else on the whole of the Northwest Coast.

"So you prefer the northern style," Bill said in his slow, clearly enunciated style.

"It's the Athens of the Indian world," I said, using a fancy expression I sometimes applied to the Inuit art of Cape Dorset.

"Yes, Haida art is very skillful, very thoughtful," Bill agreed, "quite a lot like the art of ancient Rome or Greece."

"Very carefully done," I added, "like the art of Michelangelo and Leonardo da Vinci."

"Is that the only kind of art you like?" Bill asked me. I was still busy thinking that one over when he added, "Does that mean you dislike French Impressionism?"

"Hell, no!" I laughed. "Vincent Van Gogh, Gauguin, Matisse, Toulouse Lautrec are all favorites of mine. So is Pablo Picasso."

"Good," he said. "I thought you might be willing to reach beyond that cold Haida perfection. Consider the Kwakiutl of Alert Bay on Vancouver Island. They're a people full of passion. They've been known to hack out a mask-sized piece from a cedar tree in the morning, carve it into a mask in the afternoon, then dance in it dripping wet with paint during a feast that night."

"Yes, I've heard that, and it is something to consider," I admitted. "That's passion, all right."

"Sure, it is." Bill smiled at me. "It sounds like an account of Van Gogh painting at Arles – one good-sized canvas every day for about a month, catching everything in the form and color that impressed him most."

"God, I'm impressed with your selective way of thinking about the differences in Northwest Coast Indian art," I said. "I'll bet you've got it right. But seeing their art the way you do, I find it odd that you're the very person who wrote and illustrated Northwest Coast Indian art in *An Analysis of Form*. That book taught these artists the absolute importance of the accuracy involved in the ovoid curve of the eye, the wings, the joints, everything. That's what I'd call highly formalized art, not impressionist art, wouldn't you?"

"Well, the Edenshaws and others had formalized the Haida style before the turn of the century," Bill said. "But the importance of getting all that information organized was something I cared about, something worth passing on to the younger generation of carvers and printmakers, as well as any students interested in studying the forms of Northwest Coast Indian art."

"Do you still support the rigid formality of the Haida carving?" I asked.

"Of course." Bill laughed. "One should never be too narrow. Both the northern style and the more southern, Salish styles – they each have separate virtues of their own. Taken all together or separately, they have certainly created one of the world's great arts."

"Who could argue with that?" I agreed.

Next day, I heard an Indian singing the praises of Bill Holm. "Only Indians came to that class Bill was teaching," he said, "only Northwest Coast Indians could really understand him. He's a professor who really understands the inside meanings of our art."

"He's great," I said, "but he's not an Indian. Bill is blonde and blue-eyed, very much of Scandinavian stock."

"What do you mean Bill Holm's not an Indian?" he frowned at me. "He's a lot more Indian than a helluva lot of Indians I know. Bill's got what I'd call good Indian sense. He's warm-hearted and wise-headed. And he knows our ways a lot better than most folks do."

Next day in the bright afternoon, I was wandering along a street in Alaska with Bill Holm, whom I consider to be about the wisest man I'll ever know in the field of Northwest Coast art. We saw a small antique store with an Aleut kayakman's gut-sewn garment hanging in the window, along with a few less impressive Indian and Ipiutak odds and ends.

Bill headed for the door. "You never know what's just come out of someone's attic in Alaska. It makes antique hunting here exciting."

A pleasant-looking older man was leaning against his counter, blowing smoke rings. He had a few Canadian Inuit carvings, some of which I recognized from Cape Dorset, and others from the West Coast of Hudson Bay, both old haunts of mine. One of them was a Kiawak and really good. I asked how much. I didn't buy it, but I didn't mind that the price was spectacularly high. We both continued looking, trying not to miss anything worthwhile. Finally, when we were just about to go, the dealer said, "I've got something special here that might interest you two."

He bent down and from beneath his counter he displayed a Hudson's Bay trade flintlock, a smooth-barreled musket with the big trigger guard to accommodate a mitted hand.

"About 1810 or '20, I'd judge," the dealer said.

But what caught our eyes was the elaborate Tlingit-type, Northwest Coast carving that covered the wooden stock.

"I ain't showing this," the dealer mumbled, "because it gets some of the locals too damned excited. Some claim it's their great-grandfather's and swear that others in the family had no right to sell it to me or anyone else, but they surely did. I got a copy of the goddamned sales slip kicking around here somewhere."

He handed it to Bill. I was surprised that he looked at it so casually and so quickly handed it over to me. I collect some flintlocks, muskets, and powder horns, largely because I wrote a book about the French and Indian Wars called *Ghost Fox*, and another entitled *Eagle Song*, about the Nootka. I had only seen one musket with its butt and forearm carved like this, and that was in a museum. I had never dared to hope that I might own one.

"How much?" I asked, and the dealer quoted an enormous price, then added, "If you've got a dealer's number, I could do a little better."

"It's closing time here," said Bill, "and we've got a meeting. Jim, you could come back here when this store opens in the morning."

When we went outside, it was snowing big, soft flakes.

"What meeting?" I asked Bill as we pulled up our hoods.

"Our meeting right now," said Bill. "I know where you could buy one of the Hudson's Bay Company trade muskets plain for about five hundred dollars."

"Sure," I agreed, "but what about all that terrific carving?"

"Not so terrific," he answered me. "You didn't look hard enough. There are carvers around here who could have done that yesterday. Hold onto your money, friend. You'll need it in your old age."

Ivory amulet

51

Alaskan Gold

For a while, it was legal to smoke marijuana in the state of Alaska. During a midwinter conference there, I availed myself of the chance, for I am not one to willingly miss any of the legitimate thrills, or even sometimes the illegitimate thrills, that this world has to offer.

On the first night that I tried marijuana, we were in one of those small, intimate Alaskan living rooms – all of us shoeless and stocking-footed following the local custom. The room had a deep, deep, shaggy purple rug, with a huge blue down-filled sofa that would take you down but would allow you to stand up again only after a terrible struggle. Around the room and along the hall were pieces of thick, homemade pottery – you know the kind – as well as huge pink wine glasses shaped more or less as if some spaced-out person blew them. There was a gigantic stereo system, and pictures, large and small, by local artists hung one over the other, covering almost every inch of brightly papered walls.

I took my first puff of pot and waited. Nothing happened. But I could tell it was the real thing. It made your eyes water and the smell was so unique. The experienced smokers watched me with a knowing smile.

"Take another good puff, buddy."

Still nothing happened. I more or less finished the joint and then lied to the hostess, saying I felt great. I drank a little Russian vodka on the rocks and suddenly everything really started feeling great – being with these Alaskans and the temperature outside hanging at forty below zero, both Fahrenheit and Celsius, the only time they register together. There was inch-thick silver frost glowing on the windowpanes, and that should make anyone swoon with love for the Arctic world.

I took a puff or two from someone else's joint next night and noticed that once again it did nothing for me.

On the third night, while we were visiting another writer's house, a Swedish-looking girl said, "Try mine, it's half southern Californian and half pure Alaskan gold."

I took three deep puffs, expecting nothing at all. But as I rose to get a drink, I passed a small, square mirror enhanced by an elaborate, golden picture frame. I paused to look at myself, and as I did, I saw the picture frame and glass grow deeper and deeper as its golden contours seemed to ripple and cast off a magical glow. My own image retreated backwards, shrinking in size, reducing, going farther and farther away, like the rabbit in *Alice in Wonderland*. Alarmed to see that I had almost disappeared, I went into the hostess's small, glowing bathroom and splashed my face with ice-cold water, then held onto both water faucets until I settled down.

"That Alaskan gold got through to you!" the Swedish girl laughed when I returned.

The record player was doing its thing softly and the conversation had returned to Alaskan native arts and the future of the local tourist trade. Our hostess gave us Turkish coffee and smoked salmon before we stamped into our boots, flung on our parkas, and hurried off into the clear, starlit night.

As I approached the hotel, I thought of the golden mirror and the stunningly deep rabbit warren that I had entered. Years have passed since then, and I have never felt the need to go into that magic tunnel again. Perhaps that was because I started smoking much too early, maybe when I was eight or nine, when we boys thought it fashionable to smoke the dark ends of corn silk tassels wrapped in toilet paper. That, too, proved strong enough for me.

Alaska king crab

Tommy was a taxi driver, a famous character to those who lived in and around the small city of Prince Rupert on the British Columbia mainland at the mouth of the mighty Skeena River. Expecting that it would become the gateway to Canada's growing trade with the Orient, the railroads bet a lot on the town of Prince Rupert near the turn of the old century. But some townsfolk there swear that the winter rains drowned out the battle. The trans-Pacific trade developed in Vancouver and Seattle, and just grew like Topsy. Prince Rupert had to be satisfied with canning salmon.

Tommy used to drive his taxi in Rupert and would take me here and there in town, trying to find a better restaurant. It was worth the ride just to talk to him. When night was coming down and the street lights first turned on, we could see half a dozen Indians gathered in the pool of light beneath a metal light pole. One of them was whacking the pole with a heavy stick. Several others were drinking from the necks of bottles concealed in paper bags, and the others were shouting, laughing, and dancing drunkenly. We paused near them, halted by a stoplight.

"One helluva lot of noise this early on a Saturday night," Tommy called out to them, and shook his head when one of the drunks called back to him to come and have a drink.

"What do you think of all that?" he asked me.

"Well, it's never looked too good to me," I told him, "Indians raising hell and drinking out of the necks of bottles under a street light for everyone to see."

"That's the difference right there," Tommy added. "They're making a big display of themselves right beside this stoplight, using up their money on drink. Now they'll stagger home and possibly get in trouble on the way or with their wives. White folk like you and me, we don't do things like that, do we? No," he answered. "White folk gather inside one person's house or another, and sometimes fight or get so blind drunk they couldn't make it home on their own. I know. The girl at our office gets the calls and radios me. I'm the one who has to go inside the house and help to carry them out, usually too drunk to walk on their own, and get them into this cab. So you almost never see them drunk and you think they're good, sober, upright white people.

"But these Indians around here, drinking and whooping it up beside this favorite stoplight of theirs on the main drag of Prince Rupert, you probably think, 'Where the hell's the Mounted Police? Why don't they rush over here and throw the bunch of them in jail?' Well, once in a while, they do. I drive one of these Indian fishermen or loggers home sometimes when he's had too much to drink. I just see that he's got a problem walking and I stop and give him a free lift. He'll most often say to me, if he can still talk, 'Will you roll me over, Tommy, and search my pockets, man? Take the money you need for giving me this ride.' But I don't do that. I help him out of the cab and to his door. We shake hands and say good-night. If that Indian can remember it, he'll sure as hell search me out and pay me next day.

"Yeah, mister, around here it's where a man does his drinking that really counts."

Hand adze

52

Hunger

Some people look a little squeamish when they hear that I've learned to enjoy eating raw gulls' eggs with my Inuit friends in the Arctic and can easily take the taste of fish eyes and sea urchins and many other wilder, stranger things. When you think about it, island people with no outside hope for help must have known terrifying hardships, sickness, starvation, and wars that left no one alive to tell the tale. This is especially true for those who had no written language. The last one to go carried the tragedy inside them, with no one to prepare their grave.

China was a country whose early emperors employed scholars who could write. They kept careful scrolls of their historical records covering thousands of years, telling of their struggles to suppress internal rebels or foreign raiders attacking their walled cities. An early text describes a war between the armies of Sung and Chu in the year 321 BC. Because of a siege laid down by the attacking forces, Chu's walled city was almost without food. Following the old Chinese custom, an emissary was sent to discuss the situation. While standing on the city's walls, the man from Sung's army asked about conditions in Chu.

The man from Chu honestly replied that they were terrible. "Our families," he said, "are even now exchanging their children so that they, with fewer feelings, can eat the children, then burn their bones for fuel."

Now that speaks of an almost unimaginable family circumstance. Yet, how many events in North America's history of early man went unrecorded in societies where only the oral tradition in language existed? We will probably never know.

Inuit were usually interested in forming alliances among certain groups of families and their camps. War in the eastern and central

Arctic was unthinkable, so sharing food with fellow hunters and neighboring families was absolutely essential to survival.

They say a person without water out under a relentless desert sun may die of dehydration in a single day. But in the Arctic or some other cooler, northern climates, with enough water or snow to furnish the necessary liquid, persons have been known to survive without food for well over a month. Unfortunately, because they depended on the animal migrations of the seal or caribou, Inuit must have all too often been forced to put this hardship to the test.

Night winds
come billowing out of Asia,
moving and sighing
across the sunken land bridge
following the bleary paths of moonlight
into America along its coasts,
on this night
casting not a single human shadow.
But over the centuries,
they will come again and again,
find humans crowded here,
all seekers of clean water, clear air, and food.

Most North Americans live in easy times today. But who among us would really trust that *abbundanza* to last for how many more hundreds of years? It is not really sad to grow old knowing you have survived, like many others, through the severest of world depressions and the severest of wars. Survival is the key, as is expressed in an Inuit song:

There is one thing
and only one thing,
and that is
to see the new dawn
as it comes into the sky.

53
Canoeing

Alice and I have long possessed a handsome sixteen-foot, green canvas-covered, cedar canoe. We didn't use it to fish on the Tlell River, but it was light enough to portage overland when we wished to travel. I had more or less been brought up in a canoe during all my early ventures on Lake Simcoe in Ontario and later on the chains of lakes and rivers north of Grand'Mere, Quebec, when I was making a living as an artist there just after the war. The voyageurs for the Hudson's Bay Company and the North West Company from Montreal had used their large freight canoes to make their long journeys across the whole of Canada and also down the Mississippi and Missouri Rivers to explore and trade. Their French names are spread throughout Canada and the United States today. They were real canoe men.

One favorite canoe trip for us these days is from our green cottage downriver with the tide to the estuary of the Tlell where it widens and flows into the Hecate Strait. We often wait there with a bottle of wine and a picnic lunch, and we fish or nap until the tide turns, and then we easily paddle home.

Long, narrow Mayer Lake, not far north of our home, is another place we enjoy canoeing. There we begin just off the main road, launching the canoe, if it's summer, into a wide field of water lily pads. The lake has not a building nor a person living on it. It is the home of elegant blue herons, multitudes of deer, as well as ducks and geese in season. The cutthroat trout in the lake are long and dark and lean. Some say too much oil seeps into the lake, and there's evidence of that in oil-slick sinkholes around its shores. We're lucky it's part of Naikoon Provincial Park and free of oil drilling claims.

With Alice paddling in the bow, in the increasingly heavy rain we follow the small, almost hidden river through a lush green tangle of trees and bushes at the south end of Mayer Lake. If you were to persist, you could portage through and come out at Cape Ball on the island's eastern shore on Hecate Strait. During our earlier stays here, two shy girls we knew only slightly lived entirely alone at Cape Ball for three or four years, during which time they rebuilt an old log cabin. That I would consider as remote a life as one is likely to encounter, even in the Canadian Arctic. The girls would trek out once every few months to buy essential supplies – not food, I'm told, because they lived on dried fish and venison, wild berries, and all kinds of birds and eggs which, if handled in the Haida way, will last you almost through the winter. I always rather envied those two in their self-imposed isolation. "They're tough," I told Alice.

Cape Ball is not too far north of the old shipwreck of the *Pezutta*, which lies exposed on the beach, one of the most hauntingly beautiful places I've ever seen. It could be easily reached in our small canoe if the weather was favorable, which it was not. But when we traveled at sea, we always stayed very close to shore, and on landing would carefully draw up the canoe well above the high tide line. We would even upturn the canoe and put up a tent if the weather became too nasty. There are almost no cleared trails in the forest, and without them, if you try walking home in the rain, the going is tough. Getting lost in the north woods after dark in high stands of timber where the stars are hidden is as easy as falling off a log. I know, I've done it.

On this particular trip, after listening to the early morning rain on the tent roof for an hour, I got up and made some coffee and woke Alice. The tent was damp inside and cold, and the rain was driving on the wind. "Isn't this a dandy place to be? Is there any place you'd rather be right now?" I asked her.

Alice pulled up the sleeping bag and shuddered. "Well, maybe the Bahamas – far from a morning like this – wouldn't be too bad. Remember that mockingbird singing beside our window? Remember bonefishing with Cousin Mary, and the water all robin's egg blue in all that lovely winter sunshine? Would there be anything wrong with a Canadian writing his books down there?"

CAMPING NOTES BASED ON OUR MID-SEPTEMBER RIVER CAMP
Supplies for Island Travel:
Note: If traveling by canoe, do not forget lifejackets (they serve a double use as pillows), and carry a rope and small anchor. Your supplies should fit into the canoe and will give you the elegant feeling that you're a serious voyageur. Pack your food, if you don't trust nature, in large, plastic containers – waterproof them with duct tape.

- A rolled tent, and tarp if possible, and a small saw and axe – all essential – extra paddle and map.
- Take a flashlight and fresh batteries, binoculars, a compass, a whistle, dark glasses.
- All necessary fishing gear and licenses, and rain gear – rainproof pants, jackets, and hat – fly dope, sunscreen, and toilet paper.
- Fish knife and stone.
- Toothbrush and toothpaste.
- Waterproof match container (a condom is no good, you may be surprised to learn. It lets in dampness).
- First aid kit, small.
- A pot and frying pan, a thermos, a cheap folding grill, 2 tin plates, 2 tin mugs, several plastic garbage bags, and plastic wrap.
- A water container, filled, and 4 short candles.
- Cooling chest for fresh-caught fish and other food, including: 1 dozen eggs, 1 pkg. bacon, 2 tins cooked ham, 2 tins corned beef, tinned veggies, good coffee and tea, 2 lemons for fish, a tin of butter, a loaf or two of bread, a box of pilot crackers, a 3-lb. block of cheese, small jar of jam, 5 packages soup mix, powdered milk, apples and oranges, bag of carrots, green pepper, salt & pepper, fresh dill or some dried in jar, raisins and apricots, box Quaker oats or Red River cereal, sugar.
- Dry wood, fire-starting paper.
- Extra sweaters, socks.
- Two good pocket books, sketch pad, pencils, watercolors.

54
Skidegate Days

I remember two days, years apart, when I was in Skidegate. One was a fine autumn day, when the Minister of Western Economic Diversification, the Honorable Lloyd Axworthy, flew north to Haida Gwaii. His visit followed years of negotiations between the Haida and the government of Canada. On this day, a small potlatch ceremony was planned on the Skidegate Reserve to mark the final step in handing over the Gwaii Trust.

Alice and I were present at the ceremony held at the community hall on the Reserve on Thursday, September 1, 1995, starting at 4:00 p.m. Of course, in Haida fashion, it was to be a community feast. There was a proud and open invitation to everybody on the Queen Charlotte Islands. The invitation, printed in bold letters on bright yellow paper, hung on bulletin boards from Sandspit north to Masset. On the bottom line of the notice was the announcement, "Anybody is welcome to contribute to the feast by bringing a fresh garden salad, vegetables, seafood or . . . favorite dish."

The slowly measured speeches lasted until seven o'clock. Guujaaw, as usual, danced and performed with his drum. A long, central table was filled to overflowing with good food, including an abundance of delicious smoked dog, sockeye salmon, and clam stew.

We watched as Lloyd Axworthy handed over a single symbolic check for thirty-eight million dollars to the representatives from the seven Haida Gwaii communities who accepted it.

"That's only the first step," I heard the band chief whisper. "You folks wait and see!"

A second scene. During one of my early days in the Charlottes, I stood at the south end of Graham Island at Skidegate, the Haida Indian reserve, and looked north. I tried to visualize the appearance that the small village curved along the inlet must once have had, squaring it with the 1879 photo by Dr. G. M. Dawson that showed almost fifty great totem poles – potlatch poles, house poles, memorial poles – standing before the houses that ran so elegantly along the beach. On that day, the sun was breaking through the morning fog and half a dozen bald eagles sat on the water's edge, their wings widespread but drooping, for they were trying to dry their feathers.

I looked at the beach of the Skidegate Reserve again this year as I have done so many times. The last old pole was gone, but there, almost in the same place, stood Bill Reid's famous new Haida Gwaii Band Council pole, now turned a pleasant silver gray. Bill Reid is gone now, but his pole still stands. When I squint my eyes, I can imagine a new and different-looking village, one with a whole new line of family poles once more standing guard along this Skidegate beach.

Raven rattle

55

Autumn Moon

As the October moon turns from its crescent half and waxes into the hump-backed moon, the daylight diminishes fast on these northern islands, for we are not far across the Dixon entrance south of Alaska. I usually wake early in the darkness, and remain listening in our bed. I'm glad that it is still pitch black outside around our house, guarded on three sides by the tall and dripping forest. Not far away on the gravel flats beside the ever-changing tidal river, I hear a guarding gander give a short, strong, wake-up call. He is answered in an irregular pitch and broken rhythm by a half dozen of the other big Canada geese that must be sitting close to him, waiting, like me, for the first faint sign of dawn.

Farther along the river, I hear another flock answering the first in the familiar discordant way they have. That sets up a waking babble back and forth, their cries still sounding raw and sleepy. Light starts to gently gray our room. It won't be long now. I rise and quickly dress, not wishing to miss anything. I pull on pants, shirt, and a thick sweater, and go downstairs.

Careful not to put on any lights, I go out quietly and stand on the edge of the porch. Sometimes I feel that they are aware of me. Now the closer flock of Canadas calls in earnest to the farther flock, honking their message excitedly, "What about you? We're taking off." Into the air they rise – black silhouettes – and circle, then come low along the river past our house. Here they almost always veer inland over our narrow stretch of forest between the river and the ocean's beach.

I used to count them as they passed, but now I feel I instinctively know how many are in the flock. Maintaining their separation, the two flocks follow the same path. The second flock flies just above the house. I let the two lead birds pass. One should never shoot them, but in my mind's eye, just for old times' sake, I take quick aim at a big bird behind the lead, and pull my imaginary pair of triggers. In my mind's eye, I see two of the white-cheeked birds come tumbling down onto the beach. In truth, they all passed safely on to the next place where they wished to pause and feed. I have relived a moment of my former Arctic days without disturbing a feather.

I look out our back gate and stare along the dark waters of the river, in hope of seeing some silver rings left by rolling salmon. I see none. *Well, what the hell's wrong with actually getting some writing done on a misty, rainy morning like this?* I go inside, flick on the kitchen light, start fresh coffee, and begin to heat the oatmeal porridge. In my opinion, this is the second-best way for any man to start his day.

When I am comfortably settled down in the cottage in that blissful near-silence where wild geese call and no telephone rings, I often wonder why we ever left this place, or why it took so many months to return.

Now when I look back and read many of the pieces making this book, *Hideaway*, I think, *My God, how did I ever get from there to here?* Throughout the 1950s, I lived in the Canadian eastern Arctic. For years, my address was simply "James Houston, Northern Service Officer, c/o Eastern Arctic Patrol, Main Post Office, Ottawa, Canada." No postage necessary. That meant that in the million and more square miles that was the Northwest Territories before the division of Nunavut, someone would discover my Arctic whereabouts somewhere, sometime, somehow.

How different were those wild, old days. Then how different New York City was, living in the heart of Manhattan, and the gentler life on our Rhode Island farm that followed, where with Alice I continued to try to domesticate myself, along with the farm's domesticated animals. For more than thirty years we've been coming from and going to Haida Gwaii as a writing, drawing, salmon fishing retreat, and sometimes just for talking to each other and to our guests or friends on the Northwest Coast.

Now, perhaps, I've convinced you – the reader – that the Charlottes are a place you'd probably enjoy. You'll certainly remember them – the rainforests, the beaches, the animals, the birds, the fish, the people – hell, even the wind and swirling mists. It's a place unlike any other. But you won't find it easy to get there. There are several approaches, some more expensive than others, none of them really cheap. You can fly into Sandspit from Vancouver; you can take a ferry across from Prince Rupert; or you can sail in, either privately, if you're really experienced, or with a guiding company.

If you would like, you can roam around the historic Haida areas of South Moresby Island like Ninstints, which is an unforgettable experience. Getting there from Sandspit or Graham Island by boat can be difficult. To charter a float plane is expensive, and high seas may prevent you from landing. You must also seek a permit from the Haida.

If you're a rugged sort that likes kayaking and camping, that's fine, because you can kayak everywhere in the Charlottes with a commercial group. Cycling and camping are fine, too, as many young European visitors to our islands demonstrate, passing north across the Tlell bridge on the way to Masset and North Beach with their bikes loaded for sleeping out.

Camping's an especially good idea here because, while there are several parks, you must not expect a place with any luxury hotels. The Charlottes, thank God, are not like that. Motels and a few plain and simple bed-and-breakfasts are what you can expect.

I'm writing all this with a heavy conscience, because, frankly, we love the Queen Charlottes just the way they are, and we don't want to encourage any floods of tourists. But I guess it's safe to whisper this to people like you. It's not fair for me to paint a portrait of this natural world of wonders that may leave you panting to get there without telling you more or less how you can do it, because I know you'll respect this "far away stone" as some mainland Indians call Haida Gwaii.

"How did I get from there to here?" I ask Alice.

"Don't worry, we can figure that out after you've finished this book."

"I swear it's going to be my last!"

"Of course," she says, looking down the river, "I've heard that one before."

Net markers

About the Author

JAMES HOUSTON, a Canadian author-artist, served with the Toronto Scottish Regiment in World War II, 1940-45, then lived among Inuit of the Canadian Arctic for twelve years as a Northern Service Officer, and the first Administrator of west Baffin Island, a territory of 65,000 square miles. Widely acknowledged as the prime force in the development of Inuit art, he is past chairman of both the American Indian Arts Centre and the Canadian Eskimo Arts Council and a director of the Association on American Indian Affairs. He has been honoured with the American Indian and Eskimo Cultural Foundation Award, the 1979 Inuit Kuavati Award of Merit, and the 1997 Royal Geographic Society's Massey Medal, and is an officer of the Order of Canada.

Among his writings, *The White Dawn* has been published in thirty-one editions worldwide. That novel and *Ghost Fox, Spirit Wrestler,* and *Eagle Song* have been selections of major book clubs. *Running West* won the Canadian Authors Association Book of the Year Award, while his most recent novel, *The Ice Master,* also appeared in Spanish translation. Author and illustrator of seventeen children's books, he is the only person to have won the Canadian Library Association Book of the Year Award three times. His most recent children's book is *Fire Into Ice,* about creating glass sculpture. He has also written screenplays for feature films, has created numerous documentaries, and continues to lecture widely.

His drawings, paintings, and sculptures are internationally represented in many museums including the St. Petersburg Museum in

Florida and private collections including that of the King of Saudi Arabia. He is Master Designer for Steuben Glass, with one hundred and ten pieces to his credit. He created the seventy-foot-high central sculpture in the Glenbow-Alberta Art Museum. In 1999 Canada's National Museum of Civilization devoted its show "Iqqaipaa" to the art of the Arctic in James Houston's time, and he played a central role in organizing the exhibition.

He and his wife Alice now divide the year between a colonial privateer's house in New England and a writing retreat on the bank of a salmon river on the Queen Charlotte Islands in British Columbia, where he has written a large part of his trilogy of memoirs, *Confessions of an Igloo Dweller*, *Zigzag*, and *Hideaway*.

NW Coast dancer

PUBLISHED BY McCLELLAND & STEWART INC.

CONFESSIONS OF AN IGLOO DWELLER *by* James Houston
The famous novelist and superb storyteller who brought Inuit art to the
outside world recounts his Arctic adventures between 1948 and 1962. "Sheer
entertainment, as fascinating as it is charming." *Kirkus Reviews*
Memoir/Travel, 6 × 9, 320 pages, maps, drawings, trade paperback

ZIGZAG: A Life on the Move *by* James Houston
This "remarkable account" (*Books in Canada*) ranges from the Arctic to New
York and beyond and tells of Presidents, hunters, glass factory gaffers, leopards,
walrus, movies, bestselling books and 10,000-year-old meatballs.
Memoir/Travel, 6 × 9, 288 pages, drawings, trade paperback

THE ICE MASTER: A Novel of the Arctic *by* James Houston
Part sea-story (involving a mutiny and a hurricane), part Arctic saga that tells
of Inuit and Yankee whalers in the North in 1876, this rousing historical novel
is "a straight-away adventure." *Winnipeg Free Press*
Fiction, 6 × 9, 368 pages, 40 drawings, hardcover

PADDLE TO THE ARCTIC *by* Don Starkell
The author of *Paddle to the Amazon* "has produced another remarkable book"
Quill & Quire. His 5,000-kilometre trek across the Arctic by kayak or dragging
a sled is a "fabulous adventure story." *Halifax Daily News*
Adventure, 4¼ × 7, 320 pages, maps, photos, mass market

THE CANADA TRIP *by* Charles Gordon
Charles Gordon and his wife drove from Ottawa to St. John's to Victoria and
back. The result is "a very human, warm, funny book" (*Victoria Times
Colonist*) that will set you planning your own trip.
Travel/Humour, 6 × 9, 364 pages, 22 maps, trade paperback

W.O. MITCHELL COUNTRY: Portrayed *by* Courtney Milne, Text *by* W.O.
Mitchell
W.O.'s writings about the Prairies, the Foothills and the Mountains, selected by
Orm and Barbara Mitchell, have inspired Courtney Milne to produce match-
ing full-colour photographs. A feast for the eye and the mind.
Art/Photography, 10½ × 11½, 240 pages, 200 colour photographs, hardcover

FOR YOUR EYE ALONE: Letters 1976-1995 *by* Robertson Davies
These lively letters, selected and edited by Judith Skelton Grant, give an "over the shoulder" look at the private Davies, at the height of his international fame, writing family notes and slicing up misguided reviewers.
Belles lettres, 6 × 9, 400 pages, facsimile letters, notes, index, hardcover

RED BLOOD: One (Mostly) White Guy's Encounter With the Native World *by* Robert Hunter
The founder of Greenpeace looks back on a wild, hell-raising career. "Hunter acts. He does things. . . . In all his adventures humour is a companion, but he can also write angry political commentary." *Globe and Mail*
Non-fiction, 6 × 9, 280 pages, hardcover

AN EVENING WITH W.O. MITCHELL *by* W.O. Mitchell
"A collection of 31 of Mitchell's favourite stories . . . which he regularly performed with ebullience and dramatic flair to delighted audiences across the country." *Toronto Star* "An excellent performance." *Saskatoon StarPhoenix*
Anthology, 6 × 9, 320 pages, 30 photographs, trade paperback

BROKEN GROUND: A novel *by* Jack Hodgins
It's 1922 and the shadow of the First World War hangs over a struggling Soldier's Settlement on Vancouver Island. This powerful novel with its flashbacks to the trenches is "a richly, deeply human book – a joy to read." W.J. Keith
Fiction, 6 × 9, 368 pages, trade paperback

A PASSION FOR NARRATIVE: A Guide for Writing Fiction *by* Jack Hodgins
"One excellent path from original to marketable manuscript. . . . It would take a beginning writer years to work her way through all the goodies Hodgins offers." *Globe and Mail*
Non-fiction / Writing guide, 5¼ × 8½, 216 pages, trade paperback

OVER FORTY IN BROKEN HILL: Unusual Encounters in the Australian Outback *by* Jack Hodgins
"Australia described with wit, wonder and affection by a bemused visitor with Canadian sensibilities." *Canadian Press* "Damned fine writing." *Books in Canada*
Travel, 5½ × 8½, 216 pages, trade paperback

DANCING ON THE SHORE: A Celebration of Life at Annapolis Basin *by* Harold Horwood, *Foreword by* Farley Mowat
"A Canadian *Walden*" *Windsor Star* that "will reward, provoke, challenge and enchant its readers." *Books in Canada*
Nature/Ecology, 5⅛ × 8¼, 224 pages, 16 wood engravings, trade paperback

AT THE COTTAGE: A Fearless Look at Canada's Summer Obsession *by* Charles Gordon *illustrated by* Graham Pilsworth
This perennial best-selling book of gentle humour is "a delightful reminder of why none of us addicted to cottage life will ever give it up." *Hamilton Spectator*
Humour, 6 × 9, 224 pages, illustrations, trade paperback

THE SELECTED STORIES OF MAVIS GALLANT *by* Mavis Gallant
"A volume to hold and to treasure" said the *Globe and Mail* of the 52 marvellous stories selected from Mavis Gallant's life's work. "It should be in every reader's library." *Fiction, 6⅛ × 9¼ , 900 pages, trade paperback*

THE LOVE OF A GOOD WOMAN: Stories *by* Alice Munro
"Her stories *feel* like novels," writes Robert MacNeil. The power of love – and of sex – is the theme of these eight marvellous new stories by the writer who has been described by the *Washington Post* as "our Chekhov."
Fiction, 6 × 9, 352 pages, hardcover

THE BLACK BONSPIEL OF WILLIE MACCRIMMON *by* W.O. Mitchell *illustrated by* Wesley W. Bates
A devil of a good tale about curling – W.O.Mitchell's most successful comic play now appears as a story, fully illustrated, for the first time, and it is "a true Canadian classic." *Western Report*
Fiction, 4⅝ × 7½, 144 pages with 10 wood engravings, hardcover

WHO HAS SEEN THE WIND *by* W.O. Mitchell *illustrated by* William Kurelek
W. O. Mitchell's best-loved book, this Canadian classic of childhood on the prairies is presented in its full, unexpurgated edition, and is "gorgeously illustrated." *Calgary Herald*
Fiction, 8½ × 10, 320 pages, numerous colour and black-and-white illustrations, trade paperback

ACCORDING TO JAKE AND THE KID: A Collection of New Stories *by* W.O. Mitchell
"This one's classic Mitchell. Humorous, gentle, wistful, it's 16 new short stories about life through the eyes of Jake, a farmhand, and the kid, whose mom owns the farm." *Saskatoon Star-Phoenix*
Fiction, 5 × 7¾, 280 pages, trade paperback

HUGH MACLENNAN'S BEST: An anthology *selected by* Douglas Gibson
This selection from all of the works of the witty essayist and famous novelist is "wonderful . . . It's refreshing to discover again MacLennan's formative influence on our national character." *Edmonton Journal*
Anthology, 6 × 9, 352 pages, trade paperback